Standing Ground

YUROK INDIAN SPIRITUALITY
1850–1990

THOMAS BUCKLEY

UNIVERSITY OF CALIFORNIA PRESS
Berkeley   Los Angeles   London

10041799961

University of California Press
Berkeley and Los Angeles, California

University of California Press, Ltd.
London, England

For acknowledgments of permissions, please see p. 313.

Library of Congress Cataloging-in-Publication Data

Buckley, Thomas C. T.
  Standing ground : Yurok Indian spirituality, 1850–1990 / Thomas
Buckley.
    p. cm.
  Includes bibliographical references and index.
  ISBN 0-520-23358-1 (cloth : alk. paper)—ISBN 0-520-23389-1 (paper : alk.
paper)
  1. Yurok Indians—Religion.   I. Title.
  E99.Y97 B83   2002
  299'.783—dc21   2002074222

Manufactured in the United States of America

11   10   09   08   07   06   05   04   03   02

10 9 8 7 6 5 4 3 2 1

The paper used in this publication is both acid-free and totally chlorine-
free (TCF). It meets the minimum requirements of ANSI/NISO
Z39.48–1992 (R 1997) (Permanence of Paper).

To Jorunn

Contents

Acknowledgments

This book offers my present understandings of Yurok Indians and of the neighboring native peoples with whom the Yuroks continue to be richly intertwined, culturally and historically. I write about them as they were between 1850, when the California gold rush erupted in their midst, and 1991, when I last did formal anthropological research in northwestern California. Now, in the year 2002, eleven years does not seem too many to have taken to consider just what I want to say about the American Indian people there.

I lived in the lower Klamath River region in 1973–74 and returned there as a graduate student in cultural anthropology in 1976, coming back many times after that for weeks or months of research and, increasingly, simply to see my friends. In the years since 1973, almost everyone that I know, American Indian and non-Indian alike, has helped me in some way or other to bring this book about. I greet and thank all of them. To some, however, I need to give special thanks by name.

First, my respects to the memories of native Californian elders who welcomed and taught me in the 1970s and '80s. They have passed on now, but all continue to teach.

Frank Douglas, Dewey George, Ella Norris, Calvin Rube, Florence Shaughnessy, all speaking Yurok as a first language, all took important, lasting places in my life and life-aspirations. Perhaps they did not know me quite so well, but Howard Ames, Aileen Figueroa, Sam Jones, Antone (Anafey) Obee, all Yurok, and Georgina Matilton (Hupa) were generous with their time and knowledge and remain welcomed presences in my life.

I cannot imagine myself without the eleven years that I studied with my adoptive uncle, the late Harry K. Roberts (1906–81), a non-Indian raised Yurok. (I introduce him more fully in chapter 2.)

Miss these elders as we must, we are all fortunate that later generations continue on in their spirit with intelligence, determination, and creative verve. Jimmie James and Walt Lara (Yurok) and Josephine Peters (Karuk) have been helpful to me, and sometimes much more. Over these many years Chris Peters (Yurok), Julian Lang and Brian D. Tripp (Karuk), Loren Bommelyn (Tolowa), Jack Norton (Hupa-Cherokee), and Kathy Heffner McClellan (Wailaki) have been both friends and the best colleagues I could ask for.

Since long before my own first days on the Klamath River, another friend, Merk Oliver (Yurok), has been there—enduring, funny, wise to the world and generous with welcome and the fish that he is famous for catching and cooking. Ko wic'o, Merk.

Among academic scholars, Raymond D. Fogelson, Professor of Anthropology at the University of Chicago, has been of inestimable help in all that is in this book. Erudite and constant, a compassionate mentor, a teacher in the best senses of the word, Ray has many students in American Indian studies writing now only because he has supported us and our work from the very beginning. I hope that this book repays his efforts in some small part.

If I have learned anything from the native people I've mentioned, it is to value my own family. My son Jesse (who started dodging bears with me in the Siskiyou Mountains when he was still riding in a pack frame) and my wife, Jorunn Jacobsen Buckley, to whom I dedicate this book, are at the center. How could I have lived or loved without you both?

There are many others to thank: Audrey Jones for her big heart, Marcellene Norton (Hupa) for her hospitality, Bill Hunter, Victor Golla, and Alan Bramlette (Cherokee) for giving me home bases when I was on the river. Bertha Peters and Florence Walsh (both Yurok), Carol, Tom, and Lawrence O'Rourke (Yurok), and Grandma Ada Charles (Yurok) all shared their jump dance camps and tables with me at Pecwan in 1988 and 1990. The strong examples they set in performing their demanding duties have been as lasting, for me, as their warmth and humor. I also thank Paul Friedrich, Michael Silverstein, George W. Stocking, Jr., and Terry Strauss, a woman for all seasons, all at the University of Chicago; Joan Berman, Lee Davis, Victor Golla (again), Diana Heberger, Jean Perry, the late Arnold Remington Pilling, Yvonne Rand, Esther Roberts, and Ned Simmons, all devoted and energetic witnesses to life in native northwestern California; Malcolm Margolin and Peter Nabokov, writers of earned authority; and John Balaban, Tracy McCallum, Tim Sieber, Taylor Stoehr, poets. It is a wonder to be blessed with friends such as these.

Many people have commented helpfully on versions of chapters in this book. Most especially I thank the late Dorothy Dooling, Les Field, Sergei Kan, Julian Lang, Tsianina Lomawaima (Creek), Beatrice Medicine (Standing Rock Sioux), Jack Norton, Jean O'Brian (White Earth Ojibwa), Jean Perry, Nancy Riley (Karuk), Sam Stanley, Polly Strong, Lisa Sundberg (Yurok), and Dorothea Theodoratus. Special thanks also go to Taylor Stoehr (again), who read the book manuscript at a crucial point in its growth, and to Les Field and Michael Harkin, readers of the near-final draft.

Students at the University of Massachusetts, Boston, have been inspiring—without them I might quite literally have sailed away by now. More practically speaking, my thanks go to Debbie Fricke, Carrie Lilly, Kirk Gagnier, Francis Fitzgerald Denny, and Clarissa Sansone, who all assisted me in preparing tape transcriptions and bibliographies for this book.

I deeply appreciate Brian D. Tripp's permission to use his 1984 work on paper on the cover, and its name, *Standing Ground*, as the title of this book. My use of the picture and its name reflect the high esteem in which I hold both Brian and his work, and my gratitude for the inspiration both have been to me for many years.

Several organizations have supported my travels to and from the northwest coast of California and my research there at various times: the Danforth Foundation, the Whatcom Museum Foundation, the American Philosophical Society, the Callipeplon Society, Zen Center San Francisco, the University of Massachusetts, and Humboldt State University.

Finally, hearty thanks to Stanley Holwitz, my editor at University of California Press, who has been unflagging in his support of this project all along and enormously helpful in getting it to press, to Rachel Berchten, also at the Press, who steered me through the publication process, and to my copy editor, Kay Scheuer: they've been terrific.

Introduction and Note on Orthography

The eleven chapters of this book came together over the past decade, although the idea of writing a book about the Yurok Indians goes back to my first meetings with Yurok people, in 1971. The year before, I had met Harry Kellett Roberts, then living in Sonoma County, north of San Francisco. From about 1912 until the mid-1930s, Harry had been the adoptive nephew and student of Robert Spott, a Yurok man from the village of Requa, at the mouth of the Klamath River in northwestern California. By 1973 I was spending time in the Klamath region myself, eventually coming to know a fair number of Yurok, Karuk, Hupa, and Tolowa people.

It was Harry Roberts, by 1972 my own adoptive uncle and teacher, who suggested that I go back to finish college and study anthropology, so that I could "set the record straight on the Yuroks." My casual stays on the Klamath turned into graduate anthropological field work in 1976–78, and

1

then into my 1982 doctoral dissertation at the University of Chicago, "Yurok Realities in the Nineteenth and Twentieth Centuries" (the present book bears little resemblance to it). I have stayed in touch with people in northwestern California ever since, returning there when time and money allow, for weeks or months at a time when that is possible. Today I continue to visit as a friend and a witness, occasionally doing some advocacy work, but my systematic research in the area tapered off after 1990, about the same time that the Yuroks became fully engaged in achieving a federally acknowledged tribal organization. Since 1993, full federal tribal status has spurred a chain of dramatic changes in the Yuroks' material world. The period since 1993 is not of immediate concern in this book—hence the second date in its subtitle.

All along, my primary interest has been in men's and women's spiritual training, in the ways people think about the world and act in it, and in the ways that these things vary and reemerge changed through time. Finally, after these many years, I have a good sense of what I want to say about all of this and about Yurok Indian people whom I've known over the course, now, of more than half my lifetime.

By the 1980s, my work had branched out to include the study of the history of anthropology and particularly the work of Alfred Louis Kroeber (1876–1960) and his junior colleagues in California between 1900 and the Second World War. I have published much of this research elsewhere and very little of it is repeated in *Standing Ground.* Yet I came to understand that I could not write Yurok ethnography and ethnohistory without enfolding a dialogue with Kroeber within this writing. Kroeber's influence has been that powerful, both among potential readers of my work and within ever-emergent Yurok culture itself.[1]

Dialogue in fact became the dominant theme in *Standing Ground:* dialogues between Kroeber's understanding and my own, between Yurok and other regional native individuals and myself, between contemporary Yuroks and their historical past, and among Yurok individuals, particularly in ritual contexts. Indeed, dialogue provides a metaphorical basis both for my method and, by the end of the book, for a theoretical understanding of how Yurok culture has emerged through time. It is here, I believe, that *Standing Ground* pans out from a tight focus on the Yuroks (and to a lesser degree, on Kroeber's and others' "salvage" ethnology of classic—that is, pre-1849—Yurok culture in native California) to hold broader methodological and theoretical implications for the practice of cultural anthropology (see also Buckley 1987).

Standing Ground is not a particularly technical work, however. I've tried to keep stories and their tellers in the foreground. These stories range from transcribed tape recordings and extensive field notes that I compiled with Yurok teachers in the 1970s to my own stories about my times on the Klamath (although the latter are fewer than the former; this is not a confessional book). In part, my emphasis on stories, left to speak for themselves rather than to support distantiated analyses, grew out of and allowed me to center my inquiry on the relationship between individuals and the "culture" that they share. Doing this, I approach an old Boasian conundrum that Kroeber himself had struggled with: Do culture and society determine human action, or can individual human beings improvise creatively on shared cultural themes, themselves determining, to an extent, cultural and social processes? When one reconsiders Kroeber's classic Yurok ethnography, for instance, these are matters of some consequence, for Kroeber denied individuality any place in defining "culture," and yet considered the Yuroks and their neighbors "anarchic" (1925: 35). Spirituality, communally shared but grounded in the hearts of individuals, provides an arena in which the relationships between individuals and societies are especially accessible.

As much as possible I have built this book on what I have heard, observed, or participated in myself, together with received, transcribed oral native testimony and work published by native authors in the region. Kroeber himself becomes a problem in my book, rather than an assumed benchmark authority (contra Keeling 1992). I have relied on his copious field notes and many publications to fill in gaps in my own research and experience, but overall my approach is more historical and developmental than Kroeber's, in the everyday senses of those words. While Kroeber hoped to capture the "superorganic . . . fabric" of "native primitive" Yurok culture, held "in static balance" by an ethnographic present, ca. 1848 (Kroeber 1917b, 1948, 1959; cf. Buckley 1996), I am skeptical of the notion of any fixed Yurok "culture," at any time, seeing the history of Yurok spirituality as part of a history of constant cultural emergence. Culture, I conclude, is a process, not a thing. Such abstractions, however, need to be grounded in the actualities of daily life and, in *Standing Ground*, spiritual practice and training.

ONE

Pecwan is a small but ancient town on the Klamath River, straggled along a shelf within a forested mountain canyon about fifteen miles upstream from the river mouth, which is on the Pacific coast, thirty-five miles south of the California-Oregon border. The Yurok Indian jump dance at Pecwan takes place at the end of the summer, and it is often very hot during the day. I first saw a jump dance in 1988, the third time it had been made since Yuroks restored it in 1984—forty-five years after the last performance, in 1939. The dance struck me with its sheer difficulty and demand for endurance and sacrifice as much as with its extraordinary beauty. "It's not easy to fix the world," said a friend, a dancer and ceremonial singer.

In 1990 I was there again. It was a fine dance with wonderful regalia. The famous, very old, boy's head roll made entirely of the scalps of hummingbirds danced, and four brand new baskets, woven in the two years since the last dance, danced for the first time. (Regalia themselves are sentient. They are not "displayed," but "cry to dance" and dance together with the human beings who wear and carry them, before an audience that includes invisible spirit beings who "cry to see them dance.")

Dance after dance (nearly a hundred in all, over ten days), day after day, the lead singers' voices wove and intertwined in counterpoint, the sidemen steady in the deceptively simple chorus. It is singing full of yearning and sadness. The music is old, but new songs are made, and you can hear a touch of the electric blues in some good younger singers' voices today.

Overhead, in 1990, helicopters made a constant, racketing drone, state agents searching out marijuana plants in the mountains. A few beat-up cars cruised by slowly on the narrow gravel road below the dance ground. Ospreys dived on the river from the ridges in bursts of buff feathers against the sky and trees and water and rose again with the flash of silver fish in their talons.

The jump dance builds for ten days. Fasting, thirsting, waking, singing—people are cheerful, glad to be there in the heat of the sun, the smoke of the fire, the air rich with burning angelica root. "Don't say it's hot," said an elder, "say it's a wonderful day!" The prayers build—the medicine man's, the dancers', the women's prayer in the camps, the spectators' prayer, witnessing. On the last day girls join the men and boys who have already danced for nine days, and by the end of the last dance of this tenth day all of the dancers are in the pit at once with the very best of all of the regalia. Finally the single great prayer rises up and hangs in the sky above the river, luminous and powerful. Then *everybody* dances, maybe a hundred people, from the dance grounds and down across the road, along the gravel bar by the river.

As the evening cools, at feasts in the three dance camps, each led by a senior woman holding hereditary rights to offer "a fire" or "a table," people review how well it has gone, tell stories, laugh. In another two years it will be time to fix the world again, but for now everyone is happy, the human beings and the spirit beings who have been watching the dance all along, crying for the beauty of it.

The Yurok jump dance at Pecwan is for the whole world, some people say, for the planet that would have failed long since without it. This seemed likely to me in 1990, after ten days: the completed dance felt that important. At the same time, the jump dance is a local event, the prayer of a people in place. The world that it fixes is most immediately the regional, communal world of native northwestern California, its mountains and ragged coastline, its rivers, fish and fowl and many animals, large and small, its innumerable plant-forms, and also its indigenous peoples, American Indians who remain as dynamic a part of it all as they were when their ancestors first put up the dance at Pecwan, "long years ago" as the late Frank Douglas (Yurok) was fond of saying.

TWO

Mr. Douglas and other Yuroks have often been noted for their independent spirits, as individuals and families. But they are also integrated into a regional network of indigenous peoples who are at once distinct by virtue of territories and diverse languages, and are also richly intertwined through shared histories, customs, marriages, trade, ceremonial participation, ecological and political interdependency, friendship and enmity alike. In the past, when Yurok people spoke of *ʔo·lekʷeł*, "the human world," it was this regional world of interrelated peoples living in an intimately known and specific physical environment to which they referred. Today, that world includes people now called Karuk, Hupa, Tolowa, and Wiyot Indians, a world commonly known in ethnology as "native northwestern California." "Yurok" has a very real political meaning today: the Yurok Indian Tribe, with about 3,500 enrolled members, was fully, federally organized in 1993. Yet this modern organization continues to exist within a wider regional social and cultural network—a large Indian population functionally integrated with the dominant, non-Indian population yet remaining among the most culturally autonomous in contemporary native California.[2]

"Yurok" is a relatively recent name that originally derived from the word for "downriver" among these people's upstream neighbors on the Klamath, now called the Karuk Indians, "the Uprivers." Yurok became the standard appellation for the Downrivers among non-Indians in the eighteen sixties and seventies as outsiders began to constitute them as a "tribe," an objectified entity (with an evolutionary niche implied) that could be militarily supervised, bureaucratically managed, and ethnographically inscribed. As late as the *nineteen* seventies some elders joked that they couldn't remember if "Yurok" was supposed to mean Uprivers or Downrivers—Karuks or *puliklah*, one of the Yuroks' many names for themselves.[3]

Aboriginally, these *puliklah*, "Downrivers," and *nɪʔɪnyɪh*, the closely related coastal people, spoke variants of the same language, *sa·ʔagoh*, one of only two known Algonquian languages west of the Rockies. (The second is Wiyot, closely affiliated with the Yurok language and spoken by the Yuroks' neighbors to the south.) Aboriginal Yurok political organization was minimal, subtle, and implicit, focused on villages and village clusters and sometimes on single great houses within villages, all highly independent, in and out of alliances and feuds with each other and with other neighbors who spoke their own, very different languages in their own territories.

Again, A. L. Kroeber found these aboriginal people "anarchic"—a misperception as wide of the mark as calling them a "tribe." The *puliklah* and *nɹʔɹnyɹh* together were neither anarchic nor tribal but something more difficult to pin down in European terms, an emergence through time and speech and ongoing interaction. They were the "human beings," *ʔo·lek^w-oh*, "the ones who stay here" after the *wo·gey*, the Spirit People or First People, had invented culture and—for the most part—departed at the beginning of "Indian Time." Some early American visitors called these *ʔo·lek^woh* "the Allequa"; Yuroks came to call the whites *wo·gey*, pronounced, today, with an ironic twist.[4]

At the time of first contact, in 1775, the Yuroks were fishers and foragers and hunters, secure enough in their abundant estuarine world to stay in permanent settlements of redwood plank houses along the lower forty miles of the Klamath River and along the Pacific coast to either side of the river mouth, seven miles north to Tolowa country, thirty-five miles south to the Wiyots. Like these neighbors, Yuroks lived primarily by harvesting acorns and salmon, but also sturgeon, lampreys, steelhead trout, and surf fish, deer and elk and waterfowl, vegetables from sea lettuce to brodiaea bulbs, berries to grass seeds. On the coast they worked the abundant shoreline for shellfish, sea lions, the occasional stranded whale. They traded such specialty foods as well as raw materials like elk horn and fine worked goods, like redwood river canoes, far inland, bringing back dentalia shells from north along the coast, obsidian from the mountains to the east, the scalps of pileated woodpeckers from other inland mountains beyond their own territory. These things were real wealth, suitable for dancing in the great dances, *helomey-* ("to dance"), as regalia, and also for paying bride wealth, thus securing legitimate children. Strong and ambitious men amassed wealth, power, and influence, became *numi pegɹk*, "real men," tough, learned, rich, and independent, and founded "high families" that their sons tried to maintain for their own generation at least.

Often these great houses lasted a good deal longer, although it is usually hard to tell just how long in the Western sense, limited by its three dimensions. Spiritual acumen was also nurtured in these houses although spiritual leaders were not necessarily rich. Besides, the oral histories of houses and high families have often been adjusted to account for the prominence of the newly ascendant. It was a fluid system. Families rose and fell in an order that resembled a class system but was not. The system might best be conceived of as a meritocracy in which the wealthy and those with deep spiritual acumen both had an advantage and were often one and the same.

The women who became sucking doctors, *kegeyowor* (sing. *kegey*), brought in "clean money" as well in fees for the cures they accomplished and in the bride wealth their male kin demanded for them, bringing esteem and prominence to themselves, their children, and their houses alike. Other women were wealthy in the fine baskets they wove, some of the finest in North America, and other forms of women's wealth that were received for baskets in trade. While power seems, at this distance, to have been rather evenly distributed within the society, terms like "gender symmetry" threaten to obscure genuine difference. Men's and women's worlds were generally separate, socially and architecturally, and complementary rather than symmetrically balanced in terms of power (see Buckley 1988). Exceptions were found in the sucking doctors themselves and a few other females who, like doctors, were sociological males, "real men": *pegɨk*.

This is the hypothetical pre-contact Yurok world that appears in the printed records compiled by early European visitors and, most decisively, in the cumulative "salvage ethnography" reconstructed and published by Kroeber or by his literary executors between 1902 and 1976. (Kroeber's work was based primarily on field work carried out on the Klamath River between 1900 and 1907.) While Kroeber salvaged this account from the memories of the oldest surviving, primarily male Yuroks of his time, the world that he and various of his younger colleagues and protégés witnessed was, in fact, a world vastly and terribly transformed from the one that they inscribed in their salvaged ethnographic reconstruction of classic Yurok Indian culture, ca. 1849.[5]

"The end of Indian Time," as some people call it today, had come with the California gold rush. Although a few Europeans and Euro-Americans made brief visits to Yurok territory beginning in 1775, in the first three months of 1850 an estimated 10,000 prospectors poured into the lower Klamath drainage, and more followed every month after that (Heizer and Mills 1952; Bledsoe 1885). "Whiteman Time" had begun. The ensuing conflict between Yuroks (together with their allies) and the invading whites extended into the mid-1860s, a period during which new pathogens ran rampant among the region's indigenous peoples as well. By Kroeber's conservative estimate (1925: 883), approximately 81 percent of the aboriginal population of northwestern California was lost between 1850 and 1910, the nadir of demographic collapse. "The end of the world," "the time when the stars fell," "the end of Indian Time": however people name it today, it was a time of horror and the beginning of the Yuroks' modern history, a history almost entirely neglected by Kroeber himself (1925: vi ff.).

The term "genocide" is often invoked, in popular usage, to refer to a broad range of oppressive practices that are technically distinct in more legalistic international discourse. With reference to native North America, these practices include massacre, murder, involuntary manslaughter, imprisonment, the spread of disease, enslavement, dispossession, impoverishment, and ethnocide (the ideological effort to destroy cultures, rather than the physical being of the ethnic groups that bear those cultures). Some scholars have argued on the basis of contemporary international law, however, that, while comparable losses of population occurred throughout native North America after 1492, it is primarily in northern California between 1850 and 1865 that a major factor in this population decline can be legalistically and technically defined as "genocide" under 1948 United Nations Convention criteria (e.g., Norton 1979; M. Field 1993). By no means do all such scholars seek to minimize the great North American colonial tragedy, exculpating the colonists, but rather to point out the particular evil of state-sanctioned attempts to exterminate outright all Indian people in northern California. Doing so, they hope to establish a firm legal connection between what happened there, between 1850 and 1865, and widely and legally acknowledged modern genocide in places like Nazi Europe or, more recently, Rwanda and former Yugoslavia. By this means, these scholars attempt to intrude upon a general white North American historical oblivion regarding the post-contact histories of *all* native North American peoples.

The estimated 2,500 Yurok Indians of 1850 had lost at least 73 percent of their population by 1910, and estimated losses among their 4,500 close neighbors were comparable: Karuks, 47 percent; Hupas, 50 percent; Tolowas 85; Wiyots, 90. Of the 6,000 additional people of smaller, less well-defended groups peripheral to the Yurok world—Shastas, Mattoles, Chilulas, Whilcuts, Chimarikos, Nongatls, Sinkyones, Cahtos—only 3–4 percent survived beyond 1865 to be absorbed by marginally more fortunate neighboring groups.

In some cases the parents of the oldest people whom I met on the Klamath River in the 1970s had witnessed this cataclysm firsthand. One can no more understand the contemporary world of native northwestern California without coming to terms with the facts of genocide than one can, for instance, understand the contemporary state of Israel without accepting the reality of the Holocaust. There is no local Indian family whose history does not include a nineteenth-century legacy of attempted extermination, burnt houses, disease, murder, rape, kidnapping, and involuntary servitude, although many share a proud history of armed resistance as well. It is best, I think, to let native authors themselves write of these things as they see fit (chapter 3).

Ecological devastation was as much a part of the great human tragedy engendered by the white invasion and occupation of the later nineteenth century as demographic collapse. Human beings, flora, fauna, and minerals were all reduced to objects subject to commodification when possible, extermination when not, in a white rage for profit that has yet to be exhausted.

The jump dance at Pecwan and a dozen other events that Kroeber and E. W. Gifford (1949) were to lump together as a "world renewal cult" were inaugurated in a mythic "beforetime" by the wo·gey, who knew that the dances would be needed later: that greed, breaches of the law, and disease would imbalance the world once the Indians came and Indian Time began. After 1849 the world became unbalanced almost beyond the power of the dances to fix it. In Karuk, Hupa, and Yurok territories along the lower Klamath and its tributaries, the Trinity and Salmon Rivers, damage to the riverine system from hydraulic mining for gold was already so extreme by 1851 that the spring run of Chinook salmon had stopped, their spawning beds silted in. There was no longer any point in holding the First Salmon rite at the mouth of the Klamath since there was no longer a First Salmon (Kroeber and Barrett 1960).

When the gold played out the loggers came, cutting the most accessible and profitable timber first—the giant redwoods along the coastal shelf—then moving inland, eventually clearcutting thousands of square miles of Coast Range mountains for their Douglas fir, white cedar, and other old growth. Del Norte and Humboldt County timber fed the growth of the burgeoning metropolis around San Fransisco Bay and later traveled much farther, Doug' fir reduced to plywood, sacred ("he is a person") rot-resistant redwood providing picnic tables and decks and lawn chairs halfway around the world. By the 1980s, saw-logs bucked from the trunks of ancient trees were a good part of what America had to offer the Japanese in return for their newly efficient automobiles and sophisticated consumer electronics in a then-futile effort to balance international trade. (The Japanese were powerful enough, then, to refuse any milled lumber or plywood; our export of logs to them did very little to relieve chronic unemployment along the lower Klamath and on the adjacent Pacific coast.)

The Klamath River salmon stock was once among the most abundant in the world, second in North America only to the Columbia River stock. Even after the enormously destructive hydraulic mining of the 1850s and '60s stopped, however, spawning grounds continued to be destroyed by the slash, silt, and, eventually, chemical run-off created by industrial logging practices that, by the 1970s, included the defoliation of deciduous growth with herbicides containing the carcinogenic compound 2,4D. (These hardwoods compete with profit-yielding conifers.) The ecological disaster has been deepened by other factors. River waters depleted by upstream hydroelectric and flood control dams became too warm, too shallow, and too murky for salmon to spawn. International trawling fleets fishing at sea, off the mouth of the Klamath, decimated the stock before it reached the increasingly untenable spawning grounds. With salmon nearly gone and old forests going, by 1990 multinational corporations had turned once again to mineral exploitation in the ravaged coastal mountains, seeking exotic minerals to extract with ever-more powerful technologies, scraping off the last of the fat of the land.

What one sees of the north coast of California, traveling along the few major highways, is still breath-taking in its beauty—a rugged, sparsely settled region, the "Redwood Empire" of postcards and tourist brochures. Equally far removed from the San Francisco Bay area some three hundred and fifty miles to the south and Portland, Oregon, three hundred miles to the north, however, the region is chronically economically depressed. A new maximum security prison in Crescent City, once Tolowa country and the northern limit of the old Yurok world, affords a few new opportunities for employment as guards. A big shopping mall in Eureka, sixty miles south of the Klamath in what was once Wiyot territory but is now wreathed in the sulfuric stench of pulp mills, hires clerks on a regular basis. Most salmon in the markets comes frozen from distant fish farms. Along the back roads the fractured bones of the mountains jut through the earth's skin, ravaged by clearcut logging and by far smaller but equally devastating mining operations. "This place is a colony of Wall Street," Brian Tripp, the Karuk artist, said one day in Eureka.[6]

THREE

The Yurok Indians have been exploited by ethnographers and psychologists in much the same way as trees and fish and minerals have been exploited by capitalists, their lives commodified as "culture" for exchange in an academic market place. This is not a new charge, of course, nor does the argument for it need to be made by outsiders like me, today, on behalf of the people themselves. Many among them are well aware of its particulars, complexities, and ironies, and they are articulate in voicing their diverse views of anthropology, ethnohistory, and cross-cultural psychology. I come to my work under an embarrassing cloud, although one not nearly as heavy as that which occludes the memory of my very famous predecessor, A. L. Kroeber. "Yuroks generally resent the way they have been depicted in the literature of anthropology," writes Richard Keeling (1982a: 72), "and—whether he deserves it or not—they focus their bitterness on Kroeber."

Throughout his Yurok oeuvre, Kroeber insisted that "the Yurok" were doomed by 1850, that "native primitive" Yurok culture existed only as a memory artifact by the time he arrived on the Klamath in 1900, and that no authentically Yurok culture could be said to have existed since 1850, when it began to be supplanted by a "bastard" culture, neither Indian nor white (Kroeber 1948). Both Kroeber's denial of Yurok cultural survival after 1850 and the historical obliviousness toward genocide that accompanied it, at least until 1990, are profoundly resented by many native readers of now widely accessible works, such as Kroeber's monumental *Handbook of the Indians of California* (1925).

There are other sources of bitterness about Kroeber among his native readership. As his widow Theodora Kroeber Quinn put it to me in 1978, he "just wasn't very interested in religion" and this lack of interest feels like disrespect to native readers today, as does Kroeber's dismissal of Yurok polity (largely implemented through ceremonialism) as "the extreme of political anarchy" (Kroeber 1925: 830). Today, as Richard Keeling continues (1982a), "The Indians tend to feel that their traditional spirituality has not been appreciated. The first thing that an elderly Yurok or Hupa Indian wants to impress on an outsider is that 'For old-time Indians, everything used to be religion.' " In 1978 Geneva Matz (Yurok) told me somewhat the same thing. "We are the praying people, that's who we are. In the old days everything we do is pray." At about the same time—before I had learned better—I told another local woman, a brush dance doctor, that I was interested in "Yurok religion." "Well," she said with a grimace, "I guess you could call it that." Neither she nor Mrs. Matz would have, however. Among Indian people in northwestern California who are concerned with such things, "religion" tends to refer to Christianity, to beliefs and rituals that manifest institutionalized teachings. "Praying," privately or in communal rites like dances, is about something else: "our sacred ways," "the Indian Way," "the old way," sometimes, locally, "spiritualism." In this book, I will call it "spirituality."

Spirituality, of course, connotes individuality: its locus is in individual subjectivity, affect, and experience, yet it finds voice through socially shared means and, given such means, becomes communal as well as individual. Missing the central importance of spirituality to Yurok society, Kroeber fell

short in grasping Yurok social organization. "The Yurok recognizes no public claim and the existence of no community. His world is wholly an ag-
gregation of individuals. There being no society as such, there is no social
organization" (1925: 3). Working primarily with elderly high family men,
Kroeber recognized the importance of individuality among "the Yurok,"
but did not understand how these people's independence served a processual communality. His "ethnocentric" failure in this regard (Bean and Blackburn 1976: 9) was intertwined with his lack of interest in religion and his
focus on social structure, law, and material culture. Contemporary native
intellectuals are correct in understanding that a dynamic web of wealth and
spiritual acumen and competencies classically supported communal goals
and thus formed the channels through which social action was directed.
Kroeber's failure to acknowledge this web—metaphorically woven, in
myth, by Skymaker, who knotted the sky net and set it in place—reflects
his want of interest in "religion," more generally speaking.

Disappointed not only by the Yuroks' lack of formally structured social organization, Kroeber was also disappointed in them as individuals.
Making much of the traditional sucking doctors, as the most significant
among spiritual actors, he also saw these women in the negative terms of
what he found missing in them. He was disappointed that, in Yurok
"shamanism," the "idea of an association between the shaman and certain spirits personally attached to him is weakly developed" (1925: 3).
Lacking the dramatic, highly "symbolic" shamanism of North American
Indian "civilizations" that were, in his opinion, more highly developed,
the Yuroks seemed to Kroeber merely "addicted to magic" (1959). "Concepts relating to magic are as abundantly developed among the Yurok and
their neighbors as shamanism is narrowed. Imitative magic is particularly
favored and is of the most crudely direct kind" (1925: 4). Because he was
fixated on personal "magic," the extraordinary complexity and metaphysical subtlety of collective events like the jump dance at Pecwan were
quite lost on Kroeber, reduced to individual displays of profane wealth:

> the idea of organization being absent, there are no cult societies or initia-
> tions. Symbolism is an almost unknown attitude of mind except in mat-
> ters of outright magic: therefore masks, impersonations, altars, and

sacred apparatus, as such, are not employed. The tangible paraphernalia of public ceremony are objects that possess a high property value— wealth that impresses, but nevertheless profane and negotiable wealth. The dances are displays of this wealth as much as they are song and step. All life being individualized rather than socialized. . . . [1925: 3]⁷

Kroeber (after all, a sensitive and intelligent man and an expert observer) described the "song and step" of these dances in an evocative and accurate way:

The northwesterner, particularly in the music of the great dances, loves to leap upwards an octave or more to a long, powerful note, and then sink back from this by a series of slides, often in continuous tonal transition. The accompanists at times chant a rhythmic base pulse without definite melodic relation to the strain. The levels and climaxes vary enormously in pitch, in rhythm, in intensity of intonation. [1925: 96]

Yet Kroeber did not find in this remarkable and highly emotional music ("Indian blues," some people call it today) an interpretive key that might open to him the richer spiritual meanings of the dances and of the wealth that dances in them. While recognizing that this music, with its "plaintiveness" and "emotions," was the means by which the regalia owners and dancers "expressed some of their profoundest feelings," Kroeber lamented that he could not "make a single exact and intelligible remark" about it (1925: 96).

Understanding that the Yuroks were profoundly concerned with individuality, manifested as emotion expressed within contexts of communal spiritual practice, Kroeber could not subject the singers and dancers or the meanings of the regalia that danced with them to positivist reduction and objectification. This was a methodological constraint that had numerous interpretive consequences. Because Kroeber could not objectify affect, neither could he professionally communicate the ways in which Yurok individuality was the basis of a social organization that flowed from a collective spirituality, rather than the sign of an absence or lack of socialization. This is part of what contemporary native northwestern Californians mean when they say that Kroeber "got his facts right" (for which they are grateful), but that he "didn't know what anything meant" (cf. Buckley 1996).

Altogether, these lacks in Kroeber's own salvage ethnography, not in the classic Yurok culture that he reconstructed—lack of attention to nineteenth-century genocide, to spirituality, to subtle systems of community organization and polity, to individuals and their emotional lives, to cultural survival—begin to explain why native peoples in California today focus their bitterness about anthropologists on him. The focus is not arbitrary, although it is somewhat paradoxical. As a Yurok elder once remarked, without the work of the salvage ethnographers of the early twentieth century, including "that good Doctor Kroeber," Yuroks "wouldn't know a thing today about who we really are."

The Yurok jump dance makers at Pecwan in 1984, for instance, were successful in restoring that dance in part because they were able to study accounts of past dances in the works of Kroeber, Edward Gifford, T. T. Waterman, and other ethnographers who were on the river before 1939 (e.g., Kroeber and Gifford 1949). By the same token, R. H. Robins's "Yurok Language: Grammar, Texts, Lexicon" (1958) is of inestimable value in efforts to keep the Yurok language from dying, and many other, seemingly positive examples can be offered. Perhaps Richard Keeling's far more recent book (1992), incorporating many of Kroeber's unpublished field notes, will serve this same creative function in supporting cultural persistence. Yet Jack Norton was indubitably correct in calling Kroeber "ethnocentric" and in stating that Kroeber's 1925 *Handbook* should be entirely reworked (1979: 18). The real question is, by whom?

FOUR

I readily acknowledge the timeliness of Vine Deloria, Jr.'s 1969 clarion call for "anthros" to do something useful for Indian people (by tribal invitation only) or get off their reservations (cf. Deloria 1997). However, it is in part the serendipitous usefulness of ethnographies such as Kroeber and Gifford's 1949 monograph on world renewal, disdained by Deloria's critique, that Duane Champaigne (Chippewa) has more recently acknowledged. Research, Champaigne writes, need not be conducted only at the request of tribal communities. The practical and daily interests of an Indian community will rarely coincide with the research and theoretical interests of academic disciplines. That does not mean that all research should be stopped or that only research with a tangible political or economic benefit to the tribe should proceed. In that case few research projects might go forward, and considerable knowledge may be lost. [Champaigne 1998: 184]

Other native scholars have disagreed, sometimes vehemently, as Elizabeth Cook-Lynn (Crow Creek Sioux) does in calling for an end to virtually all non-Indian writing about Indians in the same volume that Champaigne uses to proclaim that "American Indian studies are for everyone" (Mihesuah 1998).

Earlier on, I looked hopefully to the native people of the lower Klamath themselves for guidance through this ethical thicket, but—quite rightly—they returned my questions to me. About ten years ago I asked the niece of one of the elders who had told me "Indian stories" in the 1970s, a tape recorder on the kitchen table between us, whether she objected to my publishing transcribed versions of her late aunt's stories. The younger woman looked at me with a particular local combination of openness and distance and said, "Auntie gave you those stories for a reason. It was between you and her. You have to decide what to do with them."

What I've decided to do with some of them is to use them in this book, not just to make my own anthropological points but to pass them on. I feel that there is little chance of harm in doing so and that the (quite wonderful) stories and much other native testimony are valuable and to be shared, most of all with native readers in northwestern California who may not have heard them all before. I think the elder would have approved: sometimes she did tell me to "turn off the machine" before continuing with something she wanted to say to me—things that are not in this book.

By the same token, however, I continue listening to the words of another Yurok Indian, equally straightforward, who told me in 1976 that "we want to do our own anthropology now."[8]

All of these apparent contradictions begin to suggest yet other complexities. Strive as he did to capture and arrest "the Yurok" in a timeless ethnographic present, ca. 1849, Kroeber did no more and no less than inscribe his own understanding of classic Yurok culture in ways that were suited to his own academic and political moment (which was a long one). All his writings on the Yuroks were "interpretations," not just the last of them (Kroeber 1959). His successes and failures in capturing "the Yurok" as a species-like "culture" rested, however, not only on his positivist's conceit but on his failure to really recognize (while cataloging individualism as a Yurok culture trait) that Yuroks were individuals, too. What Yuroks told Kroeber about "the Yurok" constituted individuals' own, personal interpretations. These are always, humanly, both varied and mutable and, in the case of the Yurok Indians that Kroeber met, may well have been unusually so. Individually independent, and collectively a people with a deep and vibrant history of intellectual engagement and argument, Yuroks have always offered outsiders diverse accounts of what became known as "Yurok culture."

What I present in this book are my own interpretations. Occasionally they are somewhat masked by attempted near-objectivity; sometimes they are transparently my own. I would like to think that I have learned something about interpreting Yurok spiritualities in a valid way from the elders who taught me in the 1970s and '80s and from contemporary intellectuals and artists in native northwestern California. I have no way of knowing, positively. Local receptions of each of my published essays have been mixed, although encouraging enough for me to rewrite and meld some of these essays together as a book. I expect no more, and certainly do not presume to speak for "the Yurok."

FIVE

The title of this book, *Standing Ground*, is taken from Brian D. Tripp, Jr.'s (Karuk) 1984 mixed media work on paper by the same name. I first saw it just after the 1990 jump dance at Pecwan, where Brian was a participant. A grateful guest, I had stood up to witness the dances themselves, rather than sitting on the benches that are provided for those that need them. Brian gave the painting "his name" while I watched, in his studio in Eureka.

"Is that 'standing *ground*,' " I asked, "or '*standing* ground'?"

"Both," Brian said, "but it's really the standing ground, the place where people stand to watch the dances, different from dancing ground."

The book for which I have borrowed the work's name pays a so-journer's homage, not only to the artist but to all of the American Indian people of northwestern California, past, present, and future. It is a view from the outside, from the standing ground, but it seeks to honor these people who have stood their ground since the myth-time.

With some exceptions, I do not explicate much theory in this book, but rather seek to allow underlying theories to emerge, often implicitly, through my treatment of history and ethnography and through my own interpretations of these. My views of the former and my selections from the latter have been profoundly influenced by my native Californian teachers and colleagues. Those within the anthropological tradition will also recognize my indebtedness to a plethora of social theorists; by and large I refrain from citing these influences in the main text or in footnotes, seeking a wider audience and hoping not to overburden the text.

Briefly, I think that Yurok Indian spirituality provides a significant field in which individual and society meet in dialogue—cooperating, resisting, negotiating, changing each other in manifold ways. Viewed historically, this dialogue has been adaptive and has been a means of cultural survival and ramification. "Culture," here, is not a thing but a process, an emergence through time. In the Yurok case, at least, the formal, structural opposition *individual : society* is but one among the great many counterpoints simultaneously tending toward wholeness, or balance, that constitute the process.

As many people have pointed out in recent years (e.g., Gill 1988), American Indian spirituality tends to manifest itself in action, rather than being articulated as "belief." It is better represented through the witness of performance than by distantiated analyses of extractable, exegetical, or ulterior meanings. Experiential spirituality is anything but fixed, as "belief" (not a category to be found in the Yurok language, by the way) must be, at least for a meaningful time. The Yurok, Hupa, Karuk, and Tolowa dancers and spectators at Pecwan in 1988 and 1990 were at the same time enacting an ancient performance and very much in their own time and specific place. It seemed to me apparent, then and now, that rather than being motivated by a received orthodoxy in which they believed, most participants were coming to *know* what was going on through their own experiences of it. The very difficulty of what they did—singing, dancing, fasting, thirsting, waking—assured this. The dances' efficacy, rooted in received tradition, was equally rooted in the spirits of individuals. The proper methodological challenge for an outsider to take up, then, is that of understanding what other people know, rather than explaining the ulterior meanings of their beliefs.

While the native northwestern Californian people that I have known insist upon their cultural and historical uniqueness, they also, simultaneously, insist upon the common humanity that they share with others. I have come to insist upon this shared humanity, too, and to accept that we can understand each other pretty well if we work at.

I'd like to leave theoretical and methodological commentary at that. With Walt Whitman, in "Song of Myself," I'd gladly sing,

> Backward I see in my own days where I sweated through fog
> with linguists and contenders,
> I have no mockings or arguments, I witness and wait.

But, an academic, I do have arguments.

SIX

I am indeed committed to the role of the ethnographer as witness, rather than explainer of ulterior *significata,* and I've certainly seen that, if we wait long enough, most theoretical contenders' sweats, fogs, and hyper-cleverness shake out eventually. Still, I do contend, I have both political and moral commitments, as well as ethnographic ones, and I am obliged to tell my academic readers more about these things. Besides, the question left hanging above is, *how* to work at it?

My wife and colleague, Jorunn Jacobsen Buckley, insists that her students in the history of religions accept from the outset that "they are smarter than you are"—that the peoples one studies have a better understanding of what they are doing than an outsider possibly can. Her students' task is to understand what those people are telling them, rather than to explain what they are "really" up to.

It is, of course, a classic hermeneutic strategy, rooted in (primarily German) jurisprudence, biblical exegesis, and philosophical phenomenology. That tradition has come down to me, not only through my philosophically trained, European wife, but also through other hermeneuts—Paul Ricoeur and Hans Georg Gadamer particularly—and, above all, the great German sociologist Max Weber. Weber remains nonpareil in the distinctions he drew between understanding (*Verstehen*) and explanation (*Erklären*), and in his demonstrations of the interrelationships between these two epistemologies. Like so many of my generation of humanistic anthropologists, I derive much of my sense of Weber's relevance to my own work through the twentieth-century American cultural anthropologist Clifford Geertz.

I first read Geertz's *Interpretation of Cultures* (1973) in my first year of graduate study, 1975, and his lasting influence on my understandings, particularly through his practice of "thick description," might be attributed either to my naiveté and need for a guiding light at that tenuous and fraught moment in my new life, or to the purity of my untutored intellectual judgment, as yet unsullied by any real knowledge of anthropological theory or sustained reflection upon it. In any case, my admiration for Geertz's approach to things—for, really, his sensibility—has remained largely undiminished by the many critics who have rethought his work in more recent years. I continue to place trust in understanding over explanation, in the sensibilities of Weber and Geertz and their intellectual heirs—against those of, say, Émile Durkheim and Edmund Leach—despite my sense that none of this will matter terribly in the long run; that what will really count, finally, will be the devotedness of our witness.

This somewhat ironic view of both theory and method developed most notably, in my own case, during the great political-intellectual-moral debates of the 1980s and early '90s that were popularized as "the culture wars" and professionalized, with more dignity if no greater descriptive power, as "the postmodern turn." Beginning in 1982, James Clifford's deconstructions of classic ethnology became as strong an influence on my thinking as Weber and Geertz continued to be. At bottom, this was so for entirely parochial reasons; Clifford's essays on ethnographic authority validated my own long-standing doubts about, especially, A. L. Kroeber's Yurok ethnography and afforded me a hermeneutic key with which I might begin establishing these doubts as containing probabilities rather than manifesting simple hunches. In league with Michel Foucault, Clifford actively demonstrated the seeming fact that all ethnography is culturally and historically located and that the objectivity of its inscription is, virtually unavoidably, compromised by the fluxes and flows of (especially, colonial and postcolonial) political-economic power. These processes must inevitably limit the positive scientific objectivity of ethnographic representation.

Influential as he has been for me, however, I early on had some reservations about Clifford's prescription for the impasse posed by the ethnographer's historical location and necessarily accompanying biases. Particularly, though Clifford called for a dialogical ethnography in which the other might speak to a located interlocutor rather than being suppressed and exploited by the ethnographer's monological authority, the ethnographer must necessarily be the final editor of the dialogue for publication. Representational authority can never be entirely relinquished, only displaced to editorship, and it is disingenuous to think that the ethnographer-editor can do otherwise (Buckley 1987). Other critiques can and have been made.

While Clifford Geertz's work has seemed to me—for whatever personal reasons—resistant to the critical challenges raised against it, James Clifford's work and that of several other postmodernists have seemed more vulnerable. These writers, particularly in the 1980s, appeared to claim a certain exceptionalism for their own consciousness, writing as though they themselves were neither culturally nor historically located nor enmeshed in the play of power (if only on the teapot field of academe). They assumed a degree of humanistic objectivity even while deconstructing scientific objectivity. It was a neat trick, largely accomplished by substituting irony for putative objectivity to infer their access to privileged truth.

Despite the use of irony as epistemological tactic, with its relinquishing of moral and political certitude, the postmodern critique of ethnology was at heart moralistic, implicitly condemning the immorality of alleged collusion between social science and colonialism even while rejecting all moralism and also, alas, the maturity of any political commitment.

Eventually, one way out of the moral and epistemological impasse posed by postmodernism that came to appeal to many of us was to fall back on perhaps the most ancient of intellectual strategies, storytelling. With its recognition—even celebration—of voice and polyphony, reportage and imagination, dialogue and contradiction, it was, after all, the principal means by which others had been demonstrating to ethnographers, all along, that they were "smarter than we are."[9]

Of those who have been exploring the use and implications (moral, political, epistemological, and aesthetic) of narrative for understanding North American Indians over the past thirty-odd years, Robin Ridington has had a particular influence on me. As Geertz's thick description and Clifford's (at bottom, commonsensical) deconstructions of scholarly authority simply struck me as right, from the outset, so did my sense of Ridington's getting it right about Indian people seem to me trustworthy from early on. One way to add thickness to description, he shows, is to let everybody tell stories—informants as much as ethnographers, this theorist as much as that, the left side of his own brain as much as the right, all taking turns, even narrating simultaneously. Such polyphonic narration creates a large pool of voices (over which, albeit, the ethnographic writer must retain editorial authority) through or upon which readers might wade or swim or walk, coming to the other side with a changed understanding (of which the writer must finally relinquish control). It is, if nothing else, a more modest undertaking than constructing a line of data and argument, straight and narrow, along which the reader is marched toward a foreordained, explanatory conclusion: "I have shown that. . . ."

This approach seems all the more right to me since it is in agreement with the approach taken by the Yurok intellectuals and storytellers whose sensibilities I have been, all along, trying to comprehend. It is an alternate sort of "ethnomethodology." And besides, I agree with Harry Roberts that non-Indians have, largely, historically failed to understand Indian people because white people tend to "explain too much." Overexplanation not only precludes, to some extent, understanding (whose tool it should be, as Weber argued, rather than an end in itself); it also, in the view of many Yurok Indians at least, "steals" people's opportunity to learn for themselves, to create their own, authentic understanding.

I have done my best to respect the importance of such opportunities, as my Yurok teachers would have wanted me to do. Some readers will undoubtedly be more annoyed than enlightened by my approach—this is inevitable in our contentious and didactic academic world. Yet I trust that other readers will put the many voices and the many stories that they tell together for themselves, in ways that authentically reflect and respond to these readers' emergent and varied comprehensions, to take pleasure in this, and to appreciate the appropriateness of representing another, historically oppressed people in this way.

An awareness of historical and, more subtly, ongoing oppression of American Indian peoples is crucial to an outsider's understanding them, although professional obliviousness to this subordination and oppression earmarks much Boasian salvage ethnology.

In 1938, as Europe braced for the great conflagration that appeared inevitable, at least to Jews, an exasperated Edward Sapir wrote to A. L. Kroeber,

> You find anchorage—as most people do, for that matter—in an imaginatively sundered system of cultural and social values in the face of which the individual has almost to apologize for presuming to exist at all. It seems to me that if people were less amenable to cultural and social mythology we'd have less Hitlerism in the world. [Sapir to Kroeber, August 25, 1938; held by Victor Golla]

Kroeber's rendering all individuals, together with their joys and sufferings, irrelevant in the face of the "superorganic" cultural "fabrics" and the grand developmental "sweeps and contours" of the history of civilizations that he had theoretically constructed (Kroeber, var: see Buckley 1996) contributed to what would later come to be called essentialism and totalization, and Sapir seems to have understood early on the latent connection between a totalizing turn of ethnological mind and political totalitarianism. Even earlier, in his later years Max Weber had condemned the sociology that he himself had significantly helped to invent as frightening in its cold rejection of concern for the minds and spirits of its individual subjects, in the arrogance of its claims to privileged, totalized social and historical truth, in its "sacrifice of love" (in Rabinow 1991).

Taking a step back, to more "careful" words and less contentious ground,[10] we should note that Kroeber's theoretical and methodological elimination of individuality as significant in ethnological representation and argument constituted his resolution of "the squabbles among the early Boasians over the individual and culture." It posited one pole in these squabbles, with Paul Radin's insistence on the primacy of individuality in cultural formation staking out the other (Fox 1991: 104–6). Yet whether individuals shape cultures or cultures shape individuals seems, today, an anachronistic question. For some time, the apparent answer for many anthropologists has been *both* (e.g., Bourdieu 1978). A better question today might be, does "a culture," in the Boasian sense, ever exist at all, as individuals undeniably do (e.g., Abu-Lughod 1991)?

Yea or nay, "culture" is, as Claude Lévi-Strauss said of totems, "good to think." The central problem in Kroeber's Yurok ethnography is not his reification of Boasian culture in his own, virtually metaphysical, typal "civilizations" so much as in the methodology that he developed in order to analyze and explain these civilizations, or cultures.

To "rework" Kroeber's Yurok ethnography, as Jack Norton called for someone to do, a new ethnographer must understand just how Kroeber's version was constructed, how it was intended to work, and to what purposes. It does not suffice simply to select from it, rephrasing these selections in a manner more pleasing by contemporary standards. In light of a now extensive body of discursive and postcolonial theory, it is necessary to ask if and, if so, how a particular model for inscribing ethnography—A. L. Kroeber's in the present case—reflects structures and processes of domination and subordination in the world inhabited by the ethnographer and her subjects (understood by Kroeber as objects) alike.

James Axtell observed that "the meaning of an event is perpetually open to revision; its meaning for successive generations will be different from its contemporary meaning" (1981: vii). This ethnohistorian's observation can be applied as appropriately to cultural epochs as to historical events. What contemporary native critics of Kroeber's salvage ethnography wish to find in a reworking of it will not necessarily be any more true to their ancestors' lives than Kroeber's account was, although it will certainly be more true to the meanings attributed to those lives today. It may be politically and morally satisfying for outsiders (spectators) to simply turn over cultural inscription to insiders (dancers), but it will not necessarily bring us all any closer to valid, historically contextualized truth, however much both parties might wish that anthros could leave off and go find more useful work elsewhere.

The continuing strains between anthropologists and native people can be understood as resulting from native awareness that ethnographers have traditionally served the interests of dominant societies rather than those of the peoples these societies have subordinated. Native American resistance to further ethnologization by white intellectuals has contributed to a more general crisis of meaning and purpose in anthropology, to which solutions have been sought through broad but coherent spectrums of critical theories and of linked ethnographic experiments, in North America as elsewhere. Addressing this ongoing crisis in anthropological representation, Richard Fox asks,

> Can we learn to celebrate encounters other than those mediated by the ethnographer on the spot? Can we textualize encounters, for example, mediated by histories of domination and resistance, which helped produce the alter egos ethnographers found when they went looking for others? New texts . . . need not, probably dare not, abandon all the conventions that characterized the fieldwork done by anthropologists and were textualized in the ethnography, especially the concern for everyday life, participant observation, cultural relativism, and most recently, self-reflection. New texts, however, can augment these conventions of fieldwork with other textual concerns, such as historical process, individual intention, and the relations from afar that structure inequality in local, everyday life. [Fox 1991: 95]

In the case of the Yurok Indians and their neighbors (that network of interdependencies called "native northwestern California"), "histories of domination" and "relations from afar that structure inequality" include the history of regional ethnographies and relations with ethnographers themselves. A "celebration" of these peoples who have stood their ground, resisting domination, and of the role of their spirituality in their physical and cultural survival needs, then, to include portions of the history of ethnology within it. While the history of anthropology is customarily viewed as a separate subdiscipline from ethnography, they need now to be brought together, in dialogue as dual orienting discourses in what George Marcus has called a "multi-sited research imaginary" (1998: 3 ff.). This is necessary for several reasons.

At the simplest level, the native northwestern Californians with whom I've had the most to do and whose lives I find most compelling understand themselves today, to a greater or lesser extent, in partial response to what has been written about them. More complexly, ethnographic and linguistic contributions function not only to support cultural persistence and vitalization but also to change cultures. Vine Deloria, Jr., long ago noted ways that the ethnologization of American Indian peoples has changed those peoples' self-understanding, nurturing an objectified, static, self-conscious notion of "culture" itself, located in social behaviors and physical objects deemed traditional (Deloria 1981). More recently, critical theorists have expanded such analyses of cultural objectification and identity politics by emphasizing the role of ethnologically inspired cultural essentialism in contemporary indigenous identity formation in the postcolonial world, including native California (e.g., Haley and Wilcoxon 1997).

Cultural essentialism rooted in ethnographic representations has been critiqued not only as a source of suspect neotraditional identity among "culturalist," "neo-Kroeberian" (L. Field 1999) California Indians, but also as the basis for assumptions that undermine outsiders' well-intentioned efforts to address very real, entirely modern suffering in native communities. Mental health care providers at Indian Health Service clinics serving Yurok Indian women, Mariana Ferreira argued, ignore Richard Fox's ongoing "relations from afar that structure inequality in local, everyday life" in treating dysfunctional native families because they assume that "the Yurok" simply *are* "bad mothers" (paper presented at the Annual Meetings of the American Anthropological Association, 1996): being a neglectful and withholding mother is a "Yurok" trait, according to, especially, Erik Erikson, the authoritative voice on Yurok psychology whose chapter on "the Yurok" in his ever-green *Childhood and Society* was written in collaboration with A. L. Kroeber (see chapter 9, below).

Various orders of feedback from ethnography to the others that ethnographers have textualized are parts of the mutually transformative dialogue between anthropologists and their subjects that has been going on in North America since the nineteenth century (Bruner 1986). Any truly new account of those others must acknowledge such cybernetics.

At yet another level, one must ask how Fox's historical process, individual intention, and relations from afar came to be omitted from one's predecessors' work, and whether these omissions reflected the structures of domination that the people the ethnographers tried to "celebrate" were themselves resisting. And how have such omissions and unacknowledged resistance fed back into the lives and self-understandings of the native people that one would textualize now? Before addressing the last two parts of this question, we also have to ask how our predecessors' texts have conditioned our own scholarly work, which, by definition as scholarship, must both build on and respond to these texts. If self-reflection is indeed among the anthropological conventions that we dare not abandon (Fox), it is not, I agree, "the self-scrutinizing author's voice in recent ethnographic writing [that] often seems to me simple narcissism designed to obviate dialectical critique and mask unconsidered subtexts that needs to be saved" (Whiteley 1998: 195). Rather, it is dialectical critique itself, an effort to come to terms with the ways in which other anthropologists (and academic professionalism itself) have come to dominate our own thinking and the ways in which we have come to resist them, both, since resistance can foster as much distortion in our accounts of third-party others as the domination of earlier experts that we resist.

Clifford Geertz compared doing ethnography to entering a "hall of mirrors" in which (native) interpretations of (native) interpretations of (native) interpretations . . . *n*, reflect and refract and repeat. Somehow, the ethnographer, as meta-interpreter of culture, must sort all of this out. Certainly this is true in native northwestern California, where collective spirituality is so largely verbalized in varying individual interpretations of individual experiences of it (a fact that Kroeber himself never fully grasped). But here, in northwestern California as in a great many other American Indian networks that were visited by salvage ethnographers at the beginning of the twentieth century, the images reflected and refracted and repeated in the hall of mirrors include the images previous ethnographers have made and, too, images of those ethnographers themselves.

Once again, "the Yurok," as "a culture" were originally created by ethnographers as an epistemic object for empirical study (Powers 1877[1976]). That object has been (culturally!) coherent with the objectives of colonial domination and the prerequisites for management of indigenous populations by colonial bureaucrats. The first, failed federal attempts to treat with a few of the peoples who were to become "the Yurok" were signed, in 1851, with personal marks by the independent headmen of five quite different and independent villages (Heizer 1972). It was only with the greatest reluctance and resistance that the descendants of those headmen and of the people they claimed to represent finally capitulated, one hundred and forty years later, and agreed to become the fully organized Yurok Indian Tribe. By then, this was the only means by which these peoples could retain control of the remnants of their aboriginal land base or a modicum of political autonomy. It was also the only means through which they could compete with other regional "tribes" (which were all constructed through similar histories) for the federal funds that had become necessary to assure moderate well-being during the intervening century and a half of systematic impoverishment under colonial domination. "The Yurok," then, as a culture and as a society are not truly an indigenous people but the creation of colonial bureaucrats and ethnologists, and the reflections of *both* sorts of actors are included among contemporary Yurok interpretations of their own spirituality.

The reflections of past ethnologists are not merely reflections of these men and women's times, I would add, but of *their* individualities as well. A. L. Kroeber was not simply a token of an Edwardian positivist and Boasian anthropological type. Rather, his omission of, specifically, Fox's "historical process, individual intention, and the relations from afar that structure inequality in local, everyday life" in his account of "the Yurok" (whom he had a very strong hand in inventing) reflects his own individual theoretical intentions as much as the shared objectivism and liberal progressivism of his scientific era in Germanophile America. The line between historicist analysis and ad hominem interpretation has never been as well defined as we might have liked it to be nor is it, necessarily, illuminating to insist upon it.

We cannot disregard Kroeber's (or Richard Keeling's, or my own) individual intentions, then, any more than we can continue to disregard the individual intentions of native northwestern Californians as Kroeber himself so adamantly did. The hall of mirrors in which we perceive the latter incorporates the images of all parties concerned, including ourselves. There is nowhere else to stand but in our own consciousness, however much we might reduce its subjectivity through methodological objectivity, or irony. This is the sort of dialectical critique (Whiteley), it seems to me, that is necessary at the beginning of the twenty-first century to, finally, write anthropologically about the spirituality of Yurok Indians, manifested through and shaped by culturally mediated historical processes.

In *Standing Ground* I make no effort to wrap up Yurok history and "Yurok culture" in any complete or final way. I want, rather, to tell a story in increments, leaving plenty of room for others to revise and to fill in missing pieces that are important to them, to argue with me, and to present their own interpretations. This story is at once the Yuroks' and my own. Sometimes the latter appears as fragments of autobiography; always it is there in my interpretations. The story begins where Kroeber's left off, in 1850. It ends in 1990, the last time I saw the feathers dance at Pecwan, while the Yurok Indian Tribe was moving toward the full, federally acknowledged organization it achieved in 1993. Much has changed in Yurok life in the decade since then—materially, at least, for the better. Readers should remember that the "ethnographic present" of this book is at heart the nineteen years between 1971 and 1990. My book is, in short, already out of date.

SEVEN

Standing Ground is divided into three sections. The first, "Contexts," sketches aspects of the Yuroks' historical location, my own interpretive location, and the location of published academic anthropology.

Chapter 1 is a brief overview of the history of the Yurok Indian Reservation since 1850. This historical sketch includes two Yurok narrations, the first a poem by Florence Shaughnessy, the second a speech by Robert Spott. Thus, the chapter also introduces the polyvocal and dialogical approach that I have taken throughout the book.

Chapter 2, a history of my connections with Yurok Indians and their neighbors, begins to specify my own location as interpreter. I was first drawn to the Yuroks through another non-Indian, Harry Kellett Roberts, long before I turned to the practice of anthropology. My relationship with Harry as his student, and his with an adoptive Yurok lineage of teachers reaching deep into the nineteenth century, bring individuality, improvisation, and historical transformation all to the foreground as problems in understanding.

Chapter 3 examines books about native northwestern California written by local native authors in the twentieth century, and these works' relationships to non-Indian academic publications, like my own. In it, I survey five books published by native northwestern Californian intellectuals between 1916 and 1994. These books are interpreted as negotiating a variety of near-silences about genocide, non-native ethnographers, and spirituality. Such near-silences are imposed and are broken, through time, and the books have been locally accepted or rejected as a result of processes that parallel those shaping and reshaping academic texts by metropolitan intellectuals through time. By virtue of this parallelism and in light of anthropology's own doctrinal cultural relativism, neither indigenous nor metropolitan texts, such as the present one, may be viewed as finally definitive or as offering privileged access to truth.

The second section, "Testimonies," contains three longer chapters. The first two, on Yurok men's spiritual training and on "Indian doctors," are based in elders' narratives and testimony and make clear the place of immediate individual experience in Yurok spirituality.

Chapter 4 introduces varieties of physical and spiritual personal "training" through which Yurok individuals have nurtured experiential knowledge in the past and through which they continue to do so today. I treat these practices in a largely descriptive manner, eschewing generalized analyses of them while laying the ethnographic groundwork for a later critique of received anthropological and psychological reductions.

Chapter 5 continues in a descriptive vein, detailing a typology of communal spiritual experts—"doctors"—evoked largely through native testimony and storytelling. As in the preceding chapter, this testimony is drawn as much as possible from the period between 1907, when Kroeber's most intensive field work on the Klamath River came to an end, and 1991, the last year of my own formal research in the region.

In chapter 6 the descriptive approach followed in chapters 4 and 5 is interrogated in terms of its relationships with broader structures of colonial and postcolonial domination. Trait-based approaches to describing "a culture" are shown to be congruent with the objectification of the natural world as "resources." These theoretical concerns are explored through examining "the GO-road case" of the 1970s and '80s—a legal conflict over Indian use of mountain training sites. In this case, which ultimately reached the U.S. Supreme Court in 1984, federally supported logging companies sought to expropriate public lands in the inland mountain region that provide the environment for the highest levels of indigenous spiritual training. The case ultimately tested Yuroks' Constitutional claim to freedom of religion. My primary focus in chapter 6, however, is on federal bureaucratic culture rather than on the Yuroks, and this chapter introduces the "multi-sited" (Marcus) dialogical ethnography mentioned above.

While this second section rests very largely on narratives and storytelling, the third section, "Understandings," continues entering native testimony into the record while also including, more centrally than before, my own interpretations of that testimony. This third section contains five chapters of varying length, written in a variety of anthropological voices.

Chapters 7 and 8 are intentionally impressionistic short essays on two major themes in Yurok lives, "wealth" and "the world."

The Yuroks have long been stereotyped in the anthropological literature as acquisitive and hoarding—"primitive capitalists," as Walter Goldschmidt had it. In chapter 7, I suggest that capitalist wealth and Yurok wealth are two quite different things, and that Yurok sacred wealth, especially in the form of dance regalia, is both functionally communal and, interpretatively, emblematic of life-force itself, rather than being quintessentially material.

This life-force, "spirit," is ultimately identified with "that which exists," *ki ?wesonah*—also, "the world." Chapter 8 interprets this world as the processual outcome of the play of life and death. The "world renewal" ceremonials in which wealth is displayed are intended to achieve proper balance between these two great energies and all that they epitomize for native northwestern Californians.

There is peril in acknowledging death as the immutable equal partner to life in all existence, and that peril is commonly realized by human beings in melancholy. In chapter 9, I return to a more scholarly and analytic voice to examine the relationship between major depression and Yurok doctoring. The Kroeberian understanding of a culture as essentialized in a configuration of specific traits, shared by the psychologist Erik Erikson, emphasizes the incommensurability of different cultures. Yurok doctors' own melancholy, however, can best be understood not as a diagnostic trait identifying a discrete "Yurok culture," but as individual experience so widespread in space and time as to be, arguably, universal. (It is, for instance, an experience that Kroeber himself shared with his Yurok others.) What is culturally relative is not, I argue, the experience of depression, but the ways different individuals interpret it and the communal uses to which they do or do not put it.

In chapter 10, I take up historical aspects of Yurok spirituality more directly in an interpretation of the Indian Shaker Church that was introduced on the Klamath River in 1926 and that offered a new, historically appropriate context for Indian doctors' use of their healing powers. I argue that this Christian church was accurately understood by its adherents as a "continuation" or "evolution" of indigenous spirituality. Finally, the earlier Yurok jump dance, moribund since 1939, which reemerged in the 1980s through the efforts of individuals who viewed the Shaker Church as un-Yurok, is understood, rather, as a historically dialogical "evolution" of the church itself.

Dialogue thus becomes explicit as the theoretical trope informing my understanding of the history of Yurok Indian spirituality throughout the entire book. Chapter 11 examines the contemporary revival of the Yurok jump dance at the village of Pecwan, inaugurated in 1984 and still ongoing. I interpret the jump dance as an arena of social as well as spiritual discourse. Neither a fixed, immemorial form (or trait complex) nor an interest-based discursive innovation, the jump dance springs, every two years, from the dialogical tensions between these. The effort to resolve received form and ongoing creativity is seen as the process that fixes the social world by reaffirming and renewing spiritual experience within that world. This dynamic, narrated in Yurok creation myths, appears to be ancient. A fixed and static constellation of traits that can be totalized as "the jump dance" has never existed; indeed, the dance could neither have survived nor have had any efficacy if it did. It has always, since the myth-time, been a temporal emergence conditioned by individual agency exercised in dialogue.

Chapter 11 makes my overall interpretive orientation explicit and can be read as a "Conclusion," although in terms of my own theoretical approach, there can be no conclusion to works such as *Standing Ground: Yurok culture and the jump dance*, like cultural anthropology itself, continue to emerge through constant historical change, negotiated through communal dialogue among individuals.

NOTE ON ORTHOGRAPHY

I do not speak the Yurok language (few do today) and transcribe it only haltingly. The Yuroks have been part of an English speech community since the early years of the twentieth century (although many individuals have been multilingual all along), and I have avoided using Yurok except when it alone is appropriate, as in writing about pre-1915 communities and individuals or when quoting Yurok speakers.

Orthographies for transcribing Yurok have been contested for many years, on the river and off. The only one that I am fully familiar with and maintain confidence in is the phonemic orthography developed by R. H. Robins (1958). It is clearly superior to Kroeber's and others' phonetic transcriptions and I have retranscribed these, using Robins's phonology, when necessary.

In Robins's orthography most Yurok phonemes approximate familiar letters of the English alphabet in their phonetic effects. The following pronunciation guide covers, also approximately, only those that do not.

Robins orthography	Example	Effect	Approximate English equivalent
kʷ	kʷescinᵃ	off-glide	quiet
ʔ	wesʔonahᵇ	glottal stop	uh-oh, Hawaii
·	na·mulᶜ	prolongs a vowel	waay back
ɹ	mɹwɹsɹgɹhᵈ	vowel sound	church
ł	ta·łᵉ	lateral fricative	like Welsh ll
č	čekᶠ	soft c	champ
š	šekʷšewᵍ	soft s	she

In addition, Yurok phonology distinguishes between glottalized and non-glottalized consonants:

ḱ	ḱetḱelʰ
ṕ	ho·leṕⁱ
t́	t́olt́olʲ

ᵃstrawberry
ᵇsky
ᶜto carry a load
ᵈbeautiful
ᵉceremonial dancer
ᶠwren
ᵍclam
ʰsweet colt's foot
ⁱto investigate (must be inflected)
ʲmud, swampy ground

PART ONE Contexts

1 The Yurok Reservation

Once I saw a bunch of red currants that were just so perfect
I couldn't pick them. That's when I first began to see
all of my jewelry, for those red currants are rubies
and I leave them all for my children.

And I want to leave my children all of my garnets
the wild strawberries. I leave my gold
which is the gold in salmon berries, and my silver
the raindrops seen in the moonlight.

There are opals, too, when the moon shines on the water
which has been ruffled by the wind. The diamonds I leave
are the raindrops caught in a spider web, and my pearls
are raindrops caught in cobwebs.

My onyx is in the blackberries that grow everywhere
and the thimble berries are more rubies. My amethyst,
lavender, is the young salal berries.

I have a few more jewels but I haven't dug them up yet. I did see another golden
treasure when I was out at Doctor Rock. There's a kind of fungus there that
turns golden, and there were spider webs over it. The spider webs make all the
difference. When you get up early in the morning when it's all covered with dew,
then you see it: just a shining patch of gold under that sheet of cobwebs. Another
thing that I have observed in my lifetime is the migration of spiders, which filled
the air with silver. The spiders were on the south side of the river, and they let
out long webs that made sails like parachutes and the wind carried them across
the river. There were silver streaks all over the river.

These are the treasures that I leave for the children.

Florence Shaughnessy (Yurok), 1978

Non-Indians first settled in Yurok territory during the gold rush of 1849. Varied white interests defeated ratification of an 1851 treaty that would have created a large reservation. The ensuing armed conflict between Yuroks and whites extended into the mid-1860s.

In 1855 President Franklin Pierce, by executive order, established the Klamath River Reservation in Yurok territory, a military zone along the lower twenty miles of the river. (Thus the Yuroks were a federally recognized tribe early on.) In 1864 Congress authorized a total of four reservations in the state of California. These included the twelve-by-twelve-square-mile Hoopa Valley Reservation on the Trinity River, occupied by Hupa, Yurok, and other Indian people. In the 1880s and 1890s, the validity of the 1855 Klamath River Reservation came under attack. The dispute was resolved in 1891, when President Benjamin Harrison issued an executive order enlarging the

Hoopa Reservation by creating a "connecting strip" or "addition," joining the questionable Klamath River Reservation to the fully authorized Hoopa Valley Indian Reservation. The process resulted in the formation of an Extension to the Hoopa Square, a strip one mile wide on either side of the Klamath River running downriver from the Square at the junction of the Klamath and the Trinity River to the Pacific. The Square came to be popularly understood as a Hupa Indian reservation; the Extension was occupied primarily by Yuroks and is now called the Yurok Reservation. Three communal "rancherias" have also been granted to primarily Yurok residents on the coast, at Big Lagoon, Trinidad, and Klamath (Resighini).

In 1891 the Extension consisted of 58,168 acres. After 1892, however, lands in the Extension were allotted to Yurok families under the Dawes Act, and the putative "surplus" lands were opened to whites. Timber companies and others bought up many allotments through questionable forced fee patents, and eventually controlled 87 percent of the Extension. In 1990, only about 6,800 communal acres remained in the Yurok Reservation, although Yuroks held an additional approximately 2,000 allotted acres.

SURVIVAL

By 1910 Yurok population had reached its nadir. Although the deeply reduced surviving population slowly began to increase after 1910, Yuroks were plagued by governmental indifference and oppressed by non-Indian landholders. Salmon canneries, beginning in 1877, provided some wage labor until they were closed in 1934, when all Indian commercial fishing and subsistence gill netting were also banned. Yuroks sought relief from poverty and malnutrition through assured access to aboriginal subsistence sites alienated by the allotment process. Robert Spott, an influential speaker from Requa, at the mouth of the Klamath, described Yurok people's situation to a newly sympathetic white audience at San Francisco's Commonwealth Club in 1926:

> We are California Indians from the Klamath River, and I am here to tell you that we are almost at the end of the road. My English is broken, but

I will explain to you as near as I can. In the old time, away back, we had a place where we used to go and pick berries for our winter supply. Then again, we had a hunting ground where we killed the game for our winter supply. And again, we had a place where we used to go to gather acorns for our winter supply. Then again, we could go up along the river to where a fishing place was left to us. But today, when we go back to where we used to find our berries, there is the sign "Keep out." What are we going to do?

Then again we go to where we used to go to hunt. You see the sign again, "Keep out. No shooting allowed." All right. We go away. Then again, we go down to where we used to fish. That is taken up by white men. What are we going to do? We cannot do anything.

There is a strip along the Klamath River which you have heard is an Indian reservation. It is a mile on each side of the river. Yes, it is. There are some good lands. Do you think that we own it? No. It is homesteaded by white men.

Then again, there is the Indian reservation at Upper Klamath that they have allotted to us. The Indians are stationed in an Indian village. The surveyor comes and he says, "There is land for you. You locate over there." Well, that land is no good. We want the land where we used to pick berries. But "No. That is homesteaded already. You have to take this."

You hear that Indians will not work on their homes. But they will work if the land is good. We cannot raise anything upon rocks or in gravel.

Are we not native sons of these United States? I did make up my mind in the war that I am American and I went across overseas to fight for this country. Then the officers came to me while I was overseas and they told me, "You are alright. You fought for your country." I just gave them a smile and I thought to myself, "Where is my country when I get home?"

There are many Indian women who are almost blind, and they only have one meal a day, because there is no one to look after them. Most of these people used to live on fish which they cannot get, and on acorns, and they are starving. They hardly have any clothing to cover them. Many children up along the Klamath River have passed away with disease. Most of them from tuberculosis. There is no road into here where the Indians are. The only road they have got is the Klamath River. To reach doctors they have to take their children down the Klamath River, to the mouth of the Klamath. It is 24 miles to Crescent City, where we have to go for doctors. It costs us $25.00. Where are the poor Indians to get this money from to get a doctor for their children? They go from place to place to borrow money. If they cannot get it, the poor child dies without aid. Inside of four or five years more there will be hardly any Indians left upon the Klamath River. . . .

So I am here to tell you how we are standing up along the Klamath River. Often we see a car go past. It is the Indian Service. Do you suppose the man driving that car would stop? Always he has no time for the Indians, and the car with some one from the U.S.A. Indian Service goes past just like a tourist. When he does come to his office . . . just the minute he sees an Indian coming in he meets him by the door, and he says "I got business to do. I have not got any time for you. I will be back in two days." When he comes back the Indians will be sitting outside of that house waiting for him, and he just goes right through the Indians, and into the house, and comes right out again. But if he sees a white man there, he will stop in front of the white man and whisper to him. . . . And just the minute the Indians are waiting in front of the Government building there will be two or three white men in there talking with him. [Spott 1926: 133–35][1]

Robert Spott and others fought for greater equity through the (unacknowledged) Yurok Tribal Organization in the 1930s, but aboriginal subsistence rights were not supported until 1975, when year-round hunting rights in remaining Extension lands were restored. Salmon gill netting rights on the lower Klamath were not returned to the Yuroks until 1977.

TRIBAL ORGANIZATION

From 1932 to 1933, Hupa Indians organized as the Hoopa Valley Indian Tribe, with a tribal council duly elected and a constitution and bylaws formally accepted by the federal government in 1952. Although a federally recognized tribe and creating the Yurok Tribal Organization, the Yuroks, however, failed in their efforts to have a constitution approved and thus to achieve full federal acknowledgment. Timber companies, anxious to log the Hoopa Square, urged the Bureau of Indian Affairs (BIA) to exercise its authority to sell reservation timber. The BIA agreed to do so, but declined to distribute income from the sales until the Hoopa Valley Indian Tribe prepared a tribal roll and defined membership in its constitution. This was done between 1949 and 1955. That year, Jessie Short (Yurok-Hupa) filed suit on behalf of the Yuroks of the Square and the Extension, claiming that the Hoopa Valley Indian Tribe's membership definition was illegal, and that Yuroks had a right to a share in the timber revenues. Jessie Short *v.* United States was asserted in the United States Court of Claims in 1963. The court decided in the Yuroks' favor in 1973. The timber funds continued to be held in trust, however, pending federal acknowledgment of a Yurok tribal organization, while a number of companion or collateral suits were also brought.

In 1988 the federal Hupa-Yurok Settlement Act was passed, in part to resolve issues that arose in the Jessie Short case. The Square and its remaining timber went to the approximately 1,700 enrolled Hupa Indians, the far smaller Extension going to the more numerous Yuroks, together with exclusive Indian fishing rights in the lower Klamath. The timber trust funds (now called the Settlement Funds) were earmarked for per capita payments and for tribal use by the Yuroks when they were organized. A Yurok Transition Team was appointed by the Department of the Interior to oversee compilation of a Yurok roll and disbursement of the Settlement Funds, to set priorities for management of the Yurok Reservation, and to prepare for organization. More than 8,000 people applied for enrollment, subject to BIA approval and appeals. By the late summer of 1991, there were approximately 3,500 officially enrolled Yurok Indians. An Interim Council was elected later that year to serve for two years. It was charged with drafting a tribal constitution and overseeing the election of a Yurok Tribal Council in 1993. The Interim Council, however, did not wave Yurok rights to continue contesting the terms of the Settlement Act in court.

FORMAL EDUCATION

Yurok people at Requa were suing for the right of their children to attend public schools as early as the mid-1880s. Although some Yurok Indians were enrolled in BIA boarding schools on the Hoopa Valley Reservation and elsewhere, Yuroks did not attend public high schools in any numbers until after World War II. A very few Yurok men and women had begun seeking higher education in the San Francisco Bay area in the 1930s. In the 1960s, with the expansion of the California state higher education system, local opportunities for college and university education increased dramatically.

The first book by a Yurok author, Lucy Thompson's *To the American Indian*, was published in 1916. English had become the primary language on the Klamath River by 1915, but the late 1960s also brought grassroots efforts, led by Yurok elders, to retain the rapidly disappearing Yurok language and traditional culture through elementary, high school, and college programs.

MEDICAL CARE

The number of traditional Yurok "Indian doctors" declined rapidly after 1849, although a very few herbalists and modern Indian doctors continue to practice today. Affordable biomedical care, however, became absolutely necessary with the introduction of nonindigenous diseases. In the past century, a BIA hospital operated on the Hoopa Reservation until 1956 and was replaced briefly by a private hospital that opened in 1960. In 1974 the clinic that had grown out of that hospital came under Indian control, funded by the United Indian Health Services, Inc., which had also established the Tsurai Health Center on the Trinidad Rancheria in the late 1960s. In 1990 the Tsurai Health Center had over 5,000 active files.

By the 1980s, in addition to a variety of public health problems common on many reservations, Yurok Indians living along the Klamath became particularly concerned about the effects of herbicides containing 2,4D. These had been applied by the Forest Service and by timber companies since the 1970s to retard deciduous growth, increasing the yield of coniferous timber. The herbicides appeared to pose a serious threat to human health and reproduction, as well as to anadromous fish stocks and to supplies of acorns and other vital subsistence, medicinal, and craft resources.

ECONOMIC DEVELOPMENT

Over the past hundred years, in addition to work related to fish packing, Yuroks have found seasonal employment in the hops fields of northern

California and southern Oregon, and on the lily bulb farms of the coastal plain near the Smith River, on the California-Oregon border. Yurok men have enlisted in the armed services since World War I, many Yurok men and women have worked in the San Francisco Bay area since the years of the Great Depression, and Indian people continue to leave northwestern California, often only temporarily, in search of employment. Many Yuroks have entered the law and other professions. But above all, throughout the twentieth century logging and commercial and subsistence fishing have been central to the economic welfare of the Yuroks.

By the 1970s careless corporate logging, causing silting in of spawning beds, had proven detrimental to salmon fishing. Herbicides, overfishing by foreign and domestic commercial offshore fleets, and river water levels lowered by upstream dams also contributed to the endangerment of the Klamath and Trinity Rivers' salmon stocks. In August 1978, Indian gill netting rights, restored the previous year, were unexpectedly placed under moratorium as a conservation measure, and armed agents of the United States Fish and Wildlife Service moved in, instigating a "salmon war." The following year the federal government, attempting to restore peace, again allowed restricted gill netting, assured Indian rights to subsistence fishing, and mandated salmon harvest allocations. The allocation system worked, however imperfectly, through the 1980s, and two small Yurok-managed salmon hatcheries were established in the Extension. Still, depletion of salmon stocks continued. Furthermore, with declining timber reserves and increasingly stringent environmental regulations, logging and milling industries in the region could no longer be depended upon as reliable sources of income.

A bingo parlor was established on the Trinidad Rancheria in the 1980s, and in 1991 Big Lagoon Rancheria invested in a major hotel in Arcata, California; further economic development was still needed. For many Yuroks, building more plentiful and adequate housing, improving reservation roads and water systems, supplying electric service to the entire Extension, increasing the tribal land base through restoration of alienated portions of aboriginal territory, and securing a greater share in the sport fishing and tourism industries of the lower Klamath were all high priorities in 1991.

SPIRITUALITY AND THE ARTS

Christian missionaries had little success on the lower Klamath until the 1920s, when Protestant sects began to gain converts. In addition, in 1926 Jimmy Jack (Yurok) started proselytizing for the syncretic Indian Shaker Church. Three Shaker churches were built in Yurok territory, introducing what were to become new traditions in healing as well as other religious practices. The ongoing Shaker congregation at Johnsons, on the Yurok Reservation, was perhaps the strongest in California in 1990, and many Yuroks supported other churches. Earlier traditional ways continued as well.

In 1849 the Yuroks had six (or possibly seven) great regional renewal ceremonies, but by 1909 only three survived. The last of these, the jump dance at Pecwan, seemed to succumb in 1939, but in 1984 it was held again. The jump dance, whose purpose is to renew humanity spiritually and physically and to stamp out sickness, has been taking place at Pecwan every other year since 1984, following the traditional cycle, and by 1990 seemed firmly reestablished. Brush dances, three-day child-curing ceremonials, also still flourish as a major expression of Yurok spirituality. Former brush dance house-pits were rebuilt at Weitchpec and at Pecwan, following a disastrous flood in 1964. Another was reexcavated in 1976 and 1980 at the former site of a Yurok village now in Redwood National Park, on the south side of the mouth of the Klamath. Today, Yuroks continue making new brush dance songs, in both Yurok and English, along with new men's gambling and jump dance songs.

This creativity has included continued production of indigenous crafts. For example, excellent dance regalia, baskets, redwood canoes, and traditional cuisine are all being made today. Fine artists have emerged in recent years, some achieving national recognition for their modern improvisations rooted in local craft traditions and spirituality.

RELIGIOUS FREEDOM

From early on, Yuroks held the desecration of Indian gravesites on aboriginal lands now occupied by non-Indians to be a pressing issue. In the

1930s the Tribal Organization, under the leadership of Robert Spott, began acting to protect them. This effort took on new energy in 1970 when Milton Marks (Yurok) founded the Northwest Indian Cemetery Protective Association (NICPA), which was to be central to a legal action of profound national significance.

Beginning in 1968 many Yuroks protested USDA Forest Service plans for a high-standard logging road, called the "GO-road," running across Six Rivers National Forest and connecting major highways at Gasquet, on the Smith River, and Orleans, on the Klamath. These protests culminated in the 1988 United States Supreme Court's hearing of Lyng *v.* Northwest Indian Cemetery Protective Association. The primary issue in the case was whether or not Native American sacred sites on public lands are protected by the First Amendment guarantee of the free exercise of religion. The Court's five-to-three decision in the Forest Service's favor was a stunning blow to Yuroks, as well as to their Karuk and Tolowa Indian neighbors. The federal government eventually set aside the GO-road "high country" as a wilderness area legislatively, preserving its sacred sites, but avoiding setting a legal precedent regarding Native American First Amendment rights to religious freedom on federally managed public lands.

THE LAST DECADE OF THE TWENTIETH CENTURY

Many strands of modern Yurok history were woven together in Yurok craftsmen's painstaking recreation of a classic redwood plank hamlet in Patrick's Point State Park, south of the mouth of the Klamath. The village, called Sumēg, was dedicated in September 1990 with a three-day festival that included a new brush dance. At the same time, the solemn ten-day jump dance was getting underway upriver at Pecwan, and the Yurok Transition Team was moving into recently acquired tribal headquarters on the coast, north of the river's mouth.

Much had changed on the lower Klamath between 1910 and 1990, although some things did not change as quickly or as much as others. Between 1990 and 2000, changes came rapidly and, on the surface at least, for the better. Politically vibrant and active, Yuroks had replaced most of the first tribal council, elected in 1993, in their second election, in 1997. Practical democracy was functioning at a fundamental and creative level.

By 2000, successful casinos were operating on the Yurok rancherias at Trinidad and Resighini, a major sport fishing center at the mouth of the Klamath was in tribal control, and the tribe was investigating new, nongaming investments. Through these initiatives, together with the long-delayed disbursement of the Settlement Funds, families were better off than they had been even a decade earlier, and the tribe was investing as much in its own cultural survival as in profitable new enterprise.

At the thirty-eighth annual Salmon Festival at Klamath, California, in August 2000, parked cars spread over a solid half-mile as at least a thousand people joined together for a day of community celebration. The festival featured day-long stick-games played by age-grouped boys and young men, learning the game correctly and playing it well—something that would have seemed impossible ten years earlier. There was much talk of the upcoming Yurok deerskin dance at Weitchpec: to be started in late August, it would mark the first time this important dance had been given since 1912. All around, there was a feeling of health, confidence, and excitement in the air.

No doubt the political activism, creative economic experimentation, and cultural renaissance of the 1990s were both accompanied and, to an extent, shaped by dissent, factionalism, and competition. This book, however, is primarily concerned with spirituality, not political analysis. Throughout it, and especially in the final chapter, I view the seemingly inevitable hurly-burly of contentious dialogue as essential to creative communal life. So far, however apparently disruptive, moderate contention has served the Yurok Indians well, as the salmon festival and the upcoming deerskin dance both underscored in August of 2000.

2 Double Helix

A friend thought her life was a mess and tried a little psychotherapy to straighten it out. She went only once. "He didn't have any stories!" she exclaimed, indignantly. "How can anyone even live their *own* life if they don't have any stories?"

THE CAPTAIN

Captain Spott of Reḵʷoy and Omen Hipur was an ambitious man of no mean talents, with the high self-regard of a real gentleman, *numi pegɹk*: "an independent man who others can depend on." His enemies said he was *syałew*, "just rich," but no one could deny that he was a boss, *poy-*

weson, and however they felt, he was indeed learned, *teno·wok,* well educated in ancient ways.

It is uncertain just when the Captain was born, but it was a few years before the California gold rush brought a massive and sudden influx of white men into the Klamath River drainage.[1] Captain Spott's father was from house Haʔagonor at Omen Hipur, downstream at the Tolowa end of the world, and his mother was a doctor from house Wonau, in ReK̓ʷoy. Like this town poised on the north bank of the mouth of the Klamath River, on the Pacific Coast, a crux of the world, the Captain could have expected to be of some consequence among both *nɹʔɹnyɹh* and *puliklah,* coastal people and people of the lower Klamath. But there was a problem.

His father and his mother came from respected houses, and by the time they wanted to marry his mother had enhanced her own prestige considerably by becoming *kegey,* a doctor. Being a doctor is a two-sided thing, however. Her lover from Omen Hipur could not pay her bride price—or perhaps her father would not accept any offer—because her earning potential as a doctor made her too valuable to her father's family. The doctor and the man from Omen had a baby anyway, and the child was born disgraced—*ka·mu·ks,* a bastard. He lived at house Wonau in ReK̓ʷoy, with his mother's family.

The baby grew up to be the Captain, not one to let the circumstances of his birth get him down. He was determined to work his way back up. He was ambitious and by the time he was seven, I've heard, he had made a small bow, shot birds for their feathers, and put these feathers away carefully in a wooden box. He was already a hunter and, as far as hunting went, was recognized as a man, *pegɹk,* at an early age.[2] He needed wealth, most especially in its traditional forms—the scalps of pileated woodpeckers and dentalium shells (*ʔo·lekʷoh ci·k,* "Indian money"), rare hides, obsidian blades, and so on, but also the gold pieces and silver coins that were increasingly recognized as wealth by the 1860s. White man money, *wo·gey ci·k,* was valuable in itself and good to buy dance regalia with, respectable wealth. The young man from Wonau didn't turn it down. He started a freight service between ReK̓ʷoy and Crescent City, twenty miles to the north, freighting the white men and their goods—and Indian customers as well—back and forth in heavy seas, running an oversized red-wood river canoe with a partner, singing his ocean songs.

There are many stories about this time. One day when he had already established his leadership in Rek̓ʷoy he was on the Crescent City docks and met the master of a coastwise packet from San Francisco. The white man introduced himself as "Captain Spot." The canoe captain, learning English, said "I am a 'Captain Spott,' too," and so Captain Spott he was, from then on.

I don't know if this story is true.

Needless to say, the Captain was set on paying full bride price for his own wives. In time he became a rich man and increased his prestige further by dressing dance teams for the great dances. He could completely outfit a side of dancers at two different jump dances going simultaneously in two different places, upriver and down: an astonishing feat. He was a boss and a devout man. He played important ritual roles in the dances himself, but only to the extent that his low birth formally permitted: he had principles. He also had "a devil" they say, *ʔumaʔa*, "the mysterious thing," to defend himself against jealous rivals.[3]

Captain Spott married early, but it was only after struggling for six more years to accumulate the necessary wealth—clean money, not from blood money or gambling—that he was able to marry his second wife, Mary Ann, a high family young woman from house Wogwu ("In the Middle") at Wečpus, a powerful town at the junction of the Trinity and Klamath Rivers. They were full-married but, alas, could not have children.

ROBERT SPOTT

Mary Ann had a brother, Weitchpec Frank, who had married a woman from a fine family at house Otsu, also in Wečpus, in a display of his own power, unafraid of being accused of marrying a relative. They had several children, among whom was a young daughter, Alice, and a slightly younger son, Robert Frank, born in 1888. Captain Spott adopted both of these children, and in 1903 they went downriver to live with him and Mary Ann in Rek̓ʷoy, which by then was called "Requa." Robert called the Captain his "father."

Robert Spott, as he was called, became well known among whites after the First World War (in which he fought with distinction in France), as a spokesperson for the welfare of the Yurok Indians in government dealings, and as the anthropologist A. L. Kroeber's final great Yurok informant. Kroeber wrote of Robert Spott in the "Preface" to *Yurok Narratives*, a volume that they published together in 1942:

> More than making Robert an heir, Captain Spott and [Mary Ann] exerted themselves to give him a thorough Yurok education in addition to the American one which the government provided at the Hoopa Indian School. Their efforts fell on fertile soil. Robert is endowed with an excellent memory, his natural inclinations are intellectual, and above all he is possessed of extraordinary sensitivity to the value of his native culture.
> . . . He knows as much, on the whole, of old Yurok ways and beliefs as the men of his father's and grandfather's generation. [Spott and Kroeber 1942: vii]

Undoubtedly, family solidarity and responsibilities played a strong role in these adoptions, but Captain Spott and Mary Ann's efforts didn't necessarily "fall" on arbitrary actors in a social structure. They made those efforts on purpose. It seems most likely that the Captain adopted Alice and Robert in part *because* he recognized them as "fertile soil" and because he needed heirs (by 1903 the Captain was already at least sixty years old) suited to inherit all of his wealth—the regalia and the knowledge that went with it. Extraordinary himself, Captain Spott must easily have "spotted," as they say, these two other extraordinary beings. Adopting these children of real insiders, the Franks, people of good births and good marriages, also brought the Captain, an outsider by birth, a bit more inside and cemented trade connections at both ends of the river, at Wečpus (by that time, "Weitchpec") as well as Requa. The new family was closely bound by affection and respect as well.

True to the Captain's expectations, Robert Spott rose to be *teno·wok*, a "well-educated one," too: a "high man," very active in ceremonial and political spheres, and "the most Yurok-religious of men," as Theodora Kroeber called him (1970:157). But whether it was because of the indelible stain on his adoptive father's escutcheon, or because of his wealth and that which he had a right to borrow from upriver, or because Robert had

problems with his sexual identity (though just whose problem it was remains unclear), or a combination of all of these, Robert was both respected
and suspect, both inside and outside, like the Captain himself.

Whether Robert chose to remain largely chaste, as many of the old-time
high spiritual people are said to have done, or whether—as an elder who
had known him told me—he was "well, homosexual," is a complex matter, especially hard to figure given the cultural presuppositions underlying the question itself. However so, in Requa and Weitchpec alike, "Indian
Time" seemed to be over, ruptured by the white invasion and occupation
and the tortuous dilemmas that European mores and power posed for native peoples. Just what should be presupposed, in the interests of survival,
was no longer clear. Robert, like the Captain, was a man of ancient princi-
ple, exacting, and made concessions to no one. He knew what he knew.[4]

What he said was that there were no longer any women in the world
able to meet his standards for a wife, which were, he claimed, the standards of all real men since the beginning of Indian Time. Unmarried and
without a direct heir, Robert came to be in somewhat the same situation
that Captain Spott had faced and for a parallel reason. The Captain addressed his outsider's problem by adopting the children of insiders, for
all that he may have chosen Robert more for this new heir's own outsider's gaze than for his insider's credentials. Robert did much the same.
He adopted the son of a member of the elite. By now, however, in 1915,
there had been a profound change in who held the wealth (increasingly,
"white man money," wahgay cheek) on the Klamath—in who were the
bosses. Robert adopted the son of an accountant at the salmon cannery in
Requa as his nephew, *wekcum*.

KIN TERMS

This term, *wekcum*,[5] is referentially equivalent to the English "nephew,"
denoting the son of a sibling or spouse's sibling. In the same way, the
Yurok *cimos*, "uncle," denotes a father's or mother's male siblings or the
husbands of their female siblings. Traditional Yurok and contemporary
Euro-American kinterm systems are similar in these regards.

Captain Spott was Robert's *cimos*, uncle—his father's sister's husband—and Robert was the Captain's *wekcum*, his nephew. But the relationship became more complicated through the Captain's need for an heir, which, in keeping with the high family ideal to which he aspired, would best be served by a first-generation patrilineal descendant, a father's son. This was the formal adoptive arrangement agreed upon by Captain Spott and Weitchpec Frank, Robert's biological father.

The Spotts and the Franks remained close kin, friends, and allies, and Robert remained attached to both families. Weitchpec Frank was not an anonymous progenitor but the scion of a great house, Wogwu, which remained Robert's house. While referring to Captain Spott as "my father," in English, Robert took Wogwu as his public Indian name, and correctly so. These relatively familiar complexities took, however, a less familiar twist.

Captain Spott and Mary Ann adopted Robert and his sister Alice in part so that they could transmit to them the cultural knowledge that they commanded, the survival of which they feared was jeopardized by the increasingly necessary accculturation of surviving Yurok people to white ways. However, there is an old pattern in Yurok society of uncles teaching their nephews, after puberty, rather than fathers teaching sons: people say that fathers are too emotionally attached to their sons to exercise the necessary stringency. In actuality, Captain Spott *was* Robert's uncle and an appropriate teacher for him, as well as his sociological father by adoption.

All of this is suggested, somewhat, by Robert's concrete grave marker above the old Spott house site in Requa. It reads,

SPOTTS ROBERT FRANK

HARRY ROBERTS

The accountant's son that Robert Spott adopted was christened Harry Kellett Roberts, and when he met Robert as a young boy he took to him. Robert, perhaps recognizing Harry as another unusual person, paid Harry's father one Chinook salmon of remarkable quality for the privilege of adopting Harry as his "nephew." Much later I asked Harry why his uncle, Robert Spott, was buried as "Spotts Robert Frank."

"Was the Captain's name really Spotts?" I asked.

"Oh, that's easy," said Harry, who had adopted me as his own nephew. "When Robert was in the army he got used to hearing last names first— 'Spott, Robert.' The people who made that marker didn't know punctuation. There should be a comma after 'Spott'."

"But it isn't 'Spott'," I reminded Harry: "it's 'Spotts'."

"That's what I told you," Harry said, nonplussed. "They didn't know punctuation. There should be an apostrophe in it, because Robert belonged to the Spotts."

Did he belong to the Spotts or with the Captain? Or both?

Probably the inscription was intended as

SPOTT'S ROBERT FRANK

There are precedents for this, like "Tom's Pete," the name of a young warrior who accompanied Captain Spott and seventeen other Yurok men when, in 1889, they went to to the Indian Service Station in Requa to complain about their treatment by a non-Indian entrepreneur.[6] But the Spotts are a family, not just an individual, and no doubt the first name on the marker has been read as "Spotts' " by some, as well as "Spott's."

Harry was Spotts Robert Frank's, Robert Spott's, Wogwu's spiritual heir (this hardly exhausts the names Robert Spott bore). Harry's biological father, Harry C. Roberts, was as Irish as they come, despite persistent rumors of some connection with the Franks of Weitchpec. His mother, Ruth Kellett, never acknowledged her Seneca maternal grandmother, who seemed best forgotten in Ruth's pursuit of respectability in turn-of-the-century Bay Area society, where being any part Indian was not a paying proposition. Harry, their only child, was probably born in 1906 (there are mysteries here) and had bright red hair, which led the Indian workers in his father's cannery to call him Kokonew, "woodpecker," and to let him hang around to bring them gambling luck. His playmates in Requa called him Herk^{w}er, "rabbits," wordplay on Roberts, but his uncle Robert Spott called him "Harry" and, when gravity demanded it, "nephew," which he pronounced "naaphew." Harry, in his turn, was to call me "naaphew" and, on occasion, "son."

The Roberts family had become close friends with Robert and Alice Spott and Grandma Mary Ann, who survived the Captain by many years. They went to dances and camped together, Robert was a foremost spokesman in labor's dealings with management at the cannery, and Ruth and Alice did long and productive service together securing Yurok welfare both on the Klamath and in the Bay Area, where people from the river went to appear in federal court regarding land allotments and, increasingly as the twentieth century deepened, to work. Harry called Mary Ann "Grandmother." Robert Spott was a natural "uncle" to Harry, just as I called my own biological parents' best friends "uncle" and "aunt" as a child. But there was far more to it in Robert's and Harry's case.

When Harry was a boy he heard the First People making the Rek̓ʷoy jump dance while he was playing beneath the rock Oregos at the mouth of the river.[7] The spirit people were singing. Harry stayed until dark, learned the song, and then—after some careful thought—went to sing it for Robert Spott. Robert recognized it immediately: he had been trained as a jump dance medicine man and hoped to see the dance revived someday, although it had not been made since 1904. They'd been talking about it in Requa, but no one had gotten around to it, which is why the First People were making it themselves, on the beach. As Captain Spott had recognized Robert as "fertile soil" in which to sow the seeds of elite Yurok knowledge, so Robert now recognized Harry as a suitable heir to his own spiritual and intellectual heritage, according to Harry.

Robert needed an heir for various reasons. He had been put outside of the circle of real respectability by changing sexual mores. Again, putting his perceived homosexuality aside, at that difficult time there were not many young Indian men eager to work for the knowledge that Robert Spott commanded or whose survival-minded parents would allow it (these youngsters were to become the "shorthair" or "missing generation"). And Robert had the highest standards—was, like his adoptive father, a man of strict principles. In light of all this, Robert had been unable to find a suitable student to teach what he had learned from the Captain and the other old notables of his boyhood, real men like Old Kerner and Sregon Jim who "thought and thought" about things and knew what to say if a young man came to ask a question.[8] While Robert had found some satisfaction in trying to teach the "white doctors" who came up from Berkeley—anthropologists like A. L. Kroeber, T. T. Waterman, E. W. Gifford, and others—he'd found them to be slow learners, and when young

Harry Roberts came to him singing a jump dance song in spirit language, Robert understood that the solution was at hand. He liked Harry, and so much the better if, like the white doctors, Harry was an insider in the emergent power structure. He was the son of well-to-do, respected people, as Robert himself had been. As Captain Spott enhanced his prestige by adopting up, as it were, so did Robert, securing new ties with the dominant houses, which were now the houses of white people.

Again, of course, there was a distinct difficulty. Harry's being for all intents and purposes white put him somewhat outside the Indian community, much as the Captain's illegitimacy and Robert's perceived homosexuality excluded them from the highest ranks of the Yurok elite. The house name to which Robert clung, Wogwu, "In the Middle," was both a claim to spiritual attainment and a statement of unrealized social aspiration, as much as a birthright. By the same token, Harry's training under Robert Spott was to leave him not in the middle of society, but in between white and Indian worlds, an outsider to both, as perhaps Robert knew it must. To whatever extent, Robert recognized Harry as one who could stand the loneliness that was the price of his inheritance, a born outsider like the Captain and like Robert Spott himself.

Robert trained Harry seriously for about fifteen years, until the mid-1930s when Harry left Requa to seek his fortune elsewhere—a move that many Indian people were making at that time, too. By then Harry, the anthropologist Dale Valory wrote, had become "the last to be formally trained and initiated as a high class Yurok man" (1968: 2)—a statement that is somewhat misleading, having been written in 1968 when talk of the last this and the last that was still common among anthropologists and the fantasy of the white Indian was newly popular. However off the point Valory's claim may have been, there is no doubt that Harry Kellett Roberts became an "all-grown-up man" like Robert and like the Captain before him, and "well educated," too, with "a thorough Yurok education."

Like all "real men," Harry was both independent and dependable. He was deeply spiritual in his orientation to the world and commanded great traditional esoteric acumen, though Harry was actually less an intellectual, like Robert, and more a man of action, like the Captain. Perhaps it was the solidarity of alternate generations. Along with his high spiritual medicine and his knowledge of Indian law, Harry was a warrior and could move, as the old-timers said, "just like lightning."

MYSELF

Now, moving like lightning is not something that you can fake. I only saw Harry do it once—when he was an old man on crutches, by the way—but that was because I was only with him in a situation that called for it once. I know that he could have done it any time, "every time, on purpose" as he said a real man did everything that he really knew how to do. I know that he did have that old-time Yurok knowledge, too, because I spent many years going around to other elders checking out Harry's information. And I know that he was spiritually a profoundly developed man, a "remarkable man" in Gurdjieff's sense (1968).

Harry learned from Robert and others: he was indeed new "fertile soil" for a Yurok education. At the time I met Harry Roberts in 1970, thirty-some years later, he was living in poverty with a young wife, his fourth. He'd had a long and rousing go of it after leaving Robert and Requa, making a living as a boxer, a precision machinist, a logger, a ballroom dancer, a horticulturalist, and just about everything in between. By 1970, though, he'd had a run of bad luck and was ill and isolated and, not so much for his own sake as for his new wife's, looking for a way back in among people who might appreciate his knowledge and experience, and looking for an heir, his two sons having moved away from him.

This was a moment that found native California poised on the brink of a great and lasting renaissance of Indian ways that built during the mid-1970s, came into flower in the 1980s, and today bears rich fruits. The children of the short-haired generation had come home to claim their own ancient world, reinventing it when necessary. But 1970 was too early. Ten years later Harry probably would have found more than one dedicated Yurok Indian student among the many younger people who became determined to reclaim their culture in the 1980s, and began seeking out the few remaining elders who had hung on to old ways during the hardest years. As it was, Harry ended up with me.

At the time I was working in San Francisco as a writer and photographer and studying Buddhism under my first teacher, the late Sunryu Suzuki. I heard about Harry through a mutual friend and went to visit him where he was living then, in Sonoma County. He asked me what I wanted, and I told him that I wanted to go home. We understood each other pretty well from that first day on and, in a way that would probably not be made any more clear by explanation, understood that we belonged together, though I had not thought much about American Indians one way or another before then. After Suzuki-roshi died, in 1971, Harry adopted me as his nephew and my son as his grandson, and began teaching me in earnest.

I studied with Harry until his death ten years later, in 1981. In fact I continue doing so, listening for his voice within myself when I'm considering a difficult question, much as Harry used to listen for Robert's voice during the long nights we spent together, smoking tobacco and studying "the law" and the world, "creation." (Like everything, Harry taught, independence has two sides.)

He had moved back up to the Klamath River in 1972, going home. It was Harry who sent me off to finish college and become an anthropologist, "to set the record straight on the Yuroks," he said, and to get me away from the mouth of the river where I'd beached after a stormy divorce and was, it seemed likely, headed for more trouble—yet full of hauteur.

"Why don't you become a bishop?" he asked one day, laughing. "But Harry," I said, "I'm not a Christian." "Well, then, be a professor. That's about the same, and you seem like you might be a teacher, to me." "What would I teach?" "Why don't you become an anthro? You like Indians." Just then a rich uncle, my deceased father's eldest brother, died and left me enough money to go back to school.

By the time I finished my bachelor's degree in 1975 and got my Ph.D. in anthropology in 1982, the postmodern critique (to which I was to contribute) was suggesting that setting ethnographic records "straight" was not at all the self-evident task that A. L. Kroeber—the last anthropologist to try it in the Yurok case—had assumed. Meanwhile Harry Roberts, whom I'd loved as the father I'd lost too early, had died himself, in 1981. During the same time a new generation of Yurok and Hupa, Karuk and

Tolowa Indian intellectuals and artists and spiritual people had begun restoring the great dances (including the Yurok jump dance at Pecwan) and were also publishing books, holding symposia, curating museum shows, and generally taking charge of their own cultural affairs again. Usually I find a warm welcome among them.

Like the Captain, Robert, and Harry, however, I find my welcome sometimes constrained—the Captain a bastard, Robert a "two-spirit," Harry a white man, and I not only white but an anthro. But even anthros can have families, lineages that soften sharp boundaries across time, voices to listen for and smile to hear. When it's time for people to think about a tombstone for me, I'd just as soon they'd let it read,

ROBERTS THOMAS BUCKLEY

No apostrophe.

3 Native Authors

In 1976 I returned to northwestern California to undertake my first formal field work as a graduate student of anthropology. Since I was there, now, as a professional-in-training, I thought it best to announce myself formally. The Yurok Indians that were my first interest had no tribal council in the 1970s. I went instead to the Tri-county Development Agency in McKinleyville, a federally funded Indian service organization, where I spoke with Christopher Peters (Yurok), who was on the agency's staff. I told him about my plans to do anthropological research in the area.

"I won't try to stop you," Chris said, "but I won't help you, either. You're on your own. Maybe you'll find people who'll talk with you. We'll see." He paused, then continued: "We want to do our own anthropology now. We may not do it as well as white people from the universities, but we'll do it as well as we can."

Chris Peters's position—neither friendly nor unfriendly that day—reflected, locally, a growing sentiment and a nascent movement in native North America. Vine Deloria, Jr., had long since condemned "anthros" as necromancers and parasites, asking that they do something for living native Americans or get off the reservations (1969; cf. Deloria 1997). Delmos Jones, an African American, had called for a new, "native anthropology"—anthropological research to be carried out by marginalized peoples within their own societies (1970). Although Jones acknowledged that such practice contradicted then-common assumptions about the inability of insiders to achieve social-scientific objectivity, he argued that there were important new perspectives to be offered by "native anthropologists" and that anthropological objectivity was not all it was cracked up to be, anyway (cf. L. Field 1999). My own anthropological mentor, Raymond D. Fogelson, had noted, before 1976, the increasing numbers of published Native American–authored accounts of their authors' own culture histories that questioned the right of non-Indian historians and ethnographers to "possess" the native past (Fogelson 1974).

In 1976, Yurok and other native authors had been publishing the histories, narratives, and reconstructed ethnographies of the classic[1] Yuroks and their close neighbors for sixty years. Lucy Thompson (1916), Chief and Mrs. Eaglewing (1938), Robert Spott (Spott and Kroeber 1942), and Timm Williams (Seiter and Williams 1959) had all published books or pamphlets. Various columns in local newspapers by Yurok authors had also appeared, along with Robert Spott's "Address" to the Commonwealth Club (Spott 1926). Possibly, one could argue that this tradition of indigenous cultural representation began in 1900, when A. L. Kroeber started transcribing oral performances of Yurok myths, eventually translating a large corpus of narratives into English, naming the Yurok storytellers and writing brief biographical sketches of each. Kroeber's *Yurok Myths* was finally published posthumously in 1976—the year that I met Chris Peters (see also Goddard 1914a).

Kroeber was not oblivious to the "native anthropology" already emergent along the Klamath River during the period in which he was most directly involved in studying native California. In 1921 he reviewed Lucy Thompson's 1916 book, *To the American Indian,* for the *American Anthro-*

pologist, and in 1942 Kroeber published a collection of Yurok mythic and historical narratives together with commentaries upon them by his coauthor, Robert Spott. Kroeber, however, had been well aware of both a particular Yurok historical consciousness and of Yurok Indians' reflexive insights into their own cultural traditions long before either of these works saw publication.

He had found that, for example, despite strictures against naming the dead, Yuroks born before massive contact were quite capable of tracing genealogies five and more generations deep, largely for purposes of contracting prestigious marriages (Waterman and Kroeber 1934).[2] He also collected considerable, deep historical data on dance regalia ownership, house site occupation, and the transmission of subsistence usufruct rights through the testimony of his Yurok consultants (e.g., Spott and Kroeber 1942).

Again, Yuroks' self-consciousness of their pre-contact culture (including the Yurok language) as a symbolic system is well documented in Kroeber's field notes from 1900–1907, if not in his published work, as well as in surviving Yurok language use. A Yurok doctor, elderly when Kroeber first met her in 1905, gave him a prayer that spoke of gathering angelica root incense "from the middle of the sky." "That's not where I get it," she went on—"that's just the way I talk so that all kinds of money will come into my house." Kroeber printed the "formula" in his 1925 *Handbook of California Indians,* but not the doctor's commentary on it (Kroeber 1900–1907, 1925: 66). In the same vein, the late Ella Norris (Yurok-Tolowa) gave me, in 1978, a wonderful invocation of "God," a Yurok phrase, *wołkeloh ʔelačiʔn wegenoyʔ o·mom* (lit.: " 'morning-always-early' you are being-called"), a reflexive, metalinguistic putting-in-quotes that, she said, is "just what I call it—'Early Morning [sun]Rise'." Other examples of such cultural and linguistic reflexivity abound (see Buckley 1984b).

Kroeber was well aware at the beginning of the twentieth century, then, of Yuroks' historical consciousness and of their self-consciousness of their culture, as well as their language, as systems of signification rather than direct mirrorings of actuality. The "coauthored" 1942 "Yurok Narratives" is nonetheless somewhat frustrating to read today, because Kroeber virtually ignores Spott's (often very subtle and always very Yurok) commentaries on the traditional narratives that he himself performed, overriding them and capping each chapter with his own ethnological commentaries that, finally, spin Spott's meanings to Kroeber's own academic ends.

LUCY THOMPSON

In his 1921 review of Lucy Thompson's 1916 *To the American Indian*, Kroeber praised this early work for the many new "items" of ethnographic information to be found in it that might add to his analytic, trait-based account of "the world renewal cult." What he did not so much care for, however, was Thompson's far too post-contact glossing of ethnographic and mythological materials in terms of Masonic imagery (courtesy of her husband, Milton "Jim" Thompson, a white timber cruiser) and of biblical imagery (courtesy of, I believe, the Presbyterian ministry; see chapter 10). All of these were, for Kroeber, "extraneous" and "irrelevant," Thompson's prose "prolix" (Kroeber 1921; Kroeber and Gifford 1949), of little use in reconstructing the "native primitive culture before it went all to pieces" (Kroeber 1948: 427). Since then-contemporary Yurok culture was of little professional interest to him—was not, in fact "Yurok" in his eyes—Kroeber had little use for these "extraneous" materials (cf. Buckley 1996).

But Lucy Thompson, born in 1853, was a writer in no way un-Yurok, as Yurok culture had come to be during her lifetime. While no Yurok Indian student graduated from a public high school until the 1920s, when the segregation of Indian and white children began to ease, Thompson was literate, and her English prose—at its best, richly evocative (see chapter 7)—was but one instance of a Yurok respect for English literacy that emerged soon after massive contact in 1850.

Clearly, by 1900, it was a matter of expedience and cultural survival to become literate as the only defense against continuing white encroachment on remaining Yurok lands through the Dawes Act and other written instruments. There were other motives at play as well among these people whose aristocracy had always valued multilingual skills and taken pride in their abilities to speak Karuk, Wiyot, Tolowa, Hupa, and other of the very diverse languages of their principal neighbors. We have seen (chapter 1) that by the 1880s Yuroks from the town of Requa, with the help of a sympathetic white lawyer, were suing the local school board, seeking admission of Indian children to the public elementary school specifically in pursuit of English literacy. Upriver on the Klamath, Karuk Indians were apparently delighted to have missionary-sponsored English teachers sent to them in 1908, young and old reportedly jamming Mary Ellicott Arnold and Mabel Reed's classroom with lively enthusiasm as reading and writing English became a virtual fad around Happy Camp and Orleans, California (Arnold and Reed 1957).

While Lucy Thompson's literacy was neither anomalous nor, necessarily, a sign of destructive acculturation, heralding the loss of "real" Yurok culture, neither were her historical consciousness or her reflexivity, her awareness of her culture as a culture and her creative commentary upon it, in any way un-Yurok, or even un-pre-contact Yurok. While Kroeber rejected these commentaries as irrelevant to his salvage-ethnological work, these aspects of the 1916 book are decidedly interesting today, telling us much about Yuroks' efforts at the beginning of the twentieth century both to understand what had happened to them in the half-century since the whites came, and to gain the understanding of the people who had done this to them.

Lucy Thompson was no "native primitive" Yurok every-woman. She was trying hard to figure out how her Yurok culture might survive the cataclysm that had overtaken it, at one minute co-opting white language for purposes of resistance, like her Sioux contemporary Zitkala Sa (1921), at another chiding despairing and dissolute Yurok survivors angrily, much as Zora Neale Hurston was to do somewhat later, writing of her own African American people (1942: 213–37). On the next page still, Thompson transforms the ancient Yuroks and their mythic culture heroes into "Wandering Tribes," "Our Christ," "The Samson of the Klamath Indians," prophets and mermaids. The sacred sweathouse at the village of Pecwan, where she was born, becomes a "Lodge," its occupants a secret, mystic brotherhood led by "High Priests," sharing the "secret name" of the Deity. Despite these apologetic transformations, or reenvisionings, Thompson's writing is always proud and at once lovingly nostalgic and angry, as well as, I think, fearful of being misunderstood by a powerful and still-dangerous white audience.[3]

Lucy Thompson wrote her book partially in response to then-available published accounts of her people—most especially, I believe, the journalist Stephen Powers's *Tribes of California* (1976 [1877])—arguing for the legitimacy of her own, Indian voice as that of a Yurok aristocrat and trained cultural expert. "As there has been so much said and written about the American Indians, with my tribe, the Klamath Indians [Yuroks], included, by the white people, which is guessed at and not facts, I deem it necessary to first tell you who I am, for which please do not criticize me as egotistical" (Thompson 1991 [1916]: xxix). Yet Thompson is not antiwhite, and *To the American Indian* is not a racialist polemic. The book is dedicated to "My beloved husband, with whom all of my married life has been so pleasantly spent" (xxx). Indeed, Thompson had many other white friends besides her husband, such as the photographer Emma B. Freeman, an early, romantic bohemian sojourner in the northwest (Palmquist 1976).

Such friends most likely alerted Thompson to the growing white concern for Indian welfare spreading among liberal thinkers of the era with the—already apparent—failure of the federal allotment policy. People like Ruth Kellett Roberts, present on the lower Klamath at the time when Thompson was writing her book, were to be influential in the formation of the Indian Welfare committee of the California Women's Federation, one of the many precursors of John Collier's Indian Defense Association (Graves 1929: 101). It was the same social and political climate that nurtured Zitkala Sa and supported her early publications in the *Atlantic Monthly*, beginning in 1900.

However supportive this plural-social context, it incorporated only a minority of white northern Californians, most of whom were—in 1916—still rabidly anti-Indian (e.g., Heizer and Almquist 1971; Rawls 1984). Thompson was all too aware that the fate of the neighboring Wiyot Indians, "almost exterminated by the white man" in 1867 (Thompson 1991 [1916]: 217), could as easily have been that of the Yuroks. Yet her handling of the era of greatest conflict and Yurok population decline (1860–70) is restrained. Her Yurok people are not hapless victims, like the Wiyots, but killers of whites (and each other) as well, agents in a world unbalanced—for Indians and whites alike—by greed, the desire for revenge, and whiskey. Her most sustained treatment of the perilous world that she and her husband lived in, through mortal violence, pandemic disease, unspeakable abuse, and humiliation, is, finally, an argument for Temperance rather than an indictment of the whites (1–24). Only briefly and toward the end of her book do Lucy Thompson's grief and bitterness flash through: "Sometimes it seems hard to think of man's inhumanity, but sure as the sun goes down, the white man will suffer for his wicked treatment of the . . . Indians" (220).

Harry Roberts, Ruth Roberts's son and Robert Spott's protégé, told me more than once, in the eleven years I spent with him, to always "rehearse the good; let the bad go." In his view, which I came to believe manifested ancient tenets of "high" Yurok culture, "light is the normal course of events; darkness is only a temporary interruption." The essential nature of "creation" is "beauty," said Harry, and it is ungrateful—even rude—to talk about dirty (*kimol*) things, to cause pain with words. The dead should be mentioned only with the greatest discretion, and the world should be made beautiful with talk, not sullied by voiced recollection.

It is my feeling that this was Lucy Thompson's (aristocratic) sensibility as well. The great dances of renewal that she details bring people "together in peace and harmony as one family" and make them "feel that there is some good to live for." The regalia, dancing, singing and feasting make "one feel the love of the great Creator of all things" (Thompson 1991 [1916]: 112–19).

Thompson takes refuge from her present in richly detailed accounts of these great dances of her girlhood and the ancient stories that were her education, but protects these behind screens of biblical and Masonic comparison through which she proclaims herself human to her people's enemies, at the same time trying to appreciate those enemies' own humanity—and to explain to them in familiar terms something of what the old Indian ways meant. Overall, in this careful balancing act, it is the sacred itself, and the Yuroks' religious practices, that predominate.

NATIVE AMERICAN STUDIES

Lucy Thompson was the first northwestern California Indian to publish a full-length book, and the last to do so as sole author for another sixty-two years. During these same years more than seventy original anthropological and historical works were published by non-Indian authors on the Yuroks and their immediate neighbors—the Karuks, Tolowas, Hupas, and Wiyots. These seventy-plus scholarly works do not include a sizable duplicated but unpublished literature, largely generated by the USDA Forest Service (chapter 6), four or more unpublished doctoral dissertations on the Yuroks alone, any number of reprints and textbook syntheses, and so on. Little of this writing was readily accessible to the native audience in northwestern California before the late 1970s, when the Indian Action Library was established in Eureka.

It was not until 1978–79 that Indian names again appeared on books about native northwestern California. Two works, both by Hupa writers, were published in these years—Jack Norton's *Genocide in Northwestern California: When Our Worlds Cried* (1979) and *Our Home Forever: A Hupa Tribal History*, by Byron Nelson, Jr. (1978). While the two books came out in successive years, both were being written at the same time and reflect, I think, the same moment in Hupa and broader regional culture history— although, as we will see below, they sprang from different contexts within that moment.

It was a time in which Thompson's emphases and understatements had been reversed. Both Norton and Nelson decline discussion of indigenous spirituality and religious practice in any detail, and both place considerable emphasis on past genocide and present oppression by— among others—anthropologists.

Like Thompson, Norton begins his book in near-repudiation of received, non-Indian-authored ethnology and ethnohistory, but at far greater length and with considerably greater acrimony. For Norton, the ethnologization of native cultures in the region after 1900, by Pliny E. Goddard, Edward W. Gifford, T. T. Waterman and, especially, A. L. Kroeber, must be understood as a continuation of the catastrophe that had befallen his people beginning in 1849. Though he expresses a modicum of gratitude for the written records of the old ways that these ethnographers compiled, Norton also rejects this record as being ethnocentric and as serving the interests of the invaders, particularly in its blindness to native spirituality:

It should be stated here that Kroeber's *Handbook* should most emphatically be re-worked, and a complete history of the tribes of the region be produced. Those now reading this work are shocked and dismayed by the evidence of ethnocentrism and prejudice shown by Kroeber, the distinguished scholar. These need to be pointed out at some time soon, for they have been picked up and made a part of the educational process, and contribute greatly to the misconceptions about native peoples of California. [1979: 18]

While, like Thompson, Norton would address native spirituality as central to communal life, he is focused on what Thompson underplayed, as a prerequisite to further discussion of spirituality. The facts of nineteenth-century genocide need, in Norton's view, to be brought into the educational process before, ultimately, one turns to the sacred, so that the received ethnographic record, and especially its omission of spirituality, might be understood in context and thus be accurately reworked. To omit this terrible history is in effect to collude in perceived, ongoing ethnocide.

Ultimately, Norton's objective was not so much to berate Kroeber, or even the white perpetrators of genocide, but to restore the native peoples of northwestern California to the human race, as Lucy Thompson had done with her use of non-Indian comparative mythology and symbolism (and as I have done in chapter 9). Thompson used biblical and Masonic themes in her efforts to humanize the Yuroks for those who had dehumanized them, and to gain the understanding of the whites. In the secularized, legalistic, global (and safer) contexts within which he wrote, Norton used comparable texts and the symbols of comparable power-brokers—those of international law and of the United Nations. The final third of *Genocide in Northwestern California* is taken up with appendixes that begin with the 1948 United Nations Genocide Convention. They go on to include rosters of federal, state and local officials and military units actively engaged in the subjugation of northwestern California between 1850 and 1880, naming the hitherto unmentionable and also restoring *their* humanity, recovering these individual actors from a general and amnesiac "them."

Norton's approach compares native Californians and biblical peoples in a new and terrible way and amounts to an indictment that reaches much closer to most contemporary homes in the region than the Nuremberg trials. There are many familiar North Coast family names on the more local rosters. This begins to suggest the wider contexts of Norton's particular contribution.

Genocide in Northwestern California was written because "a great deal is now known about the injustices committed against Indians of the Plains, the Eastern seaboard, and the Southwest . . . . [But] little is known, and less is understood . . . of the genocide committed against the native people of California, particularly those of Northwestern California . . . this most inhumane of all American tragedies" (Norton 1979: vii). The local context rests within a wider, then-contemporary one—the co-optation, which Norton perceived, of the experience of genocide itself, along with the term "holocaust," by Israeli nationalists and their supporters (see also Thornton 1987). Norton was to make explicit his argument for broadening the reference of the term "holocaust" at international conferences in the 1980s.

Such native concerns crested in the United States in 1992, at the time of the Columbian quincentennial. As Norton does in his 1979 book, most popular expressions of these concerns in 1992 portrayed American Indians as innocent victims—quite differently, that is, than had Thompson, for whom Yuroks are (sometimes destructive) agents, and only the white man's rum is truly a demon.

There are many and complex reasons for the full emergence of the discourse on North American genocide in the later twentieth century, and at least one anthropologist has argued cogently that this discourse emerged among Native Americans through a shared narrative dialogue with anthropologists (Bruner 1986). In native northwestern California, one might surmise, this discourse was taken up both because traditional strictures against "rehearsing the bad" were weakening (and because the shame of violation had turned to less internalized anger), and also because it had become safer to speak the once unspeakable. As Lucy Thompson undoubtedly knew, it is not safe to remind the powerful of their crimes—it was not safe in 1916 in Del Norte and Humboldt Counties, nor was it all that safe in 1979, though enough so by then to make it a reasonable risk, even for a historian seeking tenure at a state university, as Jack Norton was. (One really needs to understand what a short time ago the 1860s were in local consciousness, both Indian and white, and the enormous investment the state of California has had in its sanitized history of intrepid pioneers, saintly Franciscans, and a single dead Indian, Ishi [e.g., T. Kroeber 1961].)

But if the silence surrounding nineteenth-century genocide in northwestern California was ready for breaking, a new reticence was emerging at the same time, in the late 1970s, regarding that about which Lucy Thompson had been most forthcoming—native spirituality and local religious practice. This new reticence is equally in evidence in Byron Nelson, Jr.'s *Our Home Forever* as in Jack Norton's book.

Norton was breaking what amounted to a local and national silence on genocide at a time when the region's Indian people were regrouping powerfully, both socially and culturally. Nowhere was this more true than at Hoopa. The Hupa Indian Tribe, fully organized, was positioning itself economically and politically for a new period of consolidation and growth. It was as determined to break a logjam of withheld federal timber payments as to reinvigorate Hupa traditional culture with reconstructed villages, a tribal museum, language programs, and continued sustenance of public spirituality, particularly through curative brush dances and the more momentous, biennial white deerskin dance. *Our Home Forever: A Hupa Tribal History* emerged from this context: a tribally authorized history by an author who has served several terms on the Hupa tribal council. It is both complementary to Norton's work and unlike it in many ways.

The tone of Nelson's history is unemotional and rooted in the canons of academic historiography. While mildly critical of received ethnographies and histories, his introductory ethnographic chapters are unabashedly based in Pliny Goddard's work, published at the turn of the century (Goddard 1903–4). Like Norton, Nelson acknowledges the central importance of spirituality in both pre-contact and contemporary Hupa culture, yet he too declines discussion of it in any detail—not because there is a prior historical experience to be understood before spirituality might be properly considered, however. In accord with the Hupa elders who have contributed to the work, Nelson holds that native spirituality should not be discussed publicly, dismissing the topic briefly: simply, he "does not try to describe those parts of the culture which are most closely interwoven with the people's religious beliefs" (Nelson 1978: 3). While Thompson sought to communicate the meanings of Yurok spirituality through analogy with Western traditions and Norton postponed discussion of these meanings until a historical, moral debt had been acknowledged, Nelson essentially says that they are no one's business outside of the Hoopa Valley. He would seem to be invoking a tribal secrecy regarding the sacred often invoked in native North America and elsewhere, and just as often attributed to native peoples by the outsiders who would describe them. Yet stereotypes are simplistic by definition, and Nelson's reticence regarding spirituality (in strong contrast to, say, Lucy Thompson) seems to me more complex in origin than a comparatively simple keeping of putatively traditional taboos.

Certainly, Nelson and the book's contributing elders were as concerned with maintaining cultural boundaries as with territorial sovereignty. But it seems likely that their defensiveness reveals something of Hupa and neighboring native peoples' insecurity regarding their own spiritual heritage. Elders at the time—a generation removed from Lucy Thompson—were generally dubious that the old Indian Way could survive, and Nelson's own, still more recent generation of spiritual students had yet to achieve the confidence in their own abilities to carry on that was to be clearly in evidence by the late 1980s. In the interim, spirituality and religion remained, sensibly enough, local knowledge closely guarded by politically acute thinkers such as Byron Nelson (though some native cynics have alleged that "people say things are 'secret' because they don't know anything about them themselves").

Forgoing cynicism, it seems more appropriate to assume that Nelson was writing in a professional manner, supported by the Hupa tribe, and taking care of business. What he deemed to be *everybody's* business (and here Nelson's book resembles Norton's appendixes) was the chronological and factual administrative and territorial history of the Hoopa Valley Indian Reservation.

In Nelson's text genocide becomes more complex than in Norton's victimized account, and more like Thompson's: there are good Indian Agents as well as bad, collaborating warriors as well as resisters and victims. Again, while Norton's crying "worlds" are cultural, spiritual, and above all moral territories, Nelson's "home" is more simply territory. His book is most useful and compelling as a finely researched and documented bureaucratic and economic reservation history, an accurate (by external academic, legal, and political standards) and valuable record that, taking care not to issue a blanket indictment, might earn the respect of non-Indian federal legislators and judiciary. (Norton's appended rosters, in contrast, include lists of U.S. presidents, senators, and representatives as well as more local officials.) *Our Home Forever* was a foundational text upon which the Hupa tribe might move ahead—toward, as it was to turn out, the congressional Yurok-Hupa Settlement Act of 1988, enormously beneficial to the Hupas in terms of land-base and economic stability, at some cost to their northern neighbors, the Yuroks.[4] In this regard, *Our Home Forever* came into being, most pertinently, within the context of the high-stakes federal tribal acknowledgment proceedings and land claims cases of the late 1970s, particularly in the eastern United States, with all of their technicalities and legal stringencies.

Raymond D. Fogelson's focus on indigenous reenvisioning of indigenous histories and revoicings of native historical theory, on "ethno-ethnohistory," takes on new complexities in this boundary-setting, competitive, fully modern discourse (Fogelson 1974, 1989). It becomes clear, for instance, that reticence may be as much a vehicle for expression of native perspectives on their own histories as voiced emphases. Pre-contact renderings of the region's history were cast very largely in terms of the sacred—a mythologized history of villages and houses, of the great dances and of the regalia that dances in them, all projected back into a be-foretime, when the creators and First People chartered the world that human beings were to inherit and steward (e.g., Kroeber 1976). This is the historical consciousness and the historical narration that Lucy Thompson centered her own narrative upon, reenvisioning and translating it here and there in terms of non-native mythologies, spirituality and hierarchies, but stating it nonetheless, while treating far more reticently the more recent and obscene, entirely human history and the grief-stricken and angry historical consciousness to which it gave rise.

Consciousness of this modern history is voiced by both Norton and Nelson, who choose, however, to communicate its spiritual concomitants through a new order of understatement, declining discussion of indigenous spirituality in the region while voicing loudly what Thompson had uttered sotto voce. These were not, I think, individual choices so much as collective ones, as, for example, A. L. Kroeber's virtual neglect of both contact history and of native women's points of view reflected collective decisions and styles in Boasian salvage ethnography (Buckley 1988, 1996).

The 1916 edition of Thompson's book is to be found, well cared for, in many Yurok houses, whose inhabitants speak of her with respect. The new edition (Thompson 1991 [1916]), published by Malcolm Margolin's Heyday Books—arguably the contemporary publisher most widely accepted as fully responsive to native Californian sensibilities—has a glowing introduction by the contemporary Karuk Indian artist/scholar Julian Lang. Nelson's reservation history is, again, a tribally authorized one, originally published by the Hupa Tribe, its author's work assisted by an acknowledged board of twenty-one "Contributing Elders." Norton's book was published by Rupert Costo (Cahuilla) and the activist, native-focal Indian Historian Press and continues to be widely read by native audiences in the region. The emphases and understatements that I have discussed were not simply individual, then, but communal and, as such, highly communicative of the northwestern California Indian community's changing historical consciousness and theories of history, as well as the changing external contexts within which history is recorded.

Norton's and Nelson's reserved approaches to the specifics of local spirituality were countermanded in 1982, however, by another native writer—although, significantly, an outsider. Robert G. Lake, Jr., is a Cherokee-Seneca scholar who came to work in the Ethnic Studies program at Humboldt State University, in Arcata, in the 1970s, marrying a Yurok woman and taking a serious interest in the region's own native peoples. Out of this conjunction came *Chilula: People from the Ancient Redwoods* (Lake 1982), an effort to reconstruct the culture of the Hupa's Athabascan neighbors and kindred to the south and west, decimated and dispossessed in the genocide that Norton detailed.

Lake sets out to write from what he calls an "endogenous perspective" (e.g., as one of Delmos Jones's "native anthropologists"), hoping to set right perceived errors and omissions in the outsider-ethnographies of Kroeber,

Goddard (1914a, 1914b) and others. To ensure validity, he enlists the aid of eleven named elders and of his wife, Tela Donahue Lake (now Star Hawk), a clairvoyant and apprentice Indian doctor. He also takes another step, augmenting and interpreting local historical consciousness with his own new "endogenous" perspective. As Thompson remythologized the Yuroks through the images of Western religions and Norton reenvisioned moral history through post–World War II international law, so Lake applied the metaphors and conceptual tools of alternative Western psychology, citing C. G. Jung, Bruno Bettelheim, the holistic therapists Kenneth Pelletier and Patricia Garfield, and other New Age thinkers, including John Lilly.

Lake is reticent about neither genocide nor Chilula spirituality. Indeed, spiritual meanings are at the center of his interpretations and exegeses of traditional Chilula culture and history and, where data are lacking, he seeks his wife's clairvoyant assistance to retrieve it, revealing through her the significance of a number of disused sacred sites. This focus was in part in response to native conflicts with the Forest Service in the GO-road case.

While Thompson speaks lovingly but in passing of the "mystic shadows of dreamland mountains" (1991 [1916]: 226) and Norton touches briefly on the "clues to possible solutions to today's environmental crises" offered by traditional native cultures (1979: 6), the environment and environmentalism are central to Lake's book, which is dedicated to many people, including the "Save the Redwoods League . . . and the ancient Redwood Trees that have an aboriginal right to live and to flourish" (Lake 1982: iii).

Lake's book, and his particular "endogenous perspective" were, then, in part products of particular local political situations and shared goals which, like Nelson's tribal history, it supported. And, too, it reflected broader contexts—in this case, the New Age movement that provided a good many of Lake's (and Norton's) students at Humboldt State University, as well as the then-florescent national environmentalist movement. However, rather than getting to publication through what amounts to an indigenous peer-review system (the Hupa Tribal Council, the Indian Historical Press, Heyday Books, etc.), Lake published *Chilula* through the University Press of America—a general academic publisher with a large catalog of author-subsidized works. And unlike

Nelson's and Norton's books, his was repudiated by local people—including the elders that Lake had consulted.

These elders, embarrassed by having their names in the book, charged that Lake broadcast (secret) sacred knowledge they had given him as a student and a seeker, never intending it for publication. There seem to me to be other problems inherent in the book as well, including the verbatim transcription of nonesoteric testimony that the elders themselves could not have intended for publication, either: "I ask, who is willing to learn the old ways for our tribe and for the Creator? . . . Most of the young people won't dance in the Sacred Dances, but they sure like to get drunk and dance the Whiteman's dances" (in Lake 1982: 164).

On the face of it, Lake reports nothing new here, and reports it not much differently than Lucy Thompson had in 1916, inveighing against drink and lamenting the dissoluteness of the young, but there are significant underlying differences. First of all, Lake edits and represents the voices of respected elders in such passages, while Lucy Thompson spoke for herself, as such an elder. (Alternatively, Nelson, while working with twenty-one contributing elders, linked none of them directly with potentially controversial information in his text.) Second, one cannot avoid the impression, in Lake's prose, that he uses his transcribed interviews to validate himself. In the passage quoted above, the elder, after all, confides in Lake, a younger man who has gone to the elder as an earnest student of the sacred, one who is not drunk and dancing "the Whiteman's dances." All of this is in contrast to Thompson's wariness of "egocentrism" and is in breach of still-regnant local manners. Finally, although a "native anthropologist" in Jones's terms, Lake was also an outsider to the environment he described and interpreted: his view was not *pertinently* endogenous, from a local point of view.

The book was rejected, locally, in the local way, largely by being met with silence. This was harsh treatment, for *Chilula* has its virtues: Lake's scholarship is detailed and careful, drawing together in a comprehensive way much of the scattered information published on the Chilulas, arriving at some provocative and valid interpretations of both received texts and new oral testimony. He collates a variety of useful environmental information and indeed sheds light on regional spirituality, new to the published literature. In most of this *Chilula* resembles both Norton's and Nelson's locally popular works. Perhaps it will be consulted more graciously by native readers once the critical dust has settled.

The local reaction to his book took Lake by surprise: somewhere, communications had broken down without his knowing it. However the misunderstandings occurred, archetypal energies, creative dreaming, holistic approaches to preventing stress disorders, clairvoyance, environmentalism, and the rest were not at issue—any more than Thompson's Masonic Lodge and biblical imagery, Norton's United Nations or Nelson's federal bureaucracy, to my knowledge, have been foci of the critiques of native readers. What was offensive was Lake's breaching of the then-contemporary community's reserve regarding specific sacred knowledge and individual privacy, and his seeming self-aggrandizement.

Lake left the region some time after *Chilula* was published. The language of depth psychology that he explored in it has found its way into ongoing discourse on the sacred among younger spiritual people in the region, but the book itself is not often mentioned. Lake now writes on healing for a New Age audience under the name of Medicine Grizzlybear.

INDIAN LOVE

A certain balance between boldness and careful recognition of regnant discursive strictures finally may be what characterizes the three locally *successful* books that I have discussed so far. Beyond native reenvisioning of indigenous histories and reconfigurations of received native historical consciousness, we would seem to leave behind the collective and communally constituted and acceptable. Over-the-line books like Lake's depart from both culture, as shared knowledge and practice, and history, as shared experience, and enter the domain of fiction or something else— sometimes "self-help," the bookstore section where we find Medicine Grizzlybear Lake's *Native Healer* today, published by Quest Books of the Theosophical Publishing House (1991).

Recognizing this distinction between the communal and the individual leaves unaddressed the question of how an ethnic group's shared historical consciousness and theory of history change. Does this occur largely in response to extrinsic, political-economic changes, as is so often the case in academic anthropology (e.g., Stocking 1992)? Or do varying theories indeed progress through innovation, as is also widely, if implicitly, assumed in mainstream academe? However so, a final example of such change remains to be mentioned: Julian Lang's *Ararapíkva, Creation Stories of the People: Traditional Karuk Indian Literature from Northwestern California*, published by Heyday Books in 1994, more than a decade after Norton's, Nelson's, and Lake's contributions.

Julian Lang (Karuk) leaves aside, finally, what had by 1994 become *de rigueur* anthro-bashing and condemnation by faint praise. More, it would seem, has been unnecessary. Rather, Lang acknowledges (in the book and elsewhere) his profound debt to the anthropological linguists who have made ongoing study of Karuk language and texts possible—J. P. Harrington, Helen Roberts, and especially William Bright (Lang 1989, 1990, 1994: 6). He does this gracefully, leaving his own Karuk language teachers and older storytellers at center stage.

It seems to me that this reorientation toward received academic texts is historically illuminating, as well as revealing of Lang's individual graciousness. (Anthro-bashing is "like swearing," he once told me, referring to the old use of the names of enemies' dead relatives as a form of insult or curse.)

During the 1980s Lang's generation of ceremonial leaders and participants had successfully reinvigorated, under the guidance of elders, many of the great "world renewal" dances of the Karuks, Yuroks, Hupas, and Tolowas, gaining considerable confidence through doing so. The contribution of such habitually castigated salvage-ethnographic texts as Kroeber and Gifford's "World Renewal" (1949) to this successful renaissance was undeniable. A new appreciation for some of the efforts of the early ethnographers together with increasing local cultural confidence (the two are not unrelated) have both nurtured a general improvement in relationships between native people and contemporary, non-Indian researchers.[5] While DeLoria's 1969 polemic still rings true for many, a large number of other native cultural and spiritual experts and activists—including Julian Lang—have arrived at more complex and nuanced views of the century-long collaboration between academics and Indian peoples. Lang's *Ararapíkva* manifests this new confidence and complexity, alike.

The book is organized around six retranscribed Karuk texts with interlinear English translations. These are filled out with portraits of the original storytellers, sections on Karuk culture and language, a glossary, photographs, and very careful suggestions as to what each story or prayer might be about: "Knowledge, which is what the story is, gives power" (Lang 1994: 45); "We live in a world created by yearning and sexuality, and every time we look at the moon and see Frog Woman there, we are reminded of this wonderful fact" (49); "wonder is at the heart of creation" (55). To an extent, Lang returns to Thompson's 1916 approach, which he admires (Lang, in Thompson 1991, xv–xxvi). Interpretation of the sacred is no longer postponed or deemed inappropriate, nor was the work locally rejected as un-Indian, to the best of my knowledge.

Lang positions himself, as author and editor, firmly within Karuk culture and culture history, reviewing, for instance, his own family's experience of the "wanton destruction" that Norton chronicles (Lang 1994: 11 ff.), but he also shifts the received discourse by delving into meanings of the sacred as Lake did, though far more discreetly. His presence as reinterpreter and innovator is felt in a single noun, "love," that occurs four times in the slim (112 pp.) volume: in the dedication "To Indian Love," in the introduction ("The power of love has been instrumental in keeping indigenous peoples together"), and again in the main text: "The affirmation of love as the greatest force on earth is balanced by the knowledge that even love has its limits: life must be lived according to the rules that have been laid down for us" (5, 13–14, 63). "Love" is not a word to be found in the ethnographies and histories of Kroeber or Goddard, nor is it used in so pervasive a way in any of the works of the other native authors that I have discussed, though Thompson, as we have seen, indeed invokes it. Yet, like spirituality and genocide, Lang implies, love is at the heart of native northwestern Californian cultures, past and present, and it is at the very center of his book.

Lang's work, reaching back into the past for its stories and its many subtle reflections of Lucy Thompson's pioneering work (much as non-Indian scholars continue to reach back toward Kroeber's oeuvre), equally reflects the new period of cultural confidence that dawned in native California in the 1980s. Lang is close to the center of this renaissance, grounded in a federally recognized tribe still holding a portion of its aboriginal territory, in command of his tribal language, participating in the traditional ceremonialism resurgent in northwestern California today. He can, in effect, fully afford to be generous, wealthy in his knowledge that "there is no love like Indian love" (personal communication, 1992). While his use of the English "love" has a Christian resonance, that resonance is rather different from Thompson's apologetic use of Christian comparisons. Lang subtly suggests that the Christian whites are not so much to be feared, as Thompson implies, or hated, as Norton needed to convey, as to be pitied for their loneliness in their secularized and alienated world.

INDIGENOUS AND METROPOLITAN SCHOLARSHIP

It seems to me that however distinct the two bodies of work may be, native-authored history and ethnography get constructed in much the same way as academic anthropology and ethnohistory, through processes of negotiation that are shaped both by cumulative traditions and by the transient historical and political contexts within which they emerge. In both cases, work is produced by authors and is evaluated by its most pertinent audiences in relation to collective but historically variable standards of appropriateness, grounded in a consensual historical and cultural consciousness that has its own historicity. What separates the two sorts of works most demonstrably is not a profound difference in the processes that shape them, but the historically emergent, culturally and class-relative styles, metaphors, and other tropes through which these processes manifest at the surfaces of texts; that, and the degree of power writers have to impose their particular representations on a broader, multicultural society.

Books are and are not like the pre-contact "cosmologies, narratives, rituals and ceremonies" in which, according to Ray Fogelson, nonliterate Indian historical consciousness and theories of history are embedded (Fogelson 1989). Books exist in a different world that books themselves have had no small part in creating. It is in part for this reason that "ethno-eth-nohistory" and a parallel ethno-ethnography, throughout the past century in native northwestern California, have developed in much the same way that elite academic anthropology and history do. Theoretical and methodological paradigms rise and fall, subject to external contexts and to communal validation, old themes are woven into new patterns, disappear, and reemerge, and certainly the native authors I have reviewed are as respectful of their "data" as any other serious scholars. If Norton, Nelson, Lake, and Lang do not invoke Lucy Thompson's biblical and Masonic analogies it is because they hold them to have been inappropriate not to her time, but to their own—when analogies with European Jewry, the criteria of federal courts, the insights of depth psychology, and the power of enduring and expanding love simply make more sense. If local readers (and native-focal publishers) rejected Lake's earnest but ill-advised breaching of local etiquette, it was because it fell outside of the disciplinary canons of their own anthropology and historiography. Such indigenous processes seem no more unusual or exotic than those of elite academic disciplines, viewed historically.

The elements entered into these processes, however, are not necessarily the elements entered into metropolitan academic developments over time. Kroeber, for example, pretty much ignored genocide and spirituality alike (not to mention Indian love), as well as the dialectical role of white society in shaping present Indian societies. On the other hand, native writers have not been much concerned with trait inventories or with social structure, or with "culture," for examples. Their theories and methods, broadly speaking, have different sources and different objectives from those of non-Indian academics.

In our time, indigenous and metropolitan concerns have come to overlap in some areas—in questioning elite ethnographic authority, for instance (Clifford 1988), and in understanding that narratives of Indian-white relations have never been truly monological, but always dialogical (Bruner 1986). These overlappings are, I believe, results of that very dialogue. In general, however, differing theoretical paradigms have prevailed. There was a virtual cottage industry in psychoanalyses of Yurok culture between 1943 and 1960, in academe (chapter 10). Native writers in northwestern California have never taken up this approach, although they have proposed parallel theories: depth psychology and a general theory of a love that is not exclusively erotic, for instance. Many non-Indian academics and nonacademic native writers would like to think that these are differences that make a difference, but I am not so sure.

Lucy Thompson's comparative use of biblical imagery in the interpretation of indigenous spirituality is, arguably, no more nor less appropriate than Erik Erikson's appropriation of Freud's Viennese mythology in the interpretation of that same spirituality (Erikson 1943), or so it would appear with the widely accepted downgrading of Freud's psychology from positive science to humanistic, even poetic interpretation. One could even argue that Thompson's analogies are more appropriate, comparing spiritual tradition to spiritual tradition, rather than reducing all such traditions through profoundly secular analysis. One could go on in this way, though such comparisons—as opposed to Thompson's and Freud's—indeed tend to be odious.

More certainly, it is clear that psychoanalysis, trait inventories, formalized studies of social structure and the rest have prevailed in metropolitan anthropology for cultural reasons that have had to do with power. Therefore the study of successive efforts in non-Indian academic descriptions and analyses of native northwestern California (such as the present book) is a study as much of Euro-American culture history and politics as of Yurok, Karuk, and Hupa Indians. We cannot easily dismiss native models for studying themselves and the analogies and metaphors embedded in these as merely "subjective," as nonscientific, as though the history of European and Euro-American models for studying those peoples had ever been anything else in any truly defining way. Chris Peters needn't have been so diffident about his colleagues' abilities to do their own anthropology in 1976. Rather than worrying that these colleagues would not "do it as well" as non-Indian academics, he might have said, "we will do it differently." Studying these differences takes us a long way toward understanding real differences between non-Indian academe and native northwestern California—toward understanding *both* sides of the cross-cultural equation better. All cultural and historical interpretation is reflective of its authors, if not always reflexively so. (In this, the Yurok

84   CONTEXTS

doctor Kroeber interviewed in 1905 was well ahead of the metropolitan anthropologists of her time.) Perhaps it is time to come up with some new terms for the operations and processes involved in this creative effort. Since we remain in dialogue, native abilities to confidently repossess their own histories and cultural accounts depend in part on non-Indians' abilities to stop segregating these accounts as hyphenated forms, as "folk-histories" and so on, suggesting their non-"objective" status.

In the chapters that follow it is not my intention to override or invalidate or surpass the contributions of Thompson, Norton, Nelson, Lake, Lang, and the other native authors who will produce new work in the years to come. My desire is to enter into dialogue with them, as I enter into dialogue with my academic anthropological predecessors, A. L. Kroeber especially. There will never be a definitive, final account of the American Indian peoples of northwestern California unless they cease to exist as living peoples. All accounts are rendered tentative and incomplete by the ongoing, immemorial diversity of native and anthropological understandings alike, and by the continuing emergence of local cultures through vital and changing historical processes. Through this book I seek to participate in a conversation that started long before I first arrived in the Klamath River region, in 1971, and that will continue long after I have passed from the scene.

PART TWO Testimony

4 Seeing with Their Own Eyes

According to the (always slightly different) accounts of Yurok speakers in the 1970s, every individual has a "purpose in life." People are "born for a reason." After a child is six weeks in the womb (or ten), its "fire" or "spark" enters its "heart," where it forms the individual's "foundation," which is also his "purpose."

This purpose, a person's "life" itself, is also her "spirit" (*wewecek̓, wewolocek̓*). It comes directly from "the Creator" or "creation," *ki ʔwesʔonah*, "that which exists," "the world." Some people think that a person's body comes from the mother, this life through the father: "that's the father's duty, to give life." At death, some say, the body returns to the earth and the spirit goes home," *wesʔonah hiwonik* (or *wesʔonewik*), "way up in the middle of the sky," to "Heaven": that is, "Indian Heaven."[1]

Younger intellectuals engaged in restoring what they see as an authentic "Indian Way," "our sacred ways," suspect that some elements in such accounts reflect a Christian influence. Undoubtedly, pre-contact and Christian ontologies have mixed by now (the transition from Yurok to English alone assured some such mixing and transformation), yet there remain important differences between local, non-Christian notions of a person's "spirit" and mainstream Christian understandings of the "soul." For example, a person's life, *wewecek*, belongs inviolably to that person and he or she is responsible to it alone, not to some extrinsic force in whose hands its fate finally rests. When a younger Karuk woman talks about "loyalty," for instance, she stresses the equal importance of loyalty to her Indian people and to her own purpose in life: the two are inextricably linked for her, two sides of a single ethic.

This woman's life, her real self, is "sacred," at once the basis of her communal role and a unique element or emergence that is not to be interfered with by others. It is, of course, an imperfect world: "the 'real world' is the world that people have made," some say, and we have to deal with it. "Freedom is the ability to live out the purpose you came here for," a younger Yurok man told me in 1990. "Some people try to take away your freedom by laying *their* purpose on you." When someone else's purpose in life is to interfere with you he must be stopped, lest you become his slave, his "pet."

Since people are born for a purpose it would be disrespectful, in a fundamental sort of way, to suppose that they don't know what they are doing or not to expect them to take responsibility for what they do. "There are no accidents," Harry Roberts insisted. "Whatever you do, you do on purpose. Don't say 'I'm sorry.' If you break my cup, go get me a new cup. I can't drink coffee out of 'I'm sorry.' " "When a man screws up he says, 'I screwed up.' Then we can laugh about it and say, 'you sure did' and he can laugh at himself and everybody has a good laugh and it's over."

Yurok people my own age whom I've talked with about such things accept responsibility as a matter of reason. Your life, says a friend, is the result of accumulated "cause and effect," of "discipline" and of a lack of it. What happens in your life can be understood—even analyzed—on this basis. "Your past doesn't go away just because you act well now. It's on the record and you have to take care of that." For those today who are concerned with "the spiritual," the ethics of individual responsibility and of self-discipline pertain especially to people's dealings with spiritual forces. These might bless them and, by the same token, can punish them or those they are close to, depending on the nature of individuals' present and past actions, on whether they've broken "the law" or kept it.

The movement from childhood and being "senseless" *(ma·łpoł)* to adulthood and responsibility is by way of discipline, from the elite perspective that I am taking here. Depending on people's purposes in life, this discipline also provides movement—as another younger man says—from "the physical" to "the mental" to "the spiritual," from what an elder called the "low," or earthly, to the "high," or spiritual. Some people are born to stay in the physical domain; perhaps most are. Some are born to move through the physical to the mental, to study "the law," for instance—"cause and effect." A few people in each generation are born to progress from the physical through the mental to the spiritual. Their purpose is to make "high medicine." According to Harry Roberts, you have to take every step, leaving nothing out, and if you do miss a step you cannot get any farther until you go back to what you omitted and start over again from that point.

Other elders that I knew in the 1970s and '80s often spoke of such progressions in fulfillment of individuals' purposes in life through the hierarchical metaphors of formal American education. They'd say "he got his high school diploma," "he graduated from college," "she went for her master's," "she got her Ph.D.," but they were talking about people who had made medicine for bravery, had learned to pray for different things, had become shamans *(kegey,* "doctor") in the high mountains where they'd "passed their final examination." These metaphors go back at least to the beginning of the twentieth century. Lucy Thompson uses them in her 1916 book, *To the American Indian,* although, as far as I have determined, the first Yurok Indian to graduate from a public high school was Antone (Anafey) Obee, in 1921. (He had to go to Oregon to do it.) These educational metaphors convey Indian self-respect, certainly, but they are also a bit misleading, since classical Yurok education is based on entirely different principles from those of the formal, American system that Indian people have long compared it to. Indigenous education is based on observation and experience, not on having things explained to you, and experience that leads to fulfillment of purpose is acquired by "training," *hohkep-,* not by passive attendance. People themselves must define what they want to know in accord with their unique purposes; it is not done for them by a school board or faculty committee. Traditional, "old-time" knowledge must still be acquired this way today.

If "religion" is a "world creating and world discovering human and cultural process," as Sam Gill writes (1988: 70), then "training" and the medicine-making that certain kinds of training culminate in are creative means of discovery: deep education. A person does not come to "believe in" his discoveries; he makes them or not, knows them by experience or remains ignorant of them, acts them out in what he does or knows nothing. A person goes as far as he can, in accord with his purpose in life. To become "well educated" *(teno·wok)* takes a long time, and few have ever gone that far.

Analytically and from outside, one might associate the "physical," "mental," and "spiritual," respectively, with an individual's "body," "mind," and "spirit" (all three clear native categories today). Doing this suggests that there is some obvious, shared cultural system here, but such a system exists only inferentially. Different individuals interpret things in different ways and phrase their interpretations differently.

As an intellectual I make systems of things, associate the various educational "degrees" that one elder talked about with the three levels of existence that another person finds useful to think with, and connect both with what a third person told me. A Tolowa friend, for instance, once said that "the creators" gave three instructions to the Indians when they came to the world: "kill to live; keep things proper; talk to me" (that is, in English, "pray"). Putting it all together I end up with three tidy columns: aspects of experience, stages of growth, and sacred teachings. I have no assurance, however, that what I've come up with is any more than what an elder once told me, when I'd laid out my understanding of something or other to him. It was, he said, "a pretty good way to explain it, to white men."

THE PHYSICAL

"Training" is a word with many possible nuances in its English usages, which can be both referential and metaphorical. Training can refer to a wide variety of practices and intentions, from purely physical training to get in shape, to acquiring a skill—training under a teacher to sing in a particular ceremony, for example—to being "in training" in solitude, practicing meditative austerities for days or weeks at a time, seeking transcendent experience. Its modern use, as an English noun, most likely reflects concepts that predate the use of English in northwestern California.

The late Frank Douglas, a Yurok speaker, used the Yurok verb *hohkep-*, "to be in training." Its stem, *hoh-*, is itself a noninflected form of the verb *hoh(kum-)*, "to make, build, repair, gather, cause" (Robins 1958: 200–201). Etymological explanations are always tricky, yet in the present instance it is not far-fetched to suggest a connection between training and "building" or "making" or "gathering," as in "gather together." Training is a process of building or making *yourself*—as an individual and as an actor in community life. "Gathering" is also pertinent to training. When a person trains he "accumulates" himself, people say, pulls together his energies and concentration.

There is a prevailing willingness among California Indians (if not all "traditional" American Indians) to simply let people be themselves, whoever they are, and to make room for all sorts of individuals as long as they are not destructive of communal life. Granting this, in native northwestern California men are expected to be strong and tough, aggressive when appropriate. (I asked a friend, "What word should I use? 'Fierce'?" "No," she said, "people might take that wrong. I'd say they have balls.") "A weakling had no place in the culture," wrote Philip Drucker of the aboriginal Tolowa society that he reconstructed ethnographically (1937: 225). Men's training at its most fundamental is usually directed toward meeting rather familiar male standards historically related to men's role as "providers" (women are often said to be "preparers"), and also as protectors. In the twentieth century being a provider came to mean being a proficient commercial timber faller more often than a good elk hunter, but the emphasis on rugged physicality remained. Most Yurok training has always had a strenuous physical component.

"Training" can be as simple as climbing the hill behind your house every day to strengthen your legs for an upcoming dance—as an acquaintance, rubbing his shins after a jump dance, said he *should* have done. But the gen-

eral idea of male training is more complex than this and may involve solitude, sweating, careful eating or no eating at all, abstaining from sex, avoiding menstruating women, drugs, and alcohol. People today tend to agree
that physical training is associated with the lowlands, particularly with the
river and the ocean, and with the wintertime, which is cold and wet on the
Klamath River. Men work upwards, both in altitude and in intensity of spirituality, usually in the summer months.

Winter is no time to be in the mountains, but it is the time to train for
strength—the dark, stormy time when the forces lending strength, bravery, and endurance are abroad in the world. A Hupa friend told me that
his own training, as a boy of nine or ten, began when his father had him
break the ice in the Trinity River and swim in the early morning. "That's
really starting 'low'!" he said. Next came running up the bank holding a
mouthful of water, and this man's training has proceeded, virtually all of
his life, uphill from there.

To an extent, such training is an extension of ideal daily life-practice,
understood as old or traditional. In the ceremonial camps at the late summer "world renewal" dances today, people, male or female, should rise
at dawn, bathe in a creek (no matter its temperature), avoid too much casual contact with the opposite sex, eat carefully, and follow other rules.
Life in these camps may be something like old-time village life, when
people were careful and saved easy living for late summer camps in the
hills, well away from the villages. In earlier village life, young men added
strength training to their daily baths, competing to see who could carry
a heavy rock the farthest along the river bank after sweating (Jimmy Jackson, Hupa, in Aaland 1978: 168). Today, barbells are probably more common. In the old days, unsuccessful hunters were expected to pack large
loads of wood back into camp in lieu of game, and carrying ten-to-fif-
teen-foot logs was itself recognized as a form of "training for strong."
The elaborate stonework around traditional houses was built up by the
efforts of men routinely packing rocks up from the river or creekbeds
each day after bathing, and some men follow this practice today as well.
Other men, more formally committed to strength training, have practiced running up a mountain every day carrying a stone from the river
below, slowly building a cairn of river rocks high in the hills as a testa-

ment to their efforts. From their first encounters, non-Indians have re-marked on the strength of Yurok men and their often striking physical development (e.g., Gibbs 1854–57).

Running seems always to have been another basic form of physical training. One Yurok myth tells of the manly culture hero and creator, Pulekukwerek, running all night with a boy he was training (Lame Billy of Wečpus, in Kroeber 1976: 118); in another, one of the First People asks a young man, "Do you think you can run?" "He is a man if he can do that," the *wo·gey* thinks. "Yes, I think I can run somewhat," answers the suitably diffident youth (ibid., 70). "When I was young, everywhere I go I run," Dewey George told me when he was old. "Everyone know that about me—I always running."

Wintertime training for strength and endurance might be simply that, but traditionally it has also often been linked to training as a warrior or an athlete. At its highest levels, training for bravery and the acquisition of specialized warrior's skills once went far beyond what we might con-sider "the physical," but young men have also long trained for fighting in exoteric ways. Yuroks and their neighbors once engaged in rock fights, as a less extreme form of conflict resolution than fighting with bows and pointed weapons or, later, guns, and practice in dodging rocks is still a common and a popular form of somewhat dangerous amusement. "When you can dodge your own shadow you're doing good!" a young man told me one day, in 1990, pausing and then adding with a twinkle in his eye, "Wait until the sun goes behind a cloud! Use your mind—your shadow doesn't have one." (He had moved from "the physical" to "the mental.")

Florence Shaughnessy told me that in the nineteenth century only men who had practiced dodging arrows went on dangerous raids, such as those among holders of large caches of dentalium shells in the far north, possibly as far as Puget Sound:

Blind Billy [Sta·wen Bill, ca. 1840–1920] told me about that. Getting shells from 'the Lands of the Fogs,' that's what he called it. He told me about people older than him that went up there to get shells. The Indians there were hostile to outsiders so only those who'd practiced dodging arrows went. They went in the summertime when it was foggy so they'd be hidden. Sometimes one got killed and the body had to be left and the others ran for miles and miles. It was dangerous!

Early reports, predating the collapse of armed Indian resistance to the white invasion of northwestern California in the mid-1860s, stressed the "turbulence of individuals" (Gibbs 1854–57: 33) and the readiness of small groups to engage in violence (e.g., various, in Heizer and Mills 1952). Yet violent aggression could be expensive, because of the institution of blood money payments, and thus it was shunted into nonlethal channels when possible. A local variant of shinny, the "stick game," is such a channel. It is a better-known public amusement than stone-dodging but, like rock fights, often a substitute for more lethal and costly forms of fighting. It was played with vigor on the river through the 1950s, underwent something of a revival in the 1970s, and in this new century is again played with vigor and skill.

"Stick" is rough and often played as a grudge match between rival groups—especially, today, between Yuroks and Hupas. Two teams of three men each face off, one-on-one, each attempting to move a pair of wooden toggles joined by a short thong through their opponent's goal at the end of a long field, using a stout playing stick usually made of yew wood to handle the toggles. There are only a few rules. You cannot use both hands to choke an opponent with your stick, for instance. The game combines running and passing with wrestling, and both running and strength training are appropriate for someone who wants to be a stick player. After a disappointing game in 1990, people said that the low quality of play and high incidence of injuries was due to the players stinting on their training. Dewey George, in 1976: "That's pretty rough. You don't go in there unless you train—no use to go in there. You can't choke, but you put your head here [up under your opponent's jaw], grab behind neck, check him around. That hurt! But easy to get away from. You gotta be fast. Hupa, they pretty good—but we [Yuroks] very fast!"

Training for "stick" might include running uphill with a mouthful of water and carrying a river stone, learning to breath through your nose and increasing your endurance, as well as other running training. According to the late Lewana Brantner (Yurok), men once went to Elk Valley, an alpine prairie of profound spiritual significance, to train for stick, running in circles around the small clearing enclosed by cedar forest until they dropped, competing to see who could last the longest.

The powers of the best stick players come not through physical training alone, but from Lightning and the Thunders—spirituals abroad in the winter. "You got to live lightning," said Frank Douglas in 1976, *"kits kege?y epek."* This means training to become both as fast as lightning and strong as thunder, but it can also mean seeking the aid of Lightning and of the ten Thunder Brothers, the spiritual allies of stick players and warriors. In 1978, Florence Shaughnessy remembered her foster-father, Jimmy Gensaw, training his sons on the river bar below the village of Requa:

> We had two brothers that were stick game players. In the wintertime, when it thundered and the lightning just kept on and on and the roll of the ocean—then they'd take a boat, and five or six fellas would come along and grab the boat and drag it down the gravel bar to see if the lightning wanted competition and if it would give them strength here on earth, so that they could make just about the same kind of noise. Now, you listen to the thunder; sometimes there's different kinds of thunder and some of it sounds like trailing gravel, [at] the end. That's when the old people would send the young people out to train: "Now you go out there and train, because now you have competition. Take the boat and drag it along the gravel bar to see if that will please the Thunder, [when he] sees that you're still practicing down here." Then he gives them part of his strength. So that's what Dad used to do to the boys. And then he'd make them run up the hill.

Physical training segues into spiritual training. At one time, for instance, some Hupas training for stick customarily slept in a cleft in a rock near the village of Matildon, a shinny stick held in the crook of the arm through the night as they sought spiritual aid in gaining speed and strength (Arnold R. Pilling, personal communication 1978). Others seeking power as stick players or warriors ran in the hills at night and knew that they'd "got it" if lightning struck and split a tree near them. A person does not undertake such things without preparation. "Everything has its price," Harry Roberts used to tell me, often. While spiritual forces might help people to accomplish their physical ends, these forces, whether personified as "spirits" or not, do not usually bring help of their own accord.

Spiritual aid or retribution is usually attracted by people's own efforts, loss or lack of it brought down by their omissions or transgressions—"breaking the law." When spirits appear unbidden, in a dream for instance, they come to announce that a person has a certain option, or potential. It is now up to that person to realize this potential through application of will power, in training, or not attain the goal at all. A person might dream of powerful beings or a place where "power" is available, for instance, but it remains to obtain the spirit's blessings and to bring them under control. Dewey George, in 1978: "There was a man, Barney, at Sregon. He play stick. Started training for stick one time. And he had a dream. He was up on a mountain where he was supposed to stay. He saw a big tree coming toward him. He get scared, run away. Then he wake up. He go up there, train, get famous."

Many men have trained to be brave, to be "big hearts," overcoming fear by confronting that which causes it. Harry Roberts considered this to be the essential, "first man medicine." He'd started training toward it at about eleven, when Robert Spott had sent him to spend the night on a downed tree that hung out over a creek, to contend with his fear of the dark and of water. Training for bravery proceeds toward spiritual dimensions from such relatively physical beginnings. A younger man in training told me that, after "getting clean," his teacher took him up into the hills one night, to a place he'd talked about. When they arrived the teacher said "Give me your pants." "Why?" asked the student. "Because when you see what's out there you're going to be so scared that shit is going to run down your legs like water and I don't want to be around you smelling like that." His teacher was right, the man told me, though he didn't tell me what he saw that night.

Jimmy Stevens (Yurok) said that a man diving in a lake on Red Mountain can encounter waterdogs (redwood salamanders) eight feet long, hear a loud noise, and jump out—with power. He also said that there are giant skeleton-ghosts, *soʔoˑ*, running in the woods at night near Klamath Glen (old Saʔał, which can also mean "ghost"), with sparks jumping from their eye-sockets. One of these ghosts said, in the beginning, "I shall be the bringer of what is bad. If a man is to have bad luck, I shall be the first to tell him" (Lame Billy of Wečpus, in Kroeber 1976: 53). However, Mr. Stevens said, in 1978, that if a man can catch one of the *soʔo·* and embrace him, with his arms all the way around the specter—not just touch him—he will become "brave." Other men once encountered other sorts of ghosts that gave them "spirit medicine," the power to deal with spirits unafraid, and to be a "brave person," *ʔwɹ·gɹyɹs*. There were giants in the hills so strong they could rip a man's arms out of their sockets.

While tales of attaining bravery through encountering dangers are familiar, not all men who were brave became trained warriors, *weskʷeloy*. Men got these fighting powers from other sorts of spirits. Certain Yurok men once acquired guardian spirits through training and medicine-making that imbued them with bravery and fighting skills not unlike Asian martial arts. They were called *weskʷeloy*, a word that made reference to the style in which they alone were privileged to wear their hair, and were considered "mean," *ɬmeyow*, "habitually ready to fight" (Kroeber, in Elmendorf 1960: 267.1). They were also *plo wicekʷs*, "big hearts."

These warriors got their powers through physical training and then vision questing in the winter, usually in the ocean near great rock formations—seastacks—or in riverine whirlpools, in lakes and other places that gave access to the Thunders. In the waters they encountered the Thunders or one of the water monsters called *ka·mes* or a *saʔaɬ*, a bad ghost-spirit that lives in a spring and brings disease. Some trained in the lower hills and mountains and in the hollow or cleft rocks there. Accounts of such encounters fit into a circumpolar, shamanistic pattern. Falling unconscious, men travel to the underworld to the house of the Thunders, overcoming ferocious guardians—panthers, rattlesnakes—and entering to be cut up into pieces, cooked, and reassembled as *weskʷeloy*. Clearly, however, visionary initiation has always been accompanied by stringent physical training.

According to Dewey George, in 1976, warrior training gave one the power to jump extraordinarily high or across very broad stretches from a standing start. Some exceptional women—like Robert Spott's sister, Alice Spott—acquired this ability as well, and with it the social status of "man," *pegɹk*. Mr. George, speaking of Alice Spott:

One night I was running on the road. He was running too, came around
the corner and saw me. He jumped straight up, over the bank, over the
fence on top.

Next day I see him, say, "I see you!"

"Oh no," he says, "you didn't see me!"

He laugh.

Every time I saw him I'd say, "I *seee* you."

He just laugh.

Harry Roberts told me that *weskʷeloy* entered trance when they fought,
like Norse *berserker,* and that once having entered their fighting trance
they could be stopped only by being killed. Kroeber noted that they were
"semi-professionals," with lower status than the prototypal shamans, the
kegey, sucking doctors (in Elmendorf 1960: 469.13, 473.20). It is clear from
elders' testimony in the 1970s that notable fighters trained for their skills,
acquired spirit allies, mastered unusual physical abilities, and developed
distinct character traits. They had to "live lightning," as Frank Douglas
said. He continued:

Training—train [for] combat or duel.

We had one relation. I guess he was the best one that ever was. They
call him Moʔloḱi.

They had him cornered in Crescent City. He jumped on a rail fence.
Three or four of them thought they had him. They didn't get him.

I saw him one time, I seen him coming. He was a tough old fella'.

You say "Watch out!" *nu koy ya·*[2] "Move aside!" And they did.

He was way over there. He got brushed slightly. He was pretty near
opposite us, say *nu koy ya·*!

Jeeze, he went just like lightning, just start from nothing. He just
swang!

He used to go up in the mountains above Harry Woods' on windy
nights.

Tenth night he was up there Chicken Hawk [spirit] hit him. From
then on they [enemies] couldn't hit him. A Chicken Hawk that was
blowing in the wind—must have knocked him down, too [in trance].

It's in the air—spirits in the air. You go out in the mountains. [Frank
Douglas, 1976]

While not of the highest social rank, these warriors needed considerable resources to pay for the deaths they caused. Older people today tend

to be deeply suspicious of such powers (in part because many see killing as habit-forming). An elder told me of a nephew who had been a prize-fighter and who had used "Indian medicine" to gain an advantage in the ring, leading to a short lifetime of trouble. She lamented that he ever got mixed up in such things.

However, Kroeber reported that the classic trance-warriors "disap-peared" sooner after massive contact than did the *kegeyowor*, sucking doc-tors, and that we therefore lack actual case histories (in Elmendorf 1960: 494.21; Spott and Kroeber 1942: 167). But this impression may have been created by the continued *existence* of *wesk^{w}eloy*, rather than their disap-pearance, and fear, in 1900, that they would be held accountable to "white-man law" for their continuing activities.[3] Mr. Douglas was talking about a time near the turn of the twentieth century when describing Mo?loḱi's exploits and those of other warriors.

There is not some magical power out there that somehow comes along and makes life easy for you: as my friend said, it's all discipline. And in somewhat the same vein, while the world is full of "spirituals," "unseen beings," mysterious things, it is still this hard world we live in, and men's physical lives remain rife with killing and death, often accompanied by no "spiritual" meaning whatsoever. It's not appropriate to talk much about the violence that too often marks and ends lives in northwestern California today. Frank Douglas's account of a feud near the turn of the twentieth century is worth setting down here, however, for its historical interest and Frank's inimitable storytelling style, but also because it gives some one-sided sense of continuing realities in the region:

> We lived at Hoṕew and we had this Long Billy, my uncle, way back—great big strapping young man. And there was a fella they called Tipsy Frank, tough fella. He could put his hand on a fence post and just jump clear over it, just put his hand on there. He'd wear fancy vests and everything like that. He was from ?Espew.
>
> So, by god he stole a horse, Tipsy Frank.
>
> So, the fella missed his horse.
>
> So, he knew Long Billy was a tough man, and he got him to redeem the horse—find it. He asked Long Billy if he knew where the horse was; says, "yeah, I know where he hid it, the fella Tipsy Frank."
>
> So, he got fifteen dollars for going to get the horse.
>
> Well, Long Billy moved to Oregon, kind of shamed of himself.

Well, those people on both sides of the river, all the way over to Weɫkʷew on the south side, said, "Well, we got to do something. He's just like to die and we won't see him no more, up to Oregon."

So, by gosh they got together and talked this all over, both sides of the river.

"Well, he likes to drink. We're going to get something for him to drink."

So, by god they went and got it, and they put up a brush dance at Weɫkʷew.

Long Billy had them old time pistols, with a cap; had two of them. So, after he got drunk they took his pistols off him and put them in the water, soaked the caps.

So, they got in a row and he shoots. Nothing happens. They just took and butchered him, let his guts hang out. He run over to that rock at Weɫkʷew with his guts a-dragging. And they shot them young fellas—Billy Williams and Jim Williams, young fellas from Hoṕew. They shot and hit George, from the north side of the river—kind of crippled him a little bit.

So, by god everybody laid low. And this fella Tucker and another shot a crow, but they were waiting for them and when they came out to pick it up they killed him. He fell right back.

But this Tipsy Frank came back, and they had a big dance at Pekʷon. He played stick with Sregon George. He was a big man, but Sregon George whipped him, and they were enemies on that account. And they was already waylaying him, waiting for him at Awe·, down the trail from Pekʷon.

So, by god after the stick game here he comes, double-breasted vest and all.

And by god them fellas, three men waiting up in the brush there, by the dump, see him coming.

So, by god they dropped him right there you know, killed him right there.

So that made it even.

kit akʔawʌer—your relation's got a pillow now, 'cause he was killed. That's how they explain that. Anything happen, in my day, you go *kit akʔawʌer*—"he's going to have a pillow," you going to kill somebody, you see? *ki akʔawʌer* means you going to make even.

Sitting by the road one day with a friend, I asked about someone who'd just passed by, whom I'd seen around but didn't know. "He walks the physical path," my friend said. "That's a hard path."

In Yurok, the word for "salmon" is *nepuy*, literally "to eat," more freely and clearly "for people to eat." To eat salmon, always the basis of life on the Klamath River, you have to kill them. "To eat" is, equally, to "kill to live," as my Tolowa friend had it, and men who are "providers" are of necessity killers. Some men may get tired of killing, tired of the eyes of dead fish staring up at them from the bottoms of boats, find some other way to sustain life, but that doesn't really change anything. A fisherman I know, famous for the beautiful eel hooks that he carves, held one up one time. "This isn't art," he said, "it's survival."

PROPRIETY

The trouble with segmenting human experience and knowledge into the physical, mental, and spiritual is that all three are interpenetrating and codeterminate. The Creators may have given three laws—kill to live, maintain propriety, pray—and warriors may set aside two while enacting the remaining one, but eventually the balance has to be restored. In the case of killings, relatives and allies have always had the option of giving the dead "a pillow," a corpse to rest his head upon, but that cannot go on for ever. There are formal litigations and proceedings that weigh culpability, in accordance with a received system of "Indian law," and levy payments that (in theory) restore local balance. Frank Douglas remembered the old-time way of settling as well as the killings that they settled.

> *wego·pe*, that's the one goes back and forth, offers money. They say, "no—go back again, see if they'll put a little more money in there." I seen that once myself when I was just a boy.
>
> Tracy Charlie and old Sam Smith—one of them borrowed a saddle and didn't return it.
>
> So they had a fight over it—hit one another.
>
> So they had a date to settle up.
>
> So my grandmother says, "Let's go over"—over there at old Johnson's store. They were lined up there—they all had guns on each side, they had guns. They had a man, going back and forth—make offer. Pretty soon, OK, they accept that money.

And by golly, everybody shake hands, laugh—they got started laughing. But we dasn't laugh.

I was a boy, you know, right close to my grandmother. It was over.

The formal ritual for such settlements—the traditional dance of two
opposing lines of armed men representing the two litigants, a neutral "go-
between" moving between their leaders—seems to have fallen from common usage by the 1930s. In 1976 the late Dewey George, who was among
the very few who remembered the "war dance" (people today emphasize
that it is actually a "peace dance") trained a group of young men and boys
to do it, taught them a few war songs, and put up the dance at a cultural
event, a "unity day" at the mouth of the Klamath, where it was recorded
on film for posterity.

> Early in the morning
> we come
> playing with human bones

But while this dance and its songs have fallen from use, demands for
"Indian payment," for settling breaches of Indian law—from insults to
thefts to killings—have not: indeed, they have become more common in
recent years as people have increasingly asserted their local identities
once again through reaffirming old practices. In fact, some elders claim
that younger people are making up *more* rules today than existed in the
past, perhaps due to insecurities about those identities. Other elders, like
the late Calvin Rube, however, understand the law as timeless: "it isn't
the old law or the new law or anything like that. It's the Creator's law."
But however intuitive, finally, that law may be, it is as much a product
of analysis and debate as of spiritual insight. People still spend time, at
night in summer fish camps, for instance, analyzing such classic cases as
the drowned child paradigm: If a child uses your boat without permission and drowns, who is at fault? Who owes whom what? (Harry Roberts
discussed the same case at length with Robert Spott, in Requa, after the
First World War.)

From an outsider's point of view, "the mental" provides a connection
between "the physical"—the realm of life and death—and "the spiritual,"

the source of life and of the rules of propriety that assure its continuation. This interpenetration of what I am taking to be the three levels of existence seems, from the outside, all-pervasive and to underlie "training" of every order. "The mental," engaged in understanding the law, is equally engaged (as will power) in physical training and (as concentration) in seeking "the spiritual."

Local people place great stress on the importance and power of the mind. Keeping thoughts disciplined and controlled, "having good thoughts," especially, is central to a well-lived life. "Don't say 'it's hot'! Say, 'It's a wonderful day!' " said the esteemed elder Howard Ames during a jump dance in 1990, when the temperature stayed in the nineties for a week. His words echoed an old myth in which one of the Thunders is on the ridges, "being thankful for the weather," though no particular weather is mentioned (Spott and Kroeber 1942: 230).

As the Yurok writer Timm Williams put it, in the good spiritual life one must try "to think only good thoughts" (Seiter and Williams 1959: 13). But spirituality is not necessarily good: "spirit is neutral," as Harry Roberts said, "like electricity." Some people find it necessary to train their thinking in completely negative ways—when seeking revenge, for instance. That's the other side of it, and "everything has two sides," as Harry said again and again. Thus, Florence Shaughnessy, talking about making bad medicine in the mountains, said that "some people go there for very bad, violent thoughts. They come out of there with worse thoughts."

Thinking is a kind of action, not a passive, purely internal process: it has real consequences in the real world of "cause and effect." Harry, for example, often stressed the importance of "doing your thinking" openly, precisely, thoroughly (Buckley 1979). This kind of thinking is a mode of training (for good or ill), too, as well as a vital aspect of all modes of training.

The English verb "to think" seems to have replaced a variety of Yurok words fairly early on among bilingual Yurok-English speakers. These include *so·*, *sɹnɹyɹh*, "perceive with the mind," *kocpoks-*, "meditate," and *has-* or *hes-*, "intend," as well as *cpɹwɹk(sim-)* and *noksim-*, "to think of or about" (Robins 1958: 296). When Robert Spott used the English "thinking" in his conversations with Sylvia Beyer he seems to refer to a combination of analysis and meditation (1933, in Kroeber Papers, Bancroft Library, University of California Berkeley):

> A brand new pipe can be used by a man who's thinking he wants to get rich. . . . He must do all of the same things as the doctor—divide with the Creator in smoking when he blows the smoke out—blowing the tobacco that is left in his hand. The Indian Doctor, as well as the one who's thinking to get rich, or the one who is thinking to get closer to the Creator Law, he always divided with the Creator. He says,
> Hiiiiiii . . . kalau kihon.
> ni i peyuh.[4]

"Thinking," as an active practice, an aspect of training, might be supported by contemplative smoking accompanied by ritual offering of tobacco, *hohkum*. This noun is from the same root as the verbs "to make," *hoh(kum-)*, and "to be in training," *hohkep-*. Etymologically, "Indian tobacco" is a building tool. It is an essential aid to men's training, both in thinking and through prayer, "talking with" the spirituals. The creator Pulekukwerek himself lived on tobacco smoke alone, never eating, staying clean—the very model of male asceticism.

The native tobacco of northwestern California is *Nicotiana biglovii* var. *exalta Setchell*. Few people grow this "Indian tobacco" today though many use pipes and cigarettes of commercial tobacco, *N. virginianica*, as aids in contemplation. According to Dewey George, cigarettes had replaced pipes of Indian tobacco in the last functioning sweathouse, at Pecwan, by 1932. Cigarettes of *N. virginianica* are commonly used in ritual contexts today, and some younger people smoke high-grade marijuana (*Cannabis sativa indicus* var. *sinsemila*) in contexts that seemingly would once have required the use of *N. biglovii*. While most elders—and many other younger people as well—criticize them for smoking "bud," it would seem that the (indeed, milder and more subtle) psychotropic effect of *N. biglovii* was itself once a central part of the arts of training and thinking: Indian tobacco helps your thinking become clear and focused.[5]

Thinking is a personal obligation for someone seeking knowledge: "I can't learn *for* you, can I?" Harry Roberts used to ask. While mainstream academic training stresses didactic explanation—teachers telling students what to think—trained native people and people in training tend to view explanation as a mode of interference with another's purpose in life, comparable to theft, "stealing a person's opportunity to learn." A younger Yurok man who has trained hard says, "If you explain everything to a person you take away their purpose for being here. Why did they come? There are two of them now, and neither has a purpose for being here."

For this reason, people tend to see asking questions in a demanding way as both impolite and unproductive of real understanding. ("What do you think I am, a *dictionary?*" said an elder to an earnest but importuning outsider who was trailing him around at a dance.) Traditionally, younger people seeking knowledge from elders have been expected to simply pay close attention to what the other is doing, over a long period of time, letting it sink in slowly. Sometimes direct teaching is appropriate, but it often comes as a story or a fragment of an old myth, without explanation. Kroeber is interesting on this point, writing about the way an elder tried to educate *him* about salmon at the beginning of the twentieth century (in Kroeber and Gifford 1949: 120):

> He told in brief outline the episode, familiar to every Yurok, of Wohpekumeu's theft of the concealed first salmon; another snatch, of the institutional myth type, about the salmon run; added some folklore not in narrative form about the great head-salmon Nepewo and his home Kowetsek across the ocean; summarized a formula, associated with Wohpekumeu, for luck in salmon fishing; went on, at somewhat greater length, to tell the story which explains the origin, or constitutes the kernel, of the formula spoken at the annual first salmon or New Year ceremony made at [Wełkʷew], at the mouth of the Klamath; and finished with interlardings of descriptions of the ritual and taboos. There is no formal unity to the account; but it seems to be much the sort of thing which a Yurok might now and then string together to tell his son or nephew as they lay in the sweathouse.

Although we did not use a sweathouse, Harry Roberts often insisted that I sleep on the floor beside his bed when I stayed at his house, because "we have a lot to talk about." He'd wake throughout the night, turn on the light, roll a cigarette, and begin talking: "I've been thinking about what you said two days ago. . . ." I think that this is how Robert Spott had taught him, in the frame "white man house" that they occasionally shared, and that it is an approach rooted in sweathouse practice (below).

Kroeber tended to see such counterdidacticism and refusal to explain things as evidence of Yurok deficiencies in intellectualization (1976: 441). Robert Spott, on the other hand, told Harry Roberts that he "tried and tried to teach Kroeber, but he just couldn't learn." "White people," Harry said, "explain too much."

Old ways of teaching have endured on the Klamath. In 1990 a friend told me that when he went to an elder for help in bringing back the jump dance at Pecwan, in 1984, the elder told him a single short myth, about Pulekukwerek and Condor and the origin of the jump dance. He had been thinking about the story ever since, particularly its last few lines which he went over again and again, mantralike.

Not all men can, or ever could, function as mentors in this way. Once, men who had acquired neither wealth nor ceremonial expertise, however respected for their age alone, were granted little attention as teachers. Sregon Jim told Robert Spott about the difference between a rich and learned man and a poor man lacking in the self-control that brought wealth (in Beyer 1933–34):

> Not every old man could tell this sort of thing. Some of them have been poor all their lives. All such men know is how to eat. When they have eaten enough, they go to sleep. In the morning they get up and want to eat more. That is how some of them do all their lives. Other men are not like that. They think and think, and want to know what they ought to do. If there is a boy in the house, they know what to tell him.

Today the transmission of esoteric knowledge has become strained by the fact of the "missing generation" that came of age in the 1930s and '40s, often educated in federal boarding schools, often raised as Christians. At home their parents, discouraged and feeling that "it just didn't pay to be Indian," tended not to teach them what they knew, even discouraging learning indigenous languages. This has made it imperative for younger people who seek traditional knowledge to be more aggressive in ferreting it out from increasingly fewer knowledgeable elders and from books as well, and some worry that it has decreased the experiential emphasis in traditional learning, increasing the didactic.

While traditionally, as Jimmie James said, it was the "grandfather's duty to teach," today, not uncommonly, it is grandsons who teach their elders. In moments of discouragement a man born in the 1940s worries that these transformations in the traditional transmission of knowledge have made spiritual education "just telling a story." He worries that personal training is no longer as important as it should be, that "religion" is being reduced to "ceremony," rote repetition without understanding, and that "it's all story now," rather than immediate experience, authentic knowledge.

Yet elders who had been at the last Pecwan jump dances in the 1930s said in 1990 that the dance that year was the best since the Yurok jump dance's renewal in 1984. In fact, some said, it was better, more powerful and more pure than the dances before the hiatus. They were confident that the dance could be brought back fully because of the strength of younger men's minds—that missing knowledge had been and could continue to be regained through stringent training and thinking. As a younger man said, "it's all about making your mind strong and having it pull you along; it pulls you toward your goal."

"Mind," here, has multiple references—to clear perception as well as to concentration, to will power as well as to conviction. Robert Spott emphasized the importance of mental discipline in decisive action and the dangers of double-mindedness (Spott and Kroeber 1942: 198). Timm Williams, also Yurok, writes that "we set our ambitions and do not stop until we achieve them" (Seiter and Williams 1959). Thinking and acting are thus intrinsically linked, as are different kinds of "thinking."

The richness and multiplicity of meanings of "the mind" and of "thinking" reflect a fairly systematic personal ontology—a shared understanding of what a human being is—that I have begun to describe above. "The mind," as an element in personal existence, is equal in importance in spiritual life to "the spirit," with which it acts interdependently. Although Jimmie James, born in 1914, stresses the importance of having your mind supported by (or founded in) your spirit ("If you can't give your heart, then don't try to give anything at all"), he emphasizes the importance of making up your mind: "The mind is so strong. It's all in the mind. When your mind is strong, it makes your heart act, and when the heart acts, it moves the Creator. There's great power in the mind. First you make your mind strong, then the rest follows." In 1978 he told me,

> Some people want to be a good singer, some to be rich. I was very sickly and I wasn't expected to live past twenty five. Now I'm sixty five. I made up my mind to have a long life.
>
> Then I took cold baths in the river every day before daylight. And I'd turn to the east and ask the Creator for what I wanted.
>
> That's our way. If you keep clean and ask like that, you'll get whatever it is you're after.

Through training a person takes responsibility for realizing his spirit's purposes by making his body strong, clarifying his thinking, and focusing his will. All training depends on strength of mind and thinking, yet its results are not intellectual but palpable: successful training brings about real changes in the real world. "People evolve when they train," a Wailaki friend says. "They change, they get different when they start. You can tell. They stop drinking and they evolve—you can just tell, even if nobody says anything." George Albert Pettitt observed that in native North America the quest for power, however locally specified, less often concerns the "acquisition of religious tenets than the acquisition of an inner conviction of self-sufficiency" (1946: 92)

Yurok *pegɨk*, "man," can also mean "an independent person." In a myth told to Kroeber by Lame Billy of Wečpus between 1900 and 1903, a powerful person who people thought was "a real man" says, "I grew alone. I will go on like that. I have people enough" (in Kroeber 1976: 87). This hero had acquired the conviction of which Pettitt speaks, and this conviction is what I speak of as a real-world, palpable effect of training. As one of William J. Wallace's Hupa informants remarked to him regarding a man who had trained to be a warrior, "A fellow like Rennert has to have confidence in himself to be brave like that" (W. Wallace 1947: 324).

The Yurok men's semi-subterranean lodge, *ʔɨʔgɨ·k*, where they once slept, spent leisure time, meditated, and purified themselves, is usually called the "sweathouse" or "men's house" in English. It was once the predominating locus of men's training, where mind, body, and spirit all were purified and strengthened. Timm Williams:

The sweat house was more than a dwelling, it had a spiritual importance to my people. In the middle of the floor was a sacred fire. In order to purify himself in mind and spirit a man lay by the fire until he became so warm he began to sweat. While he did this he tried to think only good thoughts. Then, when he felt ready, he got up, rushed outside, threw himself into the cold water, or, in winter, into a snow bank. After this experience he felt refreshed in spirit and in body. [Seiter and Williams 1959: 13]

Boys were once introduced to this "men's club" when they were as young as six or seven. The heat inside was intense when the structure was shuttered and the fire lit. In the 1970s elders like Charlie Morten, Dewey George, and Frank Douglas recalled how they had come close to panic when they were brought in to sweat for the first time, as young boys. Some boys tried to "escape," and others recalled older men striping boys' feet with soot, so that they could tell in the morning, by looking at the feet, if the boys had left during the night while their mentors slept. But sweathouses were instituted by Pulekukwerek so that people would "feel well" (Sandy of Kenek, in Kroeber 1976: 344). "Feeling well," here, is equated with being free of pollution—being "clean" or "beautiful" or "new," *mʌwʌksʌyʌh*—and also with being physically fit, lean, and focused in purpose.

To be clean is to be in accord with the fundamental nature of creation, which is imperiled by pollution, things that are "dirty" or "old," *kimołeni*. As the world can be threatened by an imbalance in its fundamental beauty, so can people: that is why so many laws are necessary, to preserve and restore balance. By the same token, people seeking to get closer to creation, as spirit, must make themselves clean first. This involves stringent austerities emphasizing rules for eating, sequestering, and continence, once focused by sweathouse practice. With the decline of sweathouse use in the twentieth century, elders have wondered if real training is possible any more. Ella Norris, in 1976:

> *pegʌk* [trained men]—they go into sweathouse.
> *mʌwʌksʌyʌh*, clean. You don't eat with everybody; you eat by
> yourself, you have your own food.
> *mʌwʌksʌh*—you clean, gotta' be clean, don't mingle with
> womenfolks.

mɹwɹksišon ["a clean man"], same thing. They have their own food,
they don't eat the same acorns, they have special food. So I don't know
how they going to do it now—they don't go to sweathouse.

Yurok sweathouses slowly went out of regular use after the white invasion. In the 1970s Charlie Morten remembered old Yurok men like
Humpback Jim using the sweathouse at Čurey (modern Trinidad) around
1912.[6] They stayed inside as long as they could stand it, Mr. Morten said,
and then ran up the hill to stand under a big spring pipe that flowed there.
By 1918, he thought, the sweathouse was gone; Humpback Jim, who died
in 1916, had been its last occupant. Some other Yurok sweathouses remained in sporadic use until the 1930s, but after that there was a long hiatus until, beginning in the 1970s, a very few traditional sweathouses were
reconstructed.

More recently, two new sweathouses have been built in the California
State Park at Patrick's Point, north of Trinidad. These are in a new Yurok
village and brush dance site called Sumēg, built through the efforts of
many groups and Yurok individuals and dedicated in 1990. One of these
two sweathouses is open to visitors, but the other, surrounded by a high
chainlink fence with a locked gate, is reserved for ritual use by qualified
men and boys. In addition, a very few people have built or rebuilt traditional sweathouses for their personal use. Perhaps more men today, however, use plastic tarp-covered, Plains-style sweat lodges for sweats, though
not, of course, as dwellings or "gentleman's clubs."

In addition to the sweathouse's role in getting "clean," gathering wood
for its fire was classically the predominant means of male spiritual training. The ritual gathering of sweathouse firewood was instituted by a
woman who defined it as a practice to which people should devote themselves single-mindedly for ten days at a time (Lame Billy of Wečpus, in
Kroeber 1976: 20). While women (with the exception of doctors) were ultimately evicted from the sweathouses even before "the Indians" arrived
at the beginning of Indian Time, the practice of gathering sweathouse
wood remained central to training after the Indians came and the First
People left. Meanwhile, ritual sweathouse wood gathering accompanied
by weeping had been established as the essential male practice—a prin-

cipal means of focusing will power (Ann of Espeu, in Kroeber 1976: 453–56; Spott and Kroeber 1942: 143–44).[7] There are, of course, endless rules regarding how to "pack" sweathouse wood and what kinds of wood are appropriate. Some people still train in this way. A man who studied with a knowledgable Yurok teacher in the 1970s:

It's best to do it during the full moon, so you can see. The spirits come with you. All along the trail there are spirits, good and bad. You tell them what you want, talk with them. The first thing to learn is to deal with your fear—not to overcome it, but to deal with it, use it in your development. Each night you go farther and farther up the trail. Ideally, on the tenth night you go all the way to the top [of the hill or mountain]. You gather your wood. You should time it so that you get back down, build up the fire, sweat, and come out to jump in the water just as the sun rises. [My mentor] says that the higher you go, the hotter your sweathouse, the more power in it, the stronger you become. You sweat, come out, greet the sun, bathe. Then you rest during the day inside the sweathouse.

A Hupa practitioner today claims ten sweats a day for ten days as an ideal, but I don't know how old this practice is or if Yuroks have shared it. A Karuk woman, training to be a doctor, told me that a person could train for thirty days total, at one time, broken into three ten-day periods. Robert Spott told Earl Count (1934: 11), that a dedicated man should train for three months straight, in the summer, "packing sweathouse wood" in order to be "in the spirit." Whether we see historical change in general cultural models or personal variations or both in these divergent accounts, as always it seems unwise to generalize from them to form a pat, generalized system.

Seemingly, however, all men once had their own sweathouse songs, private property obtained when they were running for wood. Some elders in 1990 had these songs, and a woman young at the beginning of the last century still recalled in the 1970s the loveliness of early mornings filled with their music as men returned from the hills, a nostalgic reminiscence shared by Lucy Thompson in her remarkable book (Thompson 1991 [1916]: 35).

Although sweathouse practice has undoubtedly declined since the nineteenth century, elders like Ella Norris were not entirely correct in deeming sweathouses forever gone. Their use is perhaps resurgent today, along with other aspects of traditional spiritual life once thought extinct—like the Pecwan jump dance. Still, other aspects of the practice of getting clean are more practicable today, particularly controlling one's appetites for food and for sex—essential manifestations of the discipline that younger Yurok men stress.

Sex is natural and pleasurable: "Those Indians are going to have a good time with women," said Coyote when he made sex safe for men (J. Sapir 1921: 254). Indeed, Kroeber himself suspected that even earlier anthropologists had overstressed and overgeneralized Yurok sexual asceticism (in Spott and Kroeber 1942: 51). Yet sex is dangerous, and the problem for a man in training is that if he is thinking of sex he cannot think in an appropriately single-minded way about the objective of his training. According to Harry Roberts, sexual energy must be converted into "seeking energy" by the one in training. Such sublimation offers one key to the interpretation of the old Yurok wisdom that ejaculation drives away wealth, the traditionally quintessential object of training and signifier of its success. For this reason, in the past mentors preferred to initiate their students into training between the ages of nine and twelve, before puberty and the new, particularly sexual complexities that it brings. The experience of the contemporary Tolowa cultural expert Loren Bommelyn, whose principal teacher, the late Sam Lopez, began to train him at age ten, is probably suggestive of far older patterns in the region.

Again, however, the folk-wisdom of continence in training is subject to another interpretation. Semen is polluting, and being polluted is antithetical to the acquisition of wealth and power, which comes only to those who are "clean" (e.g., Driver 1939: 66). Abstention from sex indeed keeps one focused, "seeking," but it also keeps men clean, free of contamination by, most especially, menstruation. Women, even when they are not menstruating, are "the great defilers" *because* they menstruate. (Kroeber 1976: 367.8,9; cf. Buckley 1988). All contact with them is defiling to the man in training, especially sexual contact but also more innocent relations and, most insidious, contact through food that women have prepared.

In many instances, people in training are expected to fast and thirst. In a myth narrated by Billy Werk of Wečpus, a man's tobacco pipe case speaks to him: "Keep yourself in control. Do not eat" (in Kroeber 1976:

255). Mortals, however, hold themselves to slightly less stringent standards because, I have been told, a person not only has to keep up his strength but, if he tried to fast and thirst completely for ten days, all he could think of would be food and water. Moderation, here, aids concentration. Rather than a total fast and complete abstention from fluids, people often sip very thin cold acorn soup from time to time. "You decide yourself how to fast," a woman training to doctor told me.

If they eat, the food that men eat while in training cannot have been touched by menstruating women and becomes progressively more "clean" the farther it is from menstrual pollution. Acorns picked and prepared by a woman ten days after the end of her period are "cleaner" than those fixed by a woman only five days "clean." Food—dried salmon or venison ("against the law" to eat together) and acorn soup—prepared by prepubescent girls and postmenopausal women is thus appropriate for a man in training. An older woman can assist a man in training by saying a prayer for him as she cooks his acorn soup; the prayer rises "up to the Creator" with the steam. Best of all is food that a man has gathered and prepared himself: of it alone can he be entirely sure. In addition to fasting and thirsting, a man in heavy training also sleeps as little as possible, though resting comfortably.[8]

Clean food and an unpolluted dwelling are requisite to training, to praying, and to making medicine. People find these activities especially difficult today, in the absence of functioning sweathouses and other elements of the classic support system. They must camp out alone or close up their houses and not admit visitors who might not be clean. They can prepare meals only from supplies with intimately known origins (no store-bought food, no restaurants). Since it can take ten days and more to get clean, these difficulties are insurmountable for many, particularly older men who might otherwise continue to train and make medicine.

When a man trains hard he keeps to himself, concentrating, avoiding other people because they can distract him and because of the pollution that they might inadvertently bring. Secrecy plays a part, but it is also simply to preserve the privacy within which to concentrate on his goal that, according to an elder, when a person trains he should not tell others about it or talk openly about what he is "after." Keeping his own counsel, eating alone or fasting, spending much of his time alone thinking and getting clean, a man invariably becomes lonely and the loneliness of the man in training (or of a woman training to become a doctor) is a familiar theme (cf. Valory 1970: 206–8). Men who have trained hard emphasize how lonely they get when they "lead a strict life," and one Yurok friend told me that the lack of human contact was the "hardest part" of his extended training, which he also called his "abandonment."

There are pitfalls here and sometimes suspicion of others' motives and practices. "Sometimes people keep what they're doing secret to protect what may not be happening rather than to keep from saying what is happening," says a younger man, active in spiritual training. This man also suspected another of "just living isolated, trying to acquire something but not doing anything in any programmatic way"—that is, not rigorously following prescribed routines and rituals for training.

There is a putative tradition of men—often widowers—who stay constantly in training and entirely devoted to a spiritual life. Usually they have been purported to be ceremonial specialists and highly valued as counselors. Whatever basis in fact these reports have, few have attempted this perpetual asceticism (although world renewal medicine men customarily "stayed clean" for a full year after each dance [Kroeber and Gifford 1949]). A life well balanced between training and ordinary living has always been respected and valued and, according to people today, those staying too long in training can find themselves depressed, alienated from society and from their own sexuality. This is probably why Robert Spott told Earl Count, in 1934, that after intensive periods of training, men *have* to sleep with women: that that's part of the law too. "For about two months" after hard training, "a man proceeds to live normally," Count wrote in his interview notes, going on to quote Robert Spott directly: "He must lie with girls; and also girls who want to become doctors must lie with men; because the Creator said they must or they will get sick" (Count 1934: 12). Harry Roberts told me much the same, saying that men needed sex with women to bring them back into the human world after training had taken them so far into the spiritual.

A man can train and make medicine to become lucky, like the famous Sraʔma·u whose luck—until he lost it—brought him wealth, hunting success, wives, and all sorts of good things (Spott and Kroeber 1942: 169–71).

Sra?ma·u's luck came to him through a stone talisman that he obtained from a spring in the mountains after hard training. Once men made luck medicine in other watery places as well, such as an ocean pothole near Big Lagoon. They might train specifically for hunting or fishing luck, diving down in the Klamath to touch a special rock or making medicine at a "wishing place" in the mountains, where a pure man could hear the barking of hunting dog spirits (Waterman 1920: 238, 262, 270). In 1976 Anafey Obee spoke of these dog-spirits as being *wo·*, "ancient" or "holy," saying, "You hear them barking a-way off. It's deep."[9]

While hunting and fishing luck is important, more attention always seems to have been paid to gambling luck—a subject of intense interest today as in the past. Like the stick game, gambling games often pit traditional rivals against each other—Yuroks and Karuks against Hupas, for instance. The regional version of the men's hand game is nicely described by Malcolm Margolin (1994). It is

> a game called "Many Sticks," or more commonly "Indian cards." The "deck" consists of a collection of sticks, one of which, the "ace," is specially marked. The two teams sit opposite each other, while a neutral person, known as the "counter" sits off to one side. As the game progresses, the counter will dispense "counter sticks" that are used to keep score. A team is chosen to go first. The singer takes up a song, keeping time on a square drum, and the rest of the team sings as a kind of chorus. The "dealer" hides the deck of cards behind his back, "shuffling" it and splitting it into two bundles. He displays the bundles to the other team. The singers strengthen their song, calculated to dishearten and confound their opponents. A guesser on the other team tries to penetrate the song, guessing in which bundle the ace is embedded.
>
> As David Hostler [Hupa] points out, in northern California the various teams know each other well and play against each other often. "You get to know each other's method, each other's style. There is a lot of trickery and psychology in this game." Jimmie James [Yurok] feels that the songs open the heart. "They give you something money can't buy," he says. "These games have been going on forever," says Julian Lang [Karuk]. "They are as much a part of our life as breathing."

"Indian cards" themselves, thin wooden sticks about the size and shape of "pickup sticks," might be made in the mountains, or taken up there and prayed over, or left in a spot associated with gambling power for a year or so. Men have trained hard before diving down to underwater gambling luck rocks or visiting places in the high mountains, like the "men's rock" near Doctor Rock, where men have gone to pray after training. How much training is necessary before such undertakings is subject to debate. An elder recently told me of a waterfall near Pecwan that brought gambling luck after only three days of training, while several years ago Lewana Brantner (Yurok) said that men had to stay clean for six months before seeking gambling luck at the men's rock. In any case, some say, you have to train for ten nights before a big game anyway, getting clean, whatever kind of luck you have (cf. Drucker 1937: 239).

Gambling luck can depend on having a certain degree of power, gained through training and medicine-making. A dealer can use his mind to make the guesser (or "shooter") see two marked sticks where there is only one, or see the single marked stick in the wrong hand—or a man can use his power when he's the shooter to see where the ace is in the opposing dealer's hand. He can even lend his medicine to another shooter whose side he's backing, shooting the shooter with his power. "You magnify your mind on one thing, and then it happens," says a contemporary expert. But as with all power, gambling power is neutral and can be used for good or ill—to bring one clairvoyant capacities, deemed good, or to blind an opponent, not a good thing.

Gambling is a display of personal and team power, and men's gambling songs and their drums themselves are valued for their power, which can be enhanced through certain practices and lost through spiritual abuse or pollution. So gambling, as a test of power, can be a source of male prestige. Luck and the money that it can bring, through gambling, is a matter of accumulated power, and three-day summer brush dances often end with one lead dancer challenging the other side, carrying drumsticks and gambling sticks in his sea otter dance quiver.

People want to be "lucky," to have a few "Indian things." In the past, certainly, and again today for people dedicated to "the Indian Way" or to following "the sacred ways," this means traditional wealth—dance regalia most strikingly. Regalia brings prestige and influence when it is let out to dance, and it can also be used in various sorts of payments, as bride wealth and as recompense for the results of having, as my friend said, "balls." "No Indian wants to be a nobody, wandering around with no place to go, stopping by people's houses and smelling nice steaks cooking. Everyone wants a little something, a few feathers or something. They want to be ordinary, not really rich, but not a nobody, either," said the elder Calvin Rube in 1978.

THE SPIRITUAL

As he "accumulates" himself and becomes more clean, the person in training sees himself as more and more "real" and thus the world as more and more "beautiful": a real place in experience rather than merely a setting for a "story," for intellectual knowledge. In 1865, Captain Spott, for instance, trained for many weeks as he helped the medicine man prepare for the First Salmon ceremony at the mouth of the Klamath River, as his ritual assistant. Spott was transformed through his extended participation. According to his adoptive son, Robert Spott, "the old [medicine] man sent [Captain Spott] to bring down sweathouse wood. On the way he cried with nearly every step because now he was seeing with his own eyes how it was done, when before he had never thought much about it" (in Spott and Kroeber 1942: 177; see also Robins 1958: 180).

Tears, crying, are of crucial importance in Yurok spiritual training as manifestations of personal yearning, sincerity, humility, and openness. Through having these feelings a person attracts the "pity" of the spirituals, whether personified or conceptualized as a general presence. "The spiritual" rewards the human supplicant with what he's after—wealth or understanding or power or luck or whatever.

This kind of account, however, stresses the symbolic nature of crying and in doing so is somewhat misleading, because it obscures the central fact of genuine tears: they come from genuine feeling, from a deeply experienced inner state of being in which the ego is abased and vulnerable. Crying makes you "empty," Jimmie James told me in 1978, it "opens your heart," like a song (above). "You have to get right down in the ashes when you pray," said a young man after a jump dance, when his friends kid-

ded him that he'd looked "dirty, and *old*" in the sacred sweathouse (a special structure built for the dance, not for individual training). The comment is very interesting, because "dirty and old" is a rough equivalent of
the Yurok *kimołeni*, which also means polluted. The sacred sweathouse for
the Rekʷoy jump dance, put up for world renewal, was also *kimolen
ʔɹʔgɹ·c*—"dirty old sweathouse." Dirty and old is ready to be made new,
to be fixed by the spiritual. Thus Calvin Rube said, "There's great power
in tears. You have to cry right out loud to the Creator. If you don't shed
tears your prayer won't work, and you won't get what you're after." The
spiritual will not help you, make you new. Florence Shaughnessy also
spoke to me of going into the mountains to seek the pity and aid of spiritual forces:

> Nature gather[s] every force to help you. They know you're worthy of it.
> Otherwise you wouldn't cry, there'd be no tears. You'd just be sort of
> desperate. And then you can go in there and be desperate and come out
> desperate. Nothing helps you. But if you have this feeling that the forces
> blessed you, then you're a worthy person and you understand that you
> needed their help. That's why our [Yurok] people go to these places, be-
> cause the forces are there.

"We know that we are not the good ones," said Calvin Rube; "the Creator is the good one."

There are many ways to speak of the sources of spiritual blessings—as
"spirits," as "the spiritual," as "the forces of nature," as "the Creator" and
many more. Different people speak out of different experiences and some
out of different degrees of Christian influence. For many following the
old ways today, specific things in nature—certain rocks, mountains,
plants—are themselves spirits, once personified. However individuals
think and speak of "the spirituals" or of "spirit," they speak of something
sentient and alert, something or some one or many "unseen beings" that
they can "talk to"—that will listen and respond, if addressed correctly.
That correctness, the experienced openness of heart, often, is signaled by
tears. The steep mountains rising out of the Klamath River canyon, coming closest to the sky and being farthest from the pollution of human habi-

tation, are where the spiritual forces are most accessible and where people go, after suitable training and preparation, to "talk with them." One
of the *wo·gey* instructed human beings in how to do this, before the *wo·gey*
left and Indian Time began:

> If a person wants to tell me something, let him come up (into the hills)
> and stay all night. Let him take tobacco with him and angelica root, only
> those two. And he must be careful of himself before he does that: he
> must get sweathouse wood, and drink no water, and go with no women.
> Then I shall answer him if he calls my name; but if he does not do that, I
> shall not answer him; and if I answer him he will have what he tells me
> that he wants. And he may not eat in the house with the others. He will
> have to eat his food (separately) for ten days. [Mack of Wečpus, in Kroe-
> ber 1976: 291]

Around 1920 Florence Shaughnessy was taken up into the mountains
by an uncle to bring him luck and to make "long life medicine" for herself, when she was a "pure" young woman. In 1978 she recalled what
she'd observed and learned:

> We went over to the rock where men pray. . . .
> You go there and you fast for ten days and then on the tenth day you
> go there and clap your hands and you tell this rock what you want and
> then if you hear the echo you're going to get your wish. But if you don't
> hear it you best go home because you're not going to get your wish, be-
> cause there is something you did not do right. You were not pure
> enough, you didn't prepare yourself right and there is something that
> you forgot in your prayer. There's something . . . maybe you drank too
> much water, you didn't attend to your fasting, you been cheating or
> something. Then you might as well go home.

Some men today undergo training more or less for its own sake, to purify themselves and to gain in spiritual knowledge. Often such training
is undertaken in the late summer and in association with a major ceremonial. But intensive, ten-day training has always been undertaken in
preparation for praying in the mountains. There are many ways to make
medicine in the mountains. Some people say that medicine grows
stronger the higher a person goes, and that he must work his way up

slowly, level by level. Others give less structured accounts, saying that there are many different sorts of medicines at various high, powerful places. For instance, a qualified person can go to Doctor Rock, a place associated with the most powerful shamans, to pray not only for high powers, such as those for doctoring, but for stick game prowess or for luck in hunting or in gambling. There may be different training traditions carried in different families: these are the sorts of things that people often disagree on. Most people do agree on the general outline of mountain training, however.

If you have trained properly and know the right prayers and procedures, and weep, you will get what you are after. If you don't make your medicine, it is because you or someone else has spoiled your training. (If you go to the mountains' sacred sites in an impure state or act inappropriately there, some say that you will be physically injured up there or made ill by the offended spirits upon your return.) To quote various contemporary practitioners, part of the correct procedure is "to announce yourself. Say who you are, where you're from, what you want." A man should go "where a rock runs out. [He] builds a fire out there. You sit there, you have your fire in front of you; you stay there all night." Some medicines require that a man be accompanied by his mentor as novice doctors are accompanied into the mountains by their teachers (chapter 5), and one contemporary trainee says it's best to take at least two other people along, to "cover you with prayer," "blanket you" with protection from the "residue" of the suffering of ancestors at the hands of the whites.

Harry Roberts studied with Robert Spott at Requa for several years in the 1920s and '30s. Eventually he went high in the mountains to make advanced "high medicine":

> Before I made my high medicine I was cleaned up four or five times by a doctor. I sweated for eight days more after that in a sweathouse near Kenek. [Elders] scraped the sweat off me with a flat stick and wiped it on a leaf, and they burnt the stick and sprinkled the sweat on the ashes of the fire. They prayed over me. I just had acorns and [Labrador] tea. I was alone six days and then they came and talked to me for two more days. It was twelve days in all, before I went up into the mountains. I had a vision of where I was meant to go. I took a pipe, tobacco. Robert [Spott] followed me up, about a day behind.

SEEING WITH THEIR OWN EYES 121

In other cases people go alone. Florence Shaughnessy, in 1976:

> People would go up alone, in secret. And they'd keep themselves hidden
> if anybody came around. They didn't want to be seen. They'd camp off
> in the brush, and they'd just make a small fire so nobody could see them.
> That was because they were so pure, and they didn't want anybody to
> come near and spoil it. They kept unclean people away.

(Today, at least, people sometimes take dentalia shells along, offering
them to the spirits of the place, so that they will "clear the path" into the
mountains.)

The fire is built in order to offer tobacco and, sometimes, dried angelica root. (In some usages, men pound angelica in a small stone bowl,
mix it with water, and bathe with the solution while in the mountains,
leaving the bowl for others to use.) According to elders, as a man sits
before his small fire he prays and "thinks until everything becomes clear.
Then he's given a certain power for what it is he has been praying for,
what he wants to do." In some cases, when he has attained the proper
spiritual state he claps his hands, listening for a clear, ricocheting echo:
"The men go there and sit in the [prayer] seat there. Then after a while
they clap their hands, and if the echo comes back clear they know they
have what they've prayed for. But if it isn't clear, they know they won't
have that good luck." Other men shout, listening for an echo. Perhaps
this is what the wo·gey meant when he said, "I shall answer him if he
calls my name."

Spirits are not all good. There is both creative and destructive power
in the mountains, and only proper training permits one to discriminate
between them. Florence Shaughnessy, in 1976:

> You go to the mountains to seek whatever you're seeking, and then
> you'll find it. And then some people go there for very bad, violent
> thoughts. They come out of there with worse thoughts, because there're
> forces there to help [in] whatever you're seeking.
>
> There's all kinds of powers that you can seek, and sometimes you're
> blessed with finding it. You go in humbleness and you'll find that. You
> come away, you feel akin to everything, you're humble before the beauty
> of everything.

There are many other sorts of medicines aside from the kinds made by trained men and women in the mountains that rely on a combination of plant "medicines," correctly prepared and used, and set prayers or, as Kroeber called them, "formulas." This sort of medicine-making was once dealt with as "compulsive magic" in the ethnological literature, and Richard Keeling emphasizes it in his account of native northwestern Californian spiritual practices (1992). However, Keeling is far more sensitive to the place of deeply felt human spirituality in medicine-making than his anthropological predecessors were, with their seeming desire to primitivize peoples like the Yuroks. This is appropriate, for all successful medicine-making—either the kinds of "high medicine" that Harry Roberts spoke of or less portenteous undertakings—finally seems to involve some order of vividly experienced transformation. Julian Lang, in 1991: "Anyone can make medicine—gather herbs and fix them and drink it. But not many people can really *make* medicine—turn the plants back into the [First P]eople they once were and work with them. It's the same with fixing the world. You have to talk with it."

Elders stress that people who train spiritually must go slowly, gradually "higher," step by step, learning a bit at a time and digesting it well. If a person tries to train too fast, to run before he can walk, there is a danger that, rather than acquiring the help of good spirits he will acquire a "devil," a malevolent force that will enable him to do great harm but that will also drive him crazy and eventually kill him. Sometimes, people say, a person might think that his training has brought him good powers—to heal, for instance—but he has really acquired a devil and is both dangerous and in deep peril. He didn't know whom he was talking with. Some rocks, for instance, will indeed talk with you, but they'll also "get inside your head and make you crazy."

A person who is well prepared through slow development can go into the "high country," the physically and spiritually highest mountains. He will encounter spiritual beings associated with specific places, and they will teach him—"talk to him."[10] Some of these beings are immemorial spirits, and some are the spiritual forms taken by former human beings, now deceased. There are those who say that training really ultimately means just sitting down with spiritual beings and talking with them.

Native northwestern Californian prayer, then, is not so much equivalent to the popular conception of beseeching an invisible supernatural superior as it is an expression of interdependence, social relationship and, at the highest levels, at-onement in a world of human and other-than-human people, all-together in place—ʔoˑlolekʷiš ʔoʔl, in Yurok ritual speech (Buckley 1984b). To "really make medicine," in Julian Lang's sense, is to experience this at-onement in a definitive way—again, for better or worse (though it's best, here, to emphasize the good). To understand training and medicine-making at the level of its deepest significance, we must understand them not just as use of the appropriate herbs and words, but as knowledge gained through hard training and intense personal experience.

The transformations that occur in men's and women's lives through spiritual training and practice may be immediate and of greater or lesser import, or they may be delayed. A person might meet spirits in the mountains and "sit right down and talk with them," or he might meet them after returning home, in a sort of delayed reaction. Calvin Rube, in 1978: "Maybe after you come back from the mountains, some night in your home, you wake up, maybe screaming in fear. There are spirits in the room and it's full of light. They'll teach you if you can get control of yourself."

Traditionally, men have been urged to train hard and constantly while they are young, with the expectation that they will reap the fruits of their efforts later in life, often in the form of the wealth that will naturally come to them. Consistent with this theory, some people today consider that a man's efforts in training, rather than having to be endlessly repeated, sometimes can lead to a definitive and irreversible "breakthrough," an enlightenment. This breakthrough may be realized in making high medicine—having a powerfully transformative experience or realization as a result of training—and it can also come later, at mid-life.

An elder who spoke to me at length in the 1970s had an immediately transformative experience. Going into trance in a "prayer seat" in the high mountains, he saw, as though through a tunnel, a small hole of light opening into a meadow (locally, a "prairie") in the sky (cf. chapter 5). A spiritual being took him up to this world above. He saw people there, "all in the prime of life—about thirty-five years." He could not talk with them or eat with them, lest he lose control and be unable to get back to earth.

He knew this to be the "beauty world," where the spirits of trained people go at death, waiting, he told me, for the time when they would come back to earth in new forms. He was guided back to the seat by one of the spirit beings, and when he returned to his body in the prayer seat he knew what "beauty" truly was, and "walked in beauty."

This man said an interesting thing. The spirits that he saw were not, he asserted, really there—their forms were simply the best his imagination could provide, given that "the spiritual is completely different from the material," and thus unimaginable.

"High men" and women who are doctors are said to be able to return to the mountain precincts and to the knowledge that they acquired there, later, without leaving the lowland villages, through out-of-body travel. This kind of experience is mythically chartered. In 1902, Stone of Wečpus told Kroeber about a hero who "left something like his picture at home while he traveled to the end of the world" (Kroeber 1976: 223). In 1978 another elder said that he commonly traveled out of his body to the place where his medicine was, in the inland mountains, and in 1990 yet another spoke of retrieving medicine from an inland lake while physically remaining in the sweathouse at Pecwan.

In contrast to life-changing, single peak experiences and the abilities that they bring, some people say that a trained man's transformation characteristically occurs slowly and almost of itself, becoming clear at middle age. This was said to have occurred to two elders whom I knew in the 1970s. A Yurok friend who also knew these men well and who spoke to me about their mid-life "breakthroughs" pondered the relationship between such spiritual completion and quitting drinking, which, as had these men, many men do at mid-life, if they have survived their wild years. While a newly heartfelt commitment to sobriety may well be a practical factor in the spiritual completion of older men today, the pattern itself—youthful training culminating much later in notable and apparent spiritual development—most probably predates the introduction of alcohol. Yurok myths describe figuratively the "yogi-like unconcern" of certain old, human men (Kroeber 1976: 315), and historic accounts bear interesting witness as well. The nineteenth-century Hupa Indian headman, called today "Captain John," seems to have exemplified the post-breakthrough trained man in classical northwestern California. Here, he is re-called by one who knew him:

> Captain John was a good man. He was a sort of religious fellow like a preacher and he always talked to the people. Old John told them how to act, what to say, and things like that. He was good to everyone. The other people depended on John some. He always was good to them. He knew the laws and he told the others about them. He was always telling young folks what was right and what was wrong. Anything he had he divided up with others. Sometimes he would get a whole boatload of eels or salmon and give them all away. He gave them to the old people, every one. Old John would give away the last thing he had. He was a good man, but if you got in trouble with him, look out! He didn't stand back for no one. [In W. Wallace 1947: 323]

Captain John "always talked to the people," replicating in his relation-ship with them his relationship with the Immortals who urged him to "talk to me." The boundaries between the human world and the spiritual are not fixed and impermeable, though their relationships are, always, matters of individual interpretation. A contemporary spiritual person thinking about the mysterious appearances and disappearances of Big-foot (Sasquatch—in Yurok, *rak ni u?ma?ah*) in the mountains, explained to me that "the spiritual" is a dimension of reality that parallels our fa-miliar mundane dimensions. Bigfoot simply steps out of and back into that dimension, at will and unpredictably. Human beings can enter the spiritual—get "in the spirit"—and when they do they are more like the First People than not. This metaphysical complexity was once evident in Yurok language use where a separate ritual speech register, "*wo·gey* speech," was syntactically constructed as referred speech. In it, "they" were human beings, "we" the *wo·gey* themselves, and both spirits and human beings were collapsed into single ontological category, "people" (Buckley 1984b). In recent years, skeptics have wondered if the great dances, like the jump dance at Pecwan, can really be restored since this language, once used by the medicine men who prayed in the dances, is now largely lost (chapter 11). Others (including many elders) have felt that language is not the issue: what matters is being in the spirit.

To emphasize the major life transformations that training and medicine-making can lead to may obscure less momentous transformations
that occur more frequently, when people are in the spirit, momentarily
transformed through training or prayer or dancing. Hupa people say, for
instance, that as they dance all night on the third and last night of the
brush dance they become more and more *xoche*—"real," "beautiful," "Indian." Yurok men dancing in the more serious jump dance also say that,
as they dance through ten days, the spirit grows stronger and stronger:
"sometimes that spirit is so strong it makes you just want to lie down."
There is a mystery here, as well as more familiar religious transport. The
black face paint that men wear in jump dances, people say, is to make
them look more like spirits. This is also why the faces of the dead are
striped with black: so they will be admitted to the spirit world. The black
paint of both dancers and the dead is their "passport."

The brilliant red head rolls appliquéd with fifty and more pileated
woodpecker scalps on buckskin—some of the "wealth" that people attract through being "good"—make dancers seem even more like spirit beings, who are said to be red from the eyebrows up. Some people say that,
by the end of a jump dance, they are spirituals: that all difference between
the unseen beings who have come to watch the beautiful regalia dance,
standing in an apparently empty space left free for them, and the men
who have danced with that regalia has momentarily disappeared. This
may be the end—on whatever level it happens—of the journey from the
physical to the mental to the spiritual: that all such distinctions disappear,
that the really "real world" is revealed. This real world is not a symbolic
cosmos whose structure we can all too easily wring from myth, ethnographic reconstruction, and the many, always varying accounts of different individuals. It is in the hearts of those individuals, who find themselves in a quite specific, concrete world.

5 Doctors

Kill or cure! The two functions of man.

Ford Madox Ford, *Parade's End*

There is no single word in Yurok that can reasonably be translated as "power," in the sense of a person's acquired, spiritually based potential to accomplish a desired end. What is today called "power" was formerly an unspecified, generalized presence (cf. Kroeber, in Elmendorf 1960: 522.2). My own understanding, gained through various elders, is that what we now call "power" was once perceived as no more or less than the integral energy of "creation," *ki ?wes?onah*, a movement at the heart of "the spiritual." As part of its essential nature or functioning, "power" was once inseparable as a unique thing from the rest of reality. Simply, there could be no world without it. A person could acquire the capacity to control this energy, to "do something" with it, good or bad, but the energy itself was essentially neutral. When one had that kind of control he or she had what people call "power" today.

Control, the ability to do something "on purpose, every time," as Harry Roberts used to say, is task-specific: a person spiritually acquires the ability to do this or to do that. This kind of control has been called "power" in English for a long time. Even the cultural conservative Robert Spott used the English term as early as the 1930s, perhaps picking it up from the Indian Shakers (who came to the Klamath in 1926; see chapter 10) or in the Baptist church that he occasionally attended but never joined (see Beyer 1933–34; Count 1934; Barnett 1957). Use of the term "power" probably long predates Spott's acceptance of it, although his adoptive nephew, Harry Roberts, seldom used the English word in his conversations with me and spoke it circumspectly when he did—as did other elders that I worked with in the 1970s.

Still, "power" is a word one hears more frequently among younger people in northwestern California today, and it has been a word invoked with some regularity by other anthropologists. It seems difficult to avoid it in discussing spirituality in the region, where having control of power, often and paradoxically while relinquishing oneself to its control, is a central aspect of being "in the spirit."

In the received ethnographic literature, the Yurok *kegey*, "doctor" (pl., *kegeyowor*), usually identified as a "shaman," seems the exemplar of those commanding power. Kroeber was clearly fascinated by these figures in part because they seemed once to have been almost exclusively women in what he construed as an overwhelmingly male-dominated world (cf. Buckley 1988) and in part because of the sheer exoticism of their training and practice. He wrote a considerable amount about them himself. He also directed Erik Erikson to the Yurok Indian doctor Fanny Flounder, widely regarded as the last of the very powerful "old-time" Yurok doctors, as a source of privileged insight into Yurok worldview (chapter 9), and had several of his graduate students at Berkeley salvage further information about them.[1]

Given all this attention, the *kegeyowor* came to be central to scholarly debates, primarily among psychologists, who mined and re-mined Kroeber's publications, usually with no firsthand contact with Yurok people.[2] However, Dale Keith Valory, the first anthropologist to do new sustained fieldwork on the Klamath after the last of Kroeber's immediate students had departed, twenty years earlier, reassessed somewhat the psychologists' pathologization of these over- and often misrepresented figures in his dissertation, subtitled "a study in identity, anxiety, and deviance" (Valory 1970).

Nonetheless, what is missing in all this attention is any real sense of the original contextualization of the *kegeyowor* within a broad associational field of men and women with curative and other powers to whom the *kegey* stood, in Jean Perry's accurate formulation, as a prototypical figure (personal communication, 1991). In addition, the historical fluidity of this semantic field itself—its reconfigurations and transformations through relatively recent historical experience—was vastly underplayed in Kroeber's ethnographic reconstructions and entirely ignored by the removed theorists who made psychoanalytic hay with them.

As men's training proceeds along a continuum and perhaps must be misunderstood if aspects of it are taken outside of this context, so sucking doctors arise along a continuum of people with increasing powers to "do" things, "on purpose, every time," at "higher" and higher levels. In this chapter I follow that continuum—one that continues to form an associational field in contemporary local discourse on "doctors." I begin, however, slightly outside of this field with the problematic figure of the "Indian devil," *ʔumaʔah*, an actor who is not locally associated with doctoring in my experience.

INDIAN DEVILS

People use the terms "Indian devil" and "deviling" to refer to "bad doctors"—witches and sorcerers—and their prayers or medicines. But the term "Indian devil," *ʔumaʔah*, is also frequently used to refer to transformer-sorcerers, shape-shifters who can run great distances at night, emit fiery sparks and displays, disguise themselves as various animals and birds—dogs, bears, and owls especially—and poison people by shooting them with tiny magical arrows from a foul-smelling kit, also called *ʔumaʔah*. In English, "devil" can also refer to this kit and to other malign power-objects, or medicines, so a person can "have a devil"—sometimes, they say, a phosphorescent root Yuroks obtain from Tolowas. The matter is complicated even further by the fact that the same terms and their variants, *ra·k ni ʔumaʔah* and *ka·p ni ʔumaʔah*—"creek devil" and "brush devil" (as well as "wild Indians")—also refer to the gigantic humanoid called Big Foot in English. Like "spirit," "doctor," and "medicine," "devil" can have many meanings, although in this case part of the seeming confusion is the result of recent historical change and part reflects older contradictions in Yurok mythology and the local typology of evil.

Dale Valory's dissertation chapter on the *?uma?ah* (Valory 1970: 102–50) is the best source available, and I will not repeat all that Valory says here.[3] Rather, I mention some central information on the *?uma?ah* from Valory's work and other sources, add some oral testimony that has not been previously recorded, and place this mysterious bad guy within the broader Yurok spectrum of personal powers.

The Mysterious Thing

There would seem to be at least two historical strands intertwined in the modern notion of the *?uma?ah*. The first and older of these concerns a sorcerer who has obtained a kit of twelve miniature poisonous black obsidian arrows, which empower him to sicken and kill enemies. Kroeber called this kit "the mysterious thing." It shot out showers of sparks and flames and originated in the poisonous fiery arrows of a jealous husband subdued, in myth, by the creator-hero Pulekukwerek (Kroeber 1976: 277–37). The tiny arrowheads were chipped from a magical "flint" so powerful that a flake of it would explode in a fiery eruption if not handled properly. Some people say that a man had to get this flint from a "creek devil," Big Foot, although Valory argues that finished kits were traded up from the Wiyots to the south (1970), and Kroeber says that they were available to anyone for purchase or hire (in Elmendorf 1960: 500.2).

The "Indian devil," trained in the use of his kit, his devil, shot its tiny arrows into his victim in an act that was the reverse of the "sucking doctors'" removal of introjected disease-causing "pains" (below). The twelve arrows were graded in strength and malevolence, the first causing a mild cold, the second a few days of cold with headaches, and so on up to the last four, which were lethal. The kits stank like very strong, rank angelica root, and their stench increased with use. They had, in fact, to be used frequently in order to retain their power, which was further increased by the devil's attributed grave-robbery and necromancy. Very few doctors had the power to suck out these arrows—none in the generation active between 1900 and 1940 and only four—a Tolowa, a Karuk, and two Yuroks—in the generation before that (Spott and Kroeber 1942: 164–65).

The Foot

The second historical strand in these sorcerers' attributes was the ability to run great distances at high speeds at night, while in trance. According to some, this ability resided in an anklet of drilled mussel shells, called a "foot" in English, that could be bought and sold or borrowed. Coyote borrows one, in myth, to race Water (Lame Billy of Wečpus, in Kroeber 1976: 139). Anafey Obee told of a man who'd bought one, put it on, and gone into trance:

> So he felt himself way up above Martin's Ferry somewhere, swung down to Kenek. He didn't know it. "Oh, I got scared!" he says. Took it back to the fella he bought it from, down to Blue Lake somewhere. He says, "You can't out-travel that son of a gun!"
> A foot.

Anyone could get a "foot," according to Mr. Obee: the Indian devil's running power didn't depend on having one but was more mysterious. Others disagree, and the matter is vague. Most people do agree that devils run at night, with or without a foot, and that they emit a light as they do, which some identify as their "souls." The hills above Pecwan are still famous for these "night runners,"[4] although Waterman (1920: 250) says that Meri·p, upstream from Pecwan, was once most famous for its devils. The whole matter is further complicated by the fact that running training—sometimes at night—is also associated with the warrior's and others' training regimens.

Shadows

The contemporary idea that the lights emitted by devils are from their "souls" contrasts somewhat with the seemingly older characterization of devils by their "shadows," saʔawor, rather than their life spirits, weweceḱ. A person can get rich if he can catch and hold onto a devil all night long—

no mean feat, given devils' strength and staying power. Devils send out their multiple shadows to confound their would-be captors. "You have to train to catch a Injin Devil," said Antone Obie, "they got super-strength, duration, endurance—they last all night." Some say that the devil has twelve shadows, one for each of his arrows (Valory 1970: 109), and others say five. Ella Norris, in 1978:

> At Fern Canyon, at Osegon—where they dried smelts—
> So, this fella says, "I'm gonna get rich. I'm gonna grab that Indian devil," because they pay well.
> So he train and he train and he train. Just like football players. Mohammed Ali—he's practicing all the time; I see his picture. They train the same way. They turn logs over, roots over, and train and run back and forth.
> So he's well-trained. He train for a long time. He's fasting.
> So he went.
> And he went way up in the hills there.
> And sure enough, he see a shadow five times. That's the way this Indian devil travels.
> So he sit there on that roadside: he saw a shadow.
> The fifth one, he jumped—grabbed him. They wrastled to pretty near daylight and the sun was coming out.
> So that Indian devil says, "You let me go—I'll pay you well. But don't tell."
> So he tied him up. That young fella was so stout he tied him up, tie him to a tree.
> He went home.
> He didn't tell everybody, but he told his folks. He said, "I got him. I tied him up."
> So he went back—had his breakfast, he went back.
> That fella's still sitting there, can't get off—he's tied him up.
> So he told him, he says *"ti?n wiš kem wi ?eket,"*[5] he says: "What you doing here?"
> And that Indian Devil he laugh, he says, "It's you. If it wasn't for you I wouldn't be sittin' here."
> So he paid him well.
> That's what that young fella got rich by—them woodpecker heads and arrows and different things.
> "Don't ever mention my name."[6]

There are many stories like this, and sometimes the name of the devil is given in them—often the name of someone known to have positive, "good medicine," too.

Devils are, often, oddly associated with laughter. One aspect of the Indian devil's persona is that of a mischief maker that runs around at night whistling and making noise, blowing out fires and giving people the creeps. So it seems somehow coherent that one way to kill an Indian devil is to make him laugh. Dewey George:[7]

> Used to go over that place near Big Lagoon—said that people camp—you don't camp by creek, you know—they camp above the creek.
> They know that Indian devil is in there then—they had a lot of fun then, nighttime.
> Them guys long time back, one time, in the story, they say catch salmon down here, you know. They took the guts out, hang it over there.
> You know, salmon have something like a balloon inside that lay around in there [swim bladder].
> Mr. Devil was have a lot of fun with the guy.
> This guy go pick up this balloon up there. He throw it, out there where the devil was. He hit on him in the eye—Bosh!
> And that devil fall over laughing so much he died.
> That's a true story. It's just a story.
> He laughed so hard. . . .

Transformation

All of this would seem to form one more-or-less consistent and coherent account of the ?uma?ah, Indian devil: a magical kit of fiery arrows to poison with, running medicine, multiple shadows (said by some to look like large furry balls), a secret cache of wealth earned by hiring out to cause harm. But there is an added wrinkle: the Indian devil can transform himself into another sort of creature—most often a dog, although owls and other birds have also been reported for Yurok sorcerers, and wolves and bears for Hupas.[8] One tradition has it that devils wear a sort of "mask," made from a dog's skin, and people today joke about stray dogs that are "wearing my hide for me until I need it" (cf. Cody 1942: 229–31). There is no end of stories about someone getting so-and-so (disguised as a bird or a dog) in their gunsights, but letting them off with a warning: "Don't do that again or I'll kill you." One famous story about two elders, now gone, is that the man used to come around the woman's house as a dog (she was a noted beauty). One night she got fed up, took a rifle, and shot him in the butt. *"A·gah"* (ouch!) he said, then *"a·ch"* (oops)—*"er·k er·k er·k"* (arf arf arf). He was seen limping around in his human form for some time after that. "She was a crack shot," said an old friend, concluding this story, "and never without a man."[9]

It may well be that deviling has more reality as an accusation than as an act (and that devil stories have higher entertainment value than truth value), but it has been a frequent accusation consistently framed, at least since the late nineteenth century. "People are always telling those horror stories," Harry Roberts used to say in disgust.

Valory (1970: 110–14) argues that the transformer aspect of the deviling accusations is fairly recent, resulting from Wiyot contacts with Pomo bear shamans during forced removals in the 1860s, the idea of shamanistic transformation into an animal spreading from the Wiyots to coastal Yuroks and thence upriver—an account supported, on other evidence, by Cora DuBois (1940: 5). Valory also argues that sorcery in general increased radically under the tensions of white occupation, as well as changing forms. Charges of deviling have also perhaps been given more recent stimulus, since 1926 by Shaker concerns with deviling and with driving out devils. Indeed, it seems likely that modern preoccupation with witchcraft and sorcery accusations, both within and outside of the Shaker Church, is in part a complex response to the social traumas of dispossession and oppression by an enemy far too large and powerful to address directly (cf. Valory 1970: 149). This may explain why it is so difficult, in many of the humorous stories, to tell whether people are speaking of human devils or other-than-human people—*ra·k ni ?uma?ah*, Big Foot.

Even when they hold devils and deviling as matters of mordant fun, however, many people are firmly convinced of their existence. Here is Aileen Figueroa's account of a confrontation with an Indian devil, probably around 1935. She talks about the devil's training in a way that makes it comparable to that of the warrior in Anafey Obee's account (chapter 4), and also to the training of the *kegeyowor*, "high doctors," as we'll see below. Aileen Figueroa in 1976:

ʔumaʔah—that's devil.

I've seen them. I've seen several of them, long time ago.

We was living on the ranch. The little one, he kept crying and crying. We had a dog and this dog—I went outside and I heard that dog barking down the road. I went outside and I heard that dog running—clear up into the mountains you'd hear him, and then he'd come down. And barking—sound like he was trying to grab at something at the same time. And then he'd come down. His mouth was all wet. He'd circle around, then he'd go back up into the mountains again—not far, but then he'd kind of circle down again.

I was setting down—it was kind of a side-hill. I was setting down kind of on my tiptoes there. I held a three-celled flashlight over my head and I was trying to shine it.

There's a road runs down below the house. I was shining it and all at once I see a big flame, right in the road there: big flames shooting about that high [three feet]. It was just beautiful, beautiful—you know how fire flames, shaped like that [pear-shaped]? Pretty. And right in the middle I seen two green eyes looking right out, right inside that fire.

I hollered, hollered at them [in the house] and I guess finally they heard me. I didn't want to leave. Finally they came out and went down there with the flashlight and looked all over and we didn't see anything.

I seen it.

It's a people, it's people . . .

A lot of time maybe you're mean to a certain person or something like that, and they're trying to get revenge or something like that, [get] back to you or something like that. Then they'll get themselves into different . . . maybe you'll see a great big dog or something like that out there. They can make theirselves into different things. . . .

It's the same thing like with the Indian medicine man. They go a certain time, ten days, something like that, without drinking water or eating, without sleeping with a woman or something like that. They go out and they learn that.

You can't do that now because people aren't clean.

While Indian devils themselves are both mysterious and, to an extent, outside of the doctoring domain, there are indeed "bad doctors" well within it. They are decidedly unfunny (below). But this large semantic domain includes a wide variety of people acting for good as well as ill. In the next section I begin to outline it in terms of a hierarchy of powers.

"YOU GO AND SPEAK TO IT"

Many Indian people in northwestern California have had a variety of extraordinary "powers" gained through the inheritance or purchase of set prayers—what Kroeber called "formulas" (cf. Keeling 1992). These prayers, usually used in conjunction with herbs, have been the bases for making medicine toward a variety of ends, both good and bad. Ella Norris in 1976, speaking of practitioners still active in the early years of this century: "Them days, they pray—everything they do. White people it's different—but Indians it's different. Indians, everything they do they pray, and they fast—maybe ten days."

For instance, in 1976 while we were driving together through a heavy fog, Dewey George told me about his father's medicine for dispelling fogs (paraphrased): "Once I was driving my father and we run into some heavy fog like this—couldn't see a thing. My father said, 'better do something about this.' I stopped and he got out, made medicine, prayed. Fog lift. I don't know what he did."

There must once have been a great deal of weather-medicine in the region, especially on the coast, although the Yuroks have had no specific "weather shamans" as do many California groups. Captain Spott (Robert and Alice Spott's adoptive father), who often traveled on the ocean in large canoes, was known to have had prayers embodied in songs for calming the sea when it got too rough (Kroeber 1976: 430.2). Such songs were frequently transmitted as capping songs in stories that told their origins. In 1976 Ella Norris told me the following story in Yurok, capping it with a Tolowa song used to turn the wind:

> About that seagull story—
> Seagull's supposed to have his own grandma, you know, own
> grandma. Coyote just the same way—is alway just got a grandmother.
> Anyway, this seagull he stayed with his grandma.
> So the grandma goes every morning pick strawberries. Oh, [s]he'd
> come home big basket full of strawberries, nice big ones.
> He says, "Where did you get 'em, grandma?"
> "Oh," she says, "I got 'em certain place—but don't you go get 'em."
> She says, "I don't want you bother 'round my strawberry patch. You
> stay 'way from it."

He thought, "Well, I'm gonna—"

So he sneaked 'round. He found where she could pick. (And in my days I noticed how be strawberries there too, wild strawberries—they get big you know.)

So anyhow, he comes home that day. He says, "Grandma," he says, "I got some strawberries here. Look!"

"Oh!" she says, "You found my strawberry patch!"

She grab him and put him outside, punish him. "You do no good," she says, "I told you not to get my strawberries. Here you are," she says [hits him with stick]. "I don't want nobody to find out where my strawberry patch."

So he feel so bad he went down to the beach. (This happened at Point Saint George.)[10] So he went down to the beach to look around. Think, "I better leave. I'm not going to come back. My grandma don't want me."

So he started, he kept on going towards the ocean 'cause he just got this bones, got biggest knuckles, you know, where she hit him [on knees]. That's how you see seagulls got big bumps [on their legs].

Soon enough, pretty soon he start flying.

And then he couldn't hardly make it towards the ocean, the south wind was a'blowing. So he started singing:

[*sings Seagull song*]

So he wished that wind would blow from the north so he could fly out. Sure enough, that wind turn 'round.

So he went way out in the ocean.

So if you look, you see them trying to fly. The north wind's blowing. They glide along.

There are many, many other sorts of prayers and songs. I have been told of prayers used to recover drowned bodies from the river or sea, for turning back epidemic illness, for controlling intentionally set grass fires, and for warding off ill omens, to mention but a few. The power of such praying or "talking to" can be dramatic. The following accounts, given to me by Florence Shaughnessy in 1976, offer vivid examples. The first concerns Starwin Bill. Blind in his old age and often called Blind Bill or Blind Billy, he lived with Kitty and Jimmy Gensaw (Yurok) at Requa. The time is around 1910:

If an owl ["timber" or "screech owl," *tek^{w}e?s*] came, that was one of the things we didn't like because he brought a message of something bad, always death.[11] So anyone who knows the prayer to counteract the message, you say "You go and speak to it." Then you use a special prayer to ward off the message that he brings. It brings the message only if he hoots, and a special way he hoots—not very long; sharp. Always he brings the news of death, and that's true—

[It was] eleven o'clock at night when everyone was in the house singing or telling stories or something. And the owl came. And he made his call. He was sitting on top of that old community hall—it was a big building.

So Momma [Kitty Gensaw] went in and told [Starwin Bill] what was happening out there.

So he said, "Bring me a rock, one rock."

So she found it—it had to be a certain shape. She had a lantern, so she found the rock.

So he took it into his hand and he prayed. And then he tossed the rock down, down to where the sound—where the owl was.

So early the next morning he was up and washed and said, "Go get those kids and send them down there to see if the owl is dead."

So we went down there and we found a dead owl. We couldn't bring it near the house.

Then up at my grandmother's [Ollie Serper's] the same sort of owl came, and she had a great big oak tree by her cabin, her home, just thick with limbs. And he came here.

And he was making his cry just so. He was just bouncing up and down and the leaves were dropping down.

So she went out and got a rock, and she prayed to the rock and went out there and tossed it.

So she told [my brother]—he was staying with her—"Go out and bury that owl."

So he went out and there was a dead owl, so he buried it.

My Grandmother Ollie Serper, see? The same prayer.[12]

I don't know how you would explain that, but each time there was a dead owl there the next morning. Maybe another owl came along and had a heart attack! But it's kind of weird, isn't it?

People who knew a variety of such prayers were called *teno·wok* in Yurok, "well educated." Florence Shaughnessy again:

> *teno·wok*—it means he knows all kinds of—he knows all the different ways to pray for things, because he has trained, he has been to the mountains, he has been to these different rocks.

So if anything happens you go to this person because he's well-schooled; he's studied all of this.[13]

Harry Roberts told me that when men like Robert Spott (whom Mrs. Shaughnessy mentioned as someone who was *teno·wok*) trained hard they naturally acquired some curing powers, which they could then choose to develop or not. Aileen Figueroa's recollection of her grandfather, which I recorded in 1976, suggests this. It perhaps relates a practice arising after the coming of European epidemic illness to the area, around 1830 at the earliest.

[Grandfather Jones] went out at night to pray. He was a medicine man. When the influenza was coming [winter 1918–19] he went out at night to pray and it stopped. It didn't come any closer. But there's no one can do that now.

He also used to doctor people. Not like an Indian doctor [*kegey*]—he would just sing and talk, pray for people.

Dewey George, who was known to have many prayers, also seems to have known how to do some curing. Mr. George, in 1976 (paraphrased):

There was a brush dance at Hoopa [in 1972] and ["Joe"] thought he saw a waterdog [redwood salamander] jump and try to get in his mouth. He tried to pull it out.

I heard about that and I said I knew how to cure him, but my sister didn't want me to. I'd have to lock up my house so nobody would come around. It takes a lot to make Indian medicine. My sister didn't want me to do that because it takes too much.

So he went to an Indian doctor in Redding [Flora Jones (Wintu)] and she cured him.

DEFINING DOCTORS

People once commanded many sorts of curative prayers, often used in combination with small amounts of herbal "medicine," *meskwoh*. Kroeber (in Spott and Kroeber 1942: 157) speaks of prayers to cure "snakebite, insanity, sacroiliac slip, cuts, bruises, breaks, puerperal fever, any illness [presumably, of new mothers] within 20 days of parturition, and arrow-head or bullet wounds." (To this list I can add "deer sickness" and boils.)

Ownership of such prayers sometimes entails command of practical techniques as well. In 1933 Robert Spott, for instance, gave Kroeber a complete recipe for healing bad backs which involved steaming the patient over a trench filled with hot rocks and herbs and covered with fir boughs, much as men in training sometimes steam themselves for purification. He also gave instructions on how to reset dislocated shoulders, and seems to have had the knowledge of a "bonesetter," one of several exoteric curative specialties mentioned by other consultants (Kroeber Papers. See 1900–1907).

Kroeber noted (in Elmendorf 1960: 248.1) that there is no special term in Yurok for the various prayer and practical doctors "as a profession." Today, they all tend to be called "doctors" in English, although the distinctions among them, and especially between them and "real doctors," the sucking doctors, remain important. By trying to force this loose congeries of multi-talented "doctors" (with the exception of the *kegey*) into clearly bounded categories of specialists we may risk imposing a kind of conceptual order on classic Yurok knowledge not present in classical Yurok culture itself. Yet there are several terms, perhaps best understood as designating occasionally overlapping prototypical associations rather than rigidly bounded hierarchical categories, that are generally translated as "doctor" today.

A herbalist who holds exoteric knowledge for dispensing the herbal medicines eaten or drunk to cure various simple ills was once called a *meges*. As such, the *meges* is not attributed spiritual powers, although an individual who practices as a *meges* might also command other, esoteric knowledge as well. White biomedical doctors, on the other hand, were called *meges* when they first arrived in northwestern California because they were viewed as mere dispensers of medicine, without the prayers or spiritual powers of "Indian doctors."

By contrast, it is said of Josephine Peters (Karuk), a contemporary herb doctor, that she had visions as a young girl and was first taken up into the mountains by two women, possibly doctors. She again went to the mountains when she had other visions but by the 1940s was unable to make the climb any more. It is uncertain, however, whether visionary experience was once common among herb doctors, or whether what is recounted in Mrs. Peters's story is part of the seeming modern decline of the mountain-trained *kegeyowor*, when women who formerly would have acquired the powers of a "high doctor" were unable to do so and thus settled for lesser powers— in this case, those of a herb doctor—and often shifted to the new models for therapeutic practice offered by the Indian Shaker Church. Whatever the historical process has been, there are a few people still practicing today— including Mrs. Peters—who are called "herb doctors," "herb and spirit doctors," and, especially, "Shaker doctors," a somewhat different category.

In Josephine Peters's case, extensive exoteric knowledge of herbs and their properties is accompanied by spiritual insight. In 1991 she spoke publicly of "psyching myself up" to diagnose by clairvoyance, seeing inwardly what is wrong with her patient and what herb to use. She also spoke of finding herbs to gather through psychic powers that seemed mysterious, even to her.

The practice of this contemporary herbalist, then, seems congruent with practices once apparently distinguished from the purely exoteric work of the *meges*. The practice of "prayer doctors," *kʷesʔoyeʔey*, always seems to have emphasized spiritual powers like Mrs. Peters's, exercised particularly in driving out or warding off several sorts of dangers, although these "praying doctors" often accompanied their prayers with the burning of angelica root or tobacco or the use of other herbal medicines. The group once included people who knew how to say the prayers for the dead that sent their spirits off to the next world, and how to remove the pollution from the houses in which people had died (cf. Harrington 1932: 233–34). Ella Norris, in 1978:

> *kʷesʔoyeʔey* means—see, he talks to that roots and you bathe in that roots, when somebody dies in the family. And he talks, he prays over the roots and they bathe with it and sprinkle the house to keep the spirit out, like ghosts, and it won't be haunted then.
> Be different ones used to know that. Lola [Lulu] Donelly was last one what knowed it. That's too bad. It's gone away.

(This medicine may indeed be gone today: most people now receive Christian burials, even though they may not have been believers in life.) Other specialists include midwives who have special prayers. Ella Norris:

> The midwife has to know what to do, what kind of medicines to use. Like the deer—deer medicine.

Deer has medicine because they have their young any place—and a certain kind of grass they eat.

So we have to know what kind of grass he chew on, too; got to know that deer song. There's right way and time when you giving birth why you don't have such a hard time.

(The "real doctors," *kegeyowor,* never delivered babies, probably because of the pollution inherent in the birth process. These "high doctors" had, above all, to "keep clean.")

Midwives have traditionally used infusions of herbs in water to ease birth (though some once used only prayers or even their mere presence). One of their techniques was spraying water from their mouths to stop the bleeding at the infant's navel, after the remnants of the umbilicus had fallen off (Gifford 1958: 249). This technique seems once to have been widespread. Knowledgable women used it to heal various injuries—as when Kitty Gensaw sprayed Florence Shaughnessy's arm, scalded while cooking. According to Mrs. Shaughnessy, the pain went away immediately and her arm was completely well the next day. (Kitty Gensaw was an acknowledged "doctor," though not a "real doctor," *kegey.*) This spraying of water and of herbal infusions seems to be a technique that was once utilized by a range of quite different practitioners, including the most powerful doctors (e.g., Drucker 1937: 258). The same is true of the technique of steaming.

Midwives once steamed a newborn infant in wormwood and soaproot, I've been told, protecting its vulnerable "life" for ten days until it had lodged firmly in the baby's body. Thus midwives may once have been associated with the Karuk prototype that Harrington called "steaming doctors," although Harrington said that most Karuk steaming doctors were formerly men (1932: 231–34). These practitioners steamed patients placed under wraps with infusions of herbs heated to boiling in cooking baskets by hot stones. (The effect was like that of a modern vaporizer.) Some people today think that this technique was once the most common and widespread curative practice in the region, possibly belonging to the oldest stratum of the regional culture.

Brush dance *(melo·)* doctors, *ʔumelo·yik* or "medicine women" (Kroeber, in Elmendorf 1960: 543.2) also steam their young patients in this way today and may once have been considered prototypical "steaming doctors." It is also possible, however, that they were associated with the *kegeyowor* or, finally, that they mode up a somewhat distinct group by themselves.

"Medicine women" are better known today than many sorts of traditional doctors because the child-curing brush dance is still a regular feature of life in northwestern California in the summertime—indeed, a lively, resurgent one. Bob Limes (Yurok) a man from Serperh, acted as a brush dance doctor two or three times in the past, according to Aileen Figueroa, but he's gone now, and male brush dance doctors are seldom heard of. Like sucking doctors, most have always been women as far as can be determined.

It is said that brush dance medicines are on Red Mountain, ʔokaˑ, near the mouth of the Klamath. Florence Shaughnessy, speaking in 1978 of a time around 1910:

> In the old days the [brush dance] doctor couldn't have any food, no water. She'd go up in the hills and hide all day—nobody could see her.
> She'd get the wood for the torches, the salal. If she came from upriver they'd send out scouts first, to find where things were, because she wouldn't know this country and they'd tell her where to look. But she had to go get everything herself—fir and pine to put in the fire.
> I went up with the doctor once when I was a little girl. And, oh! I wanted to come home so bad! I couldn't eat and I couldn't drink and all I could think about was if I ran home then I could get something to eat.
> When we come back down we took a [burden] basket up to the graveyard and she fastened on a feather in a certain way.
> You see, the feather stood up straight, the way she fixed it. But then she had to go back up and look the day after the dance, in the morning.[14] And if the feather had fallen over then the child would die. But if the feather still stood up, through the whole dance, then the child would get well.

Bad Doctors

Indian devils, ʔumaʔah, we've seen, with perhaps more folkloric than human life in modern times at least, given to laughter and tomfoolery, are not taken too seriously these days and stand somewhat outside of the realm

of "doctors." But there are other, truly "bad doctors," perhaps best identified as witches (as understood in anthropological literature), people who
harm primarily through mental influences rather than unsettling others
with fireworks, hoots and howls, bad smells and "the mysterious thing."
Florence Shaughnessy, in 1976:

> He's an Indian devil—a sort of human being. He dislikes people so he
> worries them. He keeps on doing things so they get sort of superstitious
> about it. They don't trust anyone any more and pretty soon it begins to
> work on their mind.
> So that's the Indian devil. But there's forces beyond that—you know,
> really bad, really bad. They can help you destroy.

People today speak of "deviling" others in reference to cursing them,
"making bad wishes," and professionals with this specialty are also called
"devils" by some people, but it is no laughing matter. Florence Shaughnessy:

> You stayed sort of away, you didn't dare touch any of their belongings.
> You shied away from a person that, you know, had "bad vibes," let's say.
> You know just by looking at a person that he cares nothing for you,
> that he'd just as soon strike you as talk to you. Then you just get away
> from a person because you don't want to force yourself on an evil thing.
> So they stayed mostly to themselves. But sometimes they'd throw
> their weight around and create a disturbance—a bad fight or something,
> because they're agitating, they're agitators. They want to see something
> going on.
> So, like if somebody should be hurt and then they die from a wound
> or something, then they come to you [the bad doctor] and say, "We'll
> pay you so much to make bad medicine because they have destroyed
> our main support," or "our third son" or something in the family.
> And that's how you got your power, because you'll be paid for doing
> this bad thing.
> And then you have to go someplace to get more power for being
> braver and nastier than you were yesterday.

Mrs. Shaughnessy was perhaps referring to grave-robbery in this last
statement, for the worst devils are thought to get bad medicine from
corpses, and some say today that they must visit the graves of those that

they have killed and must kill again every year. People talk of ill-wishers "shooting" people with bad medicine, "giving them a little present," and Frank Douglas told me of bad medicine at A·cah ("Bad Place"), in the high mountains, that could be used to make an enemy "bind up—die of constipation." Younger people tend to say that there's no one who can kill at a distance through sorcery anymore. Still, even these skeptics readily acknowledge that there are plenty of people left who can "devil" from close at hand, creating anxiety and disruption if not death. However so, I knew an older man who said he'd once accepted "five or six hundred dollars" to curse another man's enemy although, he said, he did nothing about it, considering the swindle a great joke. Given the man's reputation, however, the joke may very well have been on me.

Deviling and cursing, however people understand these notions, is "bad medicine," polluting. Harry Roberts refused to talk about such things, considering even their mention to be polluting, although readily admitting that even the "high men" of the past had to have bad medicine to defend themselves against jealous rivals. Most men, especially, who have attained considerable, positive spiritual power and the wealth that this attracts are, and always have been, suspected of having bad medicine or "devils" as well.

Wishing Doctors

Mrs. Shaughnessy, 1978 (taped):

> The evil doctor—you can hire them to put a curse on a family. That's the bad doctor. They do that. They learn the bad prayers—they go to the bad rocks to do this.
> And then the doctors come in. They're not necessarily the big doctors [kegeyowor]. They come in and have the power to see, pegahsoy ["praying" or "wishing doctor"].
> Your child is sick and he has the same symptoms every time he's sick, and each time it gets worse. Well, it means that—maybe there's been bad wishes made.
> And then they come in and they can see that. And then you have to confess and talk about it.

And then a lot of times there hasn't been anything in your family and nothing happens. And then it's time to go and get the real doctor [*kegey*], because it isn't bad wishes—it's just sick.

The *pegahsoy* is a clairvoyant doctor, usually a man, who can "see" the "shadows" of evil past deeds or attacks of bad medicine implanted in the body of the patient. Kroeber held that these shadows were generally the result of pollution engendered by breaking Indian law, often a rule associated with death (Spott and Kroeber 1942: 156–57, 189; cf. Gifford 1958: 248). This makes a certain amount of sense, since "shadows" themselves are associated with death and the "shadows" are freed from human bodies at death. (The same [taboo] Yurok term, *sa?awor*, is used for both the "shadows" that bring illness and a person's personal "shadow," his ghost-spirit, as well as for those that the Indian devil sends out.) The violations of the law that make people sick may not affect the guilty party directly, however, but rather members of his or her close family. Florence Shaughnessy (paraphrased): "There was a woman that had a child by her brother-in-law, so she strangled it. Then when that woman had children by her husband they choked to death. She lost three children that way. Then the fourth one got ill and she confessed. That child lived, and she had another that lived—two sons that lived."

Such violations may not only be perpetrated by others than those who suffer the consequences, but may also be far removed in time from the actual outbreak of illness. Dewey George, for instance, suffered from angina until he consulted a *pegahsoy* who "saw" the cause. One of Mr. George's "old-time" relatives had smoke-cured the heart of a kinsman murdered at Sregon, in order to avenge the murder by cursing the killer's family. Mr. George confessed the family secret, he said, and was cured.

Pollution—breaking Indian law—may be rather abstract in the etiology of a patient's malaise, too. For example, Gifford records a Karuk case in which illness was the result of failing to treat a dead shaman's pipe correctly (1958: 246). I witnessed a healing in 1978 in which a clairvoyant assistant saw "a [shadow of a] bear" on the patient. "What's that all about?" the doctor's assistant demanded. The patient confessed to eating black bear meat, itself "against Indian law," but the assistant was not satisfied.

"Were there women there?" she asked. "Yes." "They was menstruating. That's why that bear's on you."

The *pegahsoy* elicits such confessions by entering a light trance through singing and smoking a pipe. Once he—or a psychic assistant—has clairvoyantly seen the cause of illness and the patient or a family member has confessed, the doctor prays over the patient and then blows off the shadow that afflicts him with his or her breath. (Harrington records Karuk doctors brushing off the patient with a condor feather [1932: 229–331].) In a curing I witnessed in 1978, the *pegahsoy* prayed to *ki ?wes?onah*, "the world," and to *?o·lolekʷišo?n*, "Spirit," to help him rid the patient of everything *kimoleni*, defiled. He burned tobacco and blew on the patient, after confession, blowing away the "shadows" of misdeeds that he and his assistant, along with the "doctoring spirits" that were helping them, had seen. The patient was left feeling "empty" and "as though I'd been beaten" because, according to the doctor, the shadows had been "in" as well as "on" him.

This kind of practice is often coupled with the use of herbs, but it is clairvoyance and the ability to blow away shadows that are the most noteworthy attributes of the *pegahsoy*. The name comes from the verb *pahsoy*, "to confess," and *pegahsoy* itself, as a verb rather than a noun, means "to make a wish." Thus these doctors have sometimes been called "wishing doctors" among Yuroks—that is, doctors who "make a wish" that the "shadows" go away, after the patient has confessed—and "talking" or "singing doctors," *tcΣ:cΣ* among Tolowas (Drucker 1937: 258).

Kroeber does not seem to have taken these practitioners too seriously, being far more fascinated with the female shamans, the *kegeyowor*, and it may be that the *pegahsoy* (the plural is the same as the singular form) rose in importance during the present century, with the decline of the "big doctors," the *kegeyowor*. According to Kroeber, the lesser "wishing doctor's" power resided in "formulas" that were bought or inherited, and Gifford tells us that these prayers might be accounts of earlier confessions (Kroeber 1976: 409; Gifford 1958; Drucker 1937: 258). These observations seem to dismiss the *pegahsoys*' practice as yet more "compulsive magic" (Kroeber 1959), but there would seem to be more to it. Modern Yurok "Indian doctors" like the late Calvin Rube, for instance, do not locate their powers in prayers learned by rote, but in the assistance of spirit beings, "unseen beings" and "doctoring spirits" that are the sources of their clairvoyance and ability to cure and to prophesy. Mr. Rube said, in 1978, that "doctoring spirits come to help. The doctor can see them and work with them, and even the patient can feel them around. The spirits look [the patient] over and see what's wrong, what needs to be confessed."

According to Mr. Rube, the spirits report what they see to the doctor, who is primarily a vehicle for their power. His account echoes that of Flora Jones, the clairvoyant Wintu doctor and prophet: "The spirits use me for just a tool—something to get into to tell people what is going to happen and what they can do" (in Knudson 1975: 6).

Accounts of how these doctors acquire their powers tend to stress training, as we would expect of people who deal directly with spirits. Florence Shaughnessy:

> I know men go out to the mountains to study and pray for different things that they perform, like the *pegahsoy*. He has to go and have a vision and then he has to bring that vision out.
>
> When he goes to the mountains he generally goes to Doctor Rock and then to the men's rock to pray until everything becomes clear. And then he's given a certain power for what he's been praying for—what he wants to do.
>
> If you hurt someone it's up to you to take this force away—to restore, to make whole again. If you're the one that caused this evil thing to happen, then they [*pegahsoy*] come and confront you and say, "Now you will have to come forward and restore what you have taken away. You have to restore health, because you're the one that did it."
>
> So they know that you have done it.
>
> So there's nothing for you to do but come and try to help this person that you damaged—try to make whole again. When there's damage that you've done, bring to life.
>
> They don't use their mouths [like *kegeyowor*], they just sing and smoke their pipes, and then they see this evil vision.
>
> And then they'll talk it over.
>
> And they'll have to see which direction this evil vision comes from.
>
> And they'll pinpoint it to some village for instance, and they can almost find the person who is guilty of it.[15]
>
> Men could go into this trance and see visions—they were seekers of visions, too. But not just an ordinary person. You had to go to the mountains and pray for that power.

When inheritance is mentioned, as in the accounts of Lucy Thompson (1916: 43), it seems of secondary importance to mountain training:

> These men doctors hand down their secrets of different kinds of medicines they use and for what each kind is used, to their sons or close relatives, and before one begins to practice he goes back in the mountains to some distant and secluded place where there is a large rock or high peak, where he can look over the whole surrounding country all alone. There he prays to his God for health, strength and success. He does not drink water or eat and punishes himself as much as he can and stands up under the strain, he is gone from eight to twelve days and on his return he bathes himself, rests and sleeps, smokes his pipe for three or four weeks and then is ready to take up the calling of doctor and will go with the old doctors for quite awhile so as to make sure that he makes no mistakes in handling the cases nor in the uses of the different kinds of medicines to be used for different cases of diseases.

Calvin Rube said that he had inherited power from his mother, Nancy Rube, an "Indian doctor," and from Albert Thomas (Achumawi-Wintun), and had also gotten his own power in the mountains. According to him, a *pegahsoy* always has to work paired with a human helper (as he did), in addition to his spiritual helpers. It may be that these human helpers were once usually apprentices, as Lucy Thompson suggests. Mr. Rube, for instance, spoke somewhat bitterly of his own long and, according to him, exploitive apprenticeships under Albert Thomas and others. Mr. Rube told me that he went with Dr. Thomas on all of his cases for a year, probably around 1930. Thomas always asked the patient to give his apprentice some little gift—"an old hat or an old shirt"—as well as paying him, the doctor, in cash. One night, according to Mr. Rube, the doctor made three hundred dollars from all of the people that came to be doctored, but he got only an old shirt although he had done most of the work. Some nights he did all the work, the doctor just observing; still, he didn't get paid until he went on his own. This modern experience perhaps tells us a bit about the old-time *pegahsoy*'s training as well.

The *pegahsoy*'s powers, of course, are susceptible to violation by pollution, especially menstrual contamination. Frank Douglas, in 1976:

> *pegahsoy*—well, there's different ones, you know—man doctors sometimes, you know.

Mother was sick, you know.

There's Poker Bob, lived over at Johnsons.

We was at Johnsons. And I had two nieces, just young gals, and they was about ready to have their monthlies.

Oh, that's a bad thing you know, bad thing.

pahsoy—maybe it won't work out, you know, 'cause he [doctor] has to keep clean, you know.

So he come. He talk to my mother. He was scared of that [menstrual pollution] but he did anyhow.

The Real Doctors

Consideration of the *pegahsoy* brings us into a new realm or level of medicine, for their spirit-helpers, mountain training, trancing, and clairvoyance are all characteristic of "shamans" as usually understood and, in the Yurok case, are also characteristic of the "real doctors," the sucking doctors. Kroeber's negation of the *pegahsoy* undoubtedly reflected native views as well as his own fascination with the more exotic sucking doctors: Mrs. Shaughnessy implied that the *pegahsoy* were lesser than the "big" or "real doctors." Yet Lucy Thompson (1991 [1916]: 42–43) referred to them as "Pe-girk-kay-gay" (*pegak kegey*), "man doctors" (as Frank Douglas did in English, in the 1970s), thus associating them closely with the "real doctors," suggesting that they did indeed enjoy considerable prestige in earlier times, as they do today.

The *kegeyowor*, sucking doctors, were once higher in power and prestige than the *pegahsoy*. Kroeber restricted "shamanistic" experience and practice among Yuroks almost exclusively to these doctors, whom he identified as clairvoyant healers, almost without exception women (Kroeber 1925: 63; in Elmendorf 1960: 247.1; in Spott and Kroeber 1942: 155). On the basis of his 1900–1907 fieldwork, Kroeber noted that Yuroks "regularly English kegei as 'doctor' " (in Elmendorf 1960: 504.20).[16]

Although each recorded case is somewhat different, a general five-step pattern in the recruitment and training of *kegeyowor* seems evident (Kroeber 1925: 63) with, albeit, plenty of local and individual variation (Valory 1970: 264).

1) The *kegey* receives her potential for power, usually as a mature woman, by one of two channels: by inheritance—most often through the female line, from a mother or grandmother—or by "natural design" or

"universal destiny" (to use two contemporary expressions). The latter is more compelling: one has no choice but to accept it, and the power it brings is greater than inherited power.[17] In either case, the potential to be a *kegey* is most dramatically announced, traditionally, by a nightmare, a special shaman's dream (*ka·mił*, "to dream bad"), distinct from ordinary dreaming, *so·nił*. Dewey George: "A person would go to sleep and dream. They'd dream there was something bad working on them, and then they'd have to become a doctor. That's the way it used to work—you dream something." Some people actively sought such dreams, but not everyone who wished to have a doctor's dream was able to do so. Frank Douglas: "Some of them it don't work out; they don't get that dream."

If the dream comes, or a vision is gained through long periods of ascetic training in the hills, the novice is confronted by a guardian spirit. This may be the spirit of a dead doctor who has come back to the earth from the Spirit World to help novices, but it might also be an animal, usually in anthropomorphic form—Whale, Wolf, Chicken Hawk are all mentioned in printed sources (Spott and Kroeber 1942: 15). In the classic accounts, the spirit made the potential doctor swallow some sort of—often repulsive—object, and gave her her first doctoring song or "spirit song." The object was a *telogeł* or "pain."[18]

2) The dream or vision made the novice sick, and she was cared for by an experienced *kegey*. When she was ready she began to dance the *remoh*, "kick dance" or "doctor dance," in her family's men's sweathouse, perhaps falling unconscious and being supported by her male relatives. She was "crazy," *kełpey*—like a shaman, however, not *kerpey*, as in ordinary madness or a child's tantrum. She might foam at the mouth.

In this first kick dance, which lasted for ten days, the novice was *čeʔwis*, "clean spirit dancing." She had to learn to regurgitate the *telogeł*, deposit it in a dipper basket, *keyom*, and reingest it from across the room, sucking it in through her mouth or through a pipe, repeating this feat at will until she gained control of this first and most powerful "pain." If she could not learn to do this, and thus could not recover from her shamanic illness, experienced doctors might try to get the pain from her, augmenting their own powers and curing her but ending the novice's chance to become a doctor (and to compete with the established doctors).

3) When the novice had recovered she was taken into the high mountains in the summertime by her mentor and her male relatives (as many as ten of them). They went to a prayer seat, *cekce ʔł*, a semicircular enclosure of rock—sometimes river rock brought from below (Buckley 1986). The men established a camp a ways off, where they fasted, prayed, and burned angelica, keeping watch, according to Ella Norris. Meanwhile, the novice and her teacher swept the seat and prepared it carefully.

Florence Shaughnessy was taken to such a seat by male kin around 1930, to "make medicine for long life" rather than as a novice doctor. She described cleaning the seat as the doctors once must also have done:

> They should preserve all of that, over towards Blue Creek. That's all sacred ground. There are many prayer seats there.
> When I went up there we cleaned out the prayer seats. [An uncle] had a hatchet and he cut out the brush growing around the seats. Then we took that and some grasses and we fashioned brooms. And he said, Now you start in the middle and sweep the old leaves and twigs into the center, and I'll carry that down later.

Again, doctors' use of these seats traditionally followed considerable training and the initial acquisition of power. Thus, Dewey George told me that doctors had to have a certain degree of power even to go up to the mountain seats (paraphrase):

> The doctors used to walk up to Doctor Rock. They had power, so they walked up.
> They'd go up there and they'd dance for ten days, ten nights. Then they'd come back and they'd dance in the sweathouse for another five or six nights.
> That's if they wanted to be good doctors. They'd go up with their relations to dance.
> Good doctors go up Chimney Rock, but only the very best ones. Most went up Doctor Rock, not many to Chimney Rock. Hupa had their own place up at Trinity Summit. Orleans [Karuks] went someplace in the Marble Mountains. Smith River [Tolowas] went someplace, too. Yuroks and Katimin [Karuks] went up to Doctor Rock and Chimney Rock.

The degree of power attained in the mountain seats was related to their altitude: Chimney Rock is considerably higher than Doctor Rock. Doctors' training was once in part a gradual progression from lower to higher altitudes, from the water to the hills to the mountains, from lesser to greater power (and from winter to summer). The higher the seat, the greater the power available there, but one had to work one's way up slowly. Different spirits resided at different altitudes, and even on different parts of a single rock. Dewey George said that there were at least four different spots on Doctor Rock, in the southern Siskiyous, where doctors danced for power, although there was also a single famous place where they left their pipes and baskets and paraphernalia for others to use (a cave that has since been destroyed by blasting in the area). The spirits that came to these places were those of old doctors who had passed away long since and who spent part of their time in the spirit world, dancing, and part "inland," *heɬkew*, in the mountains, helping deserving supplicants (cf. Kroeber, in Elmendorf 1960: 518.21). Occasionally full doctors would go into the mountains, together or alone, to train and to augment their powers and knowledge through new spirit contacts. Florence Shaughnessy: "Groups of doctors used to go up there to dance and to train, or people would go up alone, in secret. . . . They kept the unclean people away."

Novice doctors also went into the mountains with their mentors and male kin, after considerable training, to be "tested" or "examined" (Thompson 1916: 39; Spott and Kroeber 1942: 160; Lindgren 1983b). The candidate danced to the different directions, dancing so hard, people often say, that her feet left the ground and she levitated. The dancer listened for the right voices among the many that she heard—those singing *remoh* songs. Other voices might have offered her evil powers ("a devil"), but she had to say, "I did not come for that" (Spott and Kroeber 1942: 161). When she heard the right voices the spirit "hit" her and she fell into a trance and became "crazy" again, running back down the mountain to her village sweathouse,[19] led by one of the *wo·gey*, some say, and protected by her male relatives—who might restrain her with a long strap, *weskul*, to keep her from hurting herself.[20]

When the novice successfully passed her mountain test she had attained new spirit helpers and songs, and she had "made her path into the mountains" through establishing a relationship with the *wo·gey* and doctors' spirits there—or, according to another interpretation, with the mountain itself. This meant that she could call on the mountain spirits (or the mountain) for assistance in her cures and could also visit her mountain seat in trance, without leaving her home, gaining control of new pains in this way. It also meant that her route had been established into the mountains, where she would abide as a spirit after death, helping novice shamans.[21] Would-be shamans who could not make the necessary spiritual connection, perhaps because they had broken the stringent rules of ascetic training, failed to pass the mountain test. Ella Norris told of a novice going into the mountains with her own aunt, Mary Williams—an established *kegey*—near the turn of the century, when it was becoming difficult to acquire the powers of a *kegey:*

Trail goes along on top, goes to Red Mountain, from Red Mountain to Doctor rock.

So, going on that steep mountain I guess, and on side there—must have been June month because they say there was blackberry vines there where it's kind of damp, way up on the hill there.

So, 'course they been fasting ten days down here, and this cousin was so hungry, and those blackberries hanging there looked good.

So she took two. She put one in her belt, one in her mouth. You not supposed to drink.

So, when they go up there, why naturally that Mary Williams she started in dancing and fasted.

And one man goes. He has fire just side of [Doctor Rock], has fire going and talks to it all the time while the doctors are dancing—facing the early morning—they get answers from there. They get their Master's degree.

Early in the morning: that beautiful—looks like abalone shell, that blue inside. It's a beautiful thing.

So, sometimes they get their answer. Someone hollers—certain sounds. They know they gotten their Master's degree, I call it, to be an Indian doctor.

So this one dance, dance, dance, dance—ten days! She never get nothing.

So they asked her, "What's the matter? What did you do?

So she confessed. She said, "I put one in my mouth."

So she never got—see how strict they were? I'm telling you.[22]

4) In the mountain test the novice acquired a second pain, if she had not already gotten it, perhaps in the first kick dance, because *telogeł* always occur in pairs, *wahpemew*—one male and one female. After she ran down the mountain, the newly tested doctor, who had been "hit" by the spirit, began dancing a second kick dance in her family's sweathouse, gaining control of both of her pains and demonstrating her ability to vomit them up and to reingest them from a distance. This second dance usually lasted only about five days. Following the second *remoh* the novice might begin her practice as an apprentice, often under harsh tutelage, "almost like a slave" to her mentor (compare *pegahsoy*, above).

5) In the old days, after the new doctor had refined and demonstrated her ability to cure she might be given a final dance, *ʔukʷɹkʷɹ*—the "pain cooking" ceremony—if her family could afford it. This took place in a dismantled family house, rather than in the less commodious sweathouse where the *remoh* had been held, since a great many people came to sing, to help the new doctor dance, and to feast. Doctors who had this final dance gained in prestige.

Having done all of this, which might take two or three years of constant training in the sweathouse with the men, together with her specific doctor's training, the new *kegey* was acknowledged as a "full" or "high doctor." Often by then she had acquired the powers of a "tracer," a finder of lost objects, together with clairvoyance and the ability to cure by sucking out a patient's paired sets of "pains." She might choose to continue avoiding sexual intercourse for a long time so that she didn't weaken her power, and many doctors went back into the mountains, physically or in trance, to regain their power after they had started having sex again.

The doctor's pains have customarily been understood as manifestations of the powers granted her by her helping spirit. Control of her *telogeł* gave the doctor both clairvoyance and the ability to suck out complementary, disease-causing pains from her patients' bodies. Smoking her pipe, singing her spirit song and dancing, the *kegey* entered trance and saw the cause of her patient's affliction.[23] This might be perceived in the form of the now familiar "shadow"—here, an image of a past deed making the patient sick, as in the *pegahsoy*'s practice, the *kegey* "half seeing the ancient act in shadowy form" (Kroeber, in Elmendorf 1960: 505.21; compare Gifford 1958: 248). Florence Shaughnessy:

> They'd get the doctors and they'd dance and they'd see a formless thing. They all see this formless thing. It is not an object—just a sort of mass of something. And they know this evil force has something to do with this person.
>
> A doctor would have a vision of something, a mass of something coming towards them. That was a memory in the family, some terrible secret they'd hidden, a "skeleton in the closet" that was affecting that person. And when it was stated, then it would go away and the person would get better.
>
> The whole family, everybody would be there. The doctor would sing in trance and she'd tell her vision. If you had knowledge of it you had to tell. After there was a confession the doctor'd fan the patient with a large basket. Then he slept. And he woke up hungry again, and in a couple of days he was well.

After hearing the patient's and family members' confessions, the doctor prayed over the patient and blew the shadow away with her breath (or a fan or feather), or perhaps sprayed the patient with an infusion of herbs from her mouth. These, of course, are methods identified primarily with the male *pegahsoy*, but also with other, lesser "herb and spirit" doctors. Again, classic Yurok doctoring occurred along a continuum of techniques and powers rather than in rigidly segmented, hierarchical categories of specialists. But while *pegahsoy* and herb doctors may share certain techniques and powers—like clairvoyance—with the *kegeyowor*, and while *pegahsoy* were often called in by *kegeyowor* to assist in diagnoses, the *kegey* once had a technique that was her own and that was not utilized by others lacking her training and qualifications. This was the technique of sucking out the patient's "pains," *teloget*, that, together with the *kegey*'s stringent training and testing, once brought the highest degree of prestige enjoyed by any Yurok doctors—and the highest fees. When the patient was not afflicted by a shadow that could be blown off or wished away, the *kegey*, entering trance, saw pairs of *teloget* in the patient's body, and sucked these out with her mouth. The pains that she had acquired from guardian spirits and learned to control through the kick dance went out and captured the patient's paired "pains" in a "blanket of slime" (Spott and Kroeber 1942: 156), allowing the doctor to extract them.

Calvin Rube, perhaps voicing an entirely modern interpretation, in 1978: "When the doctor sings it's like he's snake charming. The pains get hypnotized by the songs and start rising in the body to see what it is and when it's close enough to the surface the doctor can take it out by sucking, or with his hands." (By the 1970s, sucking had disappeared from Indian doctors' repertoires, at least temporarily.)

The pain that the doctor or her helper sees might be the result of someone else's evil-doing. Harry Roberts said that people who have made bad medicine against someone are drawn to the doctors' healing rituals as though by "cords," knowing that when the patient is cured "the poison can turn on them." If they are there when the doctor accuses them, they can confess. Then the pain can be removed easily, and cures obtained through confession, Mr. Roberts said, are the best. Otherwise, it is very difficult to remove these sorts of pains.[24]

Doctors specialized in curing different sorts of illnesses by dint of the different *telogeł* that they ingested and brought under control, and this is true today of doctors who do not suck out pains. Calvin Rube: "Doctors are like mechanics, specialists. Some mechanics are for radiators, some for transmissions. It's the same with doctors." Traditionally, these specialists sometimes worked in teams to diagnose and treat very ill patients, *pegahsoy* aiding *kegeyowor* in diagnoses, or several *kegeyowor* working together on the most difficult cases. Dewey George, in 1976 (paraphrase):

Three doctors worked on me when I was young. I was very sickly. That was seventy years ago and there were lots of doctors then. I was sick all of the time.

They used to go after the doctors on the trails, in boats. They used to say, "If you see a boat going upriver real fast they're going for the doctor." They'd go pretty fast.

We used to have lots of doctors. There're different kinds of doctors. Some press their mouths on your body. They press their mouth on your belly. They'd suck.

I saw a doctor suck out a big ball, round [golf ball sized], and it had roots coming down from it. I guess it was a cancer. I didn't have that.

They had power. They'd sing, they'd dance, they'd foam at the mouth. The foam would come out of their mouth and they'd grab that in their hand and they'd go outside. Then they'd [shake off the foam]. They take that outside.

The *teloget* that the *kegeyowor* sucked out of their patients' bodies took many forms. Victor Crutchfield (Yurok) spoke of a doctor who removed pains from his grandmother that looked like "black beetles." Afterwards, Mr. Crutchfield said, the doctor cut each witness lightly on the throat to prevent the pains from entering them. Florence Shaughnessy spoke of the famous doctor Fanny Flounder, her neighbor in Requa when Mrs. Shaughnessy was a child: "When Fanny went to cure she took baskets. She'd suck and she'd draw little things—they looked like little pieces of rock—from the body of the patient. They made a lot of noise when they were doctoring. We had to sing to help her, but it was scary and we didn't want to. But we had to." Aileen Figueroa added to this picture of the pains that Fanny Flounder extracted:

> I saw her take things out of people, sucking them with her mouth. Then she'd spit it out in her hand. I saw her spit out bees, eggs, lizards, arrows. That was real. I saw those things breathe and move. . . .
> [She'd] sing and dance. Nobody would tell her where they hurt. But she'd just go and—she'd put her mouth [there] and suck it out. Then she'd spit out in her hand and drop it on the basin [*keyom*].
> I'd see her when there'd be a bunch of them in there. They'd dance plumb around. There's a bunch of them dancing. Then she'd spit out like a little lizard—you could see it just move and kind of quiver.

Doctors were once ranked in terms of the numbers and strengh of the pains and other powers that they controlled, as well as the altitude in the mountains at which they had been tested. After the *kegey* had passed her mountain test she could acquire additional pains for treating various sorts of illnesses without going back into the mountains physically, although she might demonstrate these new powers in additional kick dances. Florence Shaughnessy remembered such a dance put up in Requa for Fanny Flounder who, it is said, ultimately acquired five sets of pains, making her one of the most powerful and wealthy sucking doctors in memory:[25]

> Doctor songs had word-pictures in them. [Fanny Flounder] would sing and spew up her vision.

Once in the middle of the night George [Meldon/Flounder] came to our [Gensaw] house and asked us all to come help Fanny, who was in great pain because of a dream she'd had. We all had to go down to the [Brooks's traditional plank] house and sing to help her. I didn't want to go because it scared me, but we were made to go to help.

Fanny wanted a kick dance, and George came to get us.

Bill Gensaw sang Jimmy Gensaw's song about a bird that had a special stump that nobody else could come near because it was full of his food. He sang and Fanny started dancing.

George said, "Don't stop singing!"

We sang and sang and she danced.

Finally she spewed up a bloody mess into a basin [*keyom*]. It looked just like a small swallow all covered with slime. I looked and I could see its little beak, the gold stripes on its shoulder. It was *breathing* there. I saw it clearly, sitting there breathing.

George put the bowl on the mantel [storage ledge of the semi-subterranean house]. Fanny got up. She was swinging around, making that sound that doctors make [below]. Then she drew on her long pipe. There was a *thud!* I can still hear it—like flesh hitting flesh. Then the basin came swirling down to the floor, empty.

She got up. ["Pete's"] grandfather and Jimmy Gensaw grabbed her and held her and she calmed right down, and she danced some more.

That bird was a new pain for her, and they said it gave her power over tumors.

(After this occasion, the swallow/*telogeł* appeared only as an oblong, black object in healing performances.)

Fanny Flounder, who died in the early 1950s at about eighty years of age, was widely regarded as having practiced a virtually aboriginal mode of doctoring. After 1850 and the white invasion it seems to have become increasingly hard for women to fully attain the powers of a *kegey*, as Fanny Flounder did. Indigenous doctoring came to be influenced by Christianity (through the Shaker Church) as well as by regional, pan-Indian doctoring styles, such as that of Albert Thomas. (I go into the subsequent history of doctoring on the river in chapter 10.)

Before the introduction of monotheistic religious concepts it is my understanding that the power through which the *kegeyowor* cured was ultimately attributed to "that which exists," "the world," *ḱi ʔwesʔonah*, as manifested by the "sky," *wesʔonah*. The energy of "creation" is visible in the waves and tides of the ocean, which are caused by the rim of the sky rising and falling upon the sea at the western edge of the earth. Fanny Flounder's first doctor's dream was of the sky-rim, that dripped with repugnant icicles of blood—one of which was to be her first *teloget*. Her spirit song was, "Where the sky moves up and down you are traveling in the air" (Spott and Kroeber 1942: 159). The waves caused by the falling sky-rim go throughout creation. Ella Norris:

> Like I said about Doctor Rock—
> I wish to goodness [the Forest Service] would leave that place alone because that's the last thing we ever own.[26] That's our Holy Land, our secret place. That's where they used to go to practice—not only to be a doctor, but there's different places, different little places—like that whale place.[27]
> And then another place where the tide goes in and out. It's a hole up there. When the tide comes in here it goes up there, and when the tide goes out it's low.

Harry Roberts, who spent time with Fanny Flounder as a young man (paraphrase):

> There was a theory. [Yuroks] thought that the ocean waves went through the body.
> You know, even in the mountains you can see the creeks rise and fall very slightly? Indians said that the ocean waves set that rhythm and that they set a rhythm in your body, too. That rhythm would come ten or twelve times a minute or as slow as four, when you're almost gone. If there's a lot of tension it might get up to eighteen or twenty—so much tension that you can't relax.
> That wave—it's not really in the water and it's not in the tissue. It's an energy wave, spirit. It comes up through your feet, all the way up to your head, then back out down through your feet and your fingers. Occasionally it goes through the top of your head but I don't know about that. That's information a doctor had.
> The doctor used this to create a current. When Fanny was curing I used to see a blue light coming off the back of her head and I could see it at the end of her fingers. You see that in a dim room. She'd create a low-keyed hum—"hmmmmmmmmmmm"—and click sticks together or clap her hands lightly. She'd go on like that for a long time, like a beehive—keep it

up for hours. Then suddenly she'd touch a tension spot on her patient's body and lead the tension off. Then she'd [wipe her hands vigorously].[28]

I don't know how you do those things. You focus your energy. You're a receiver, that's all. All energy is in the air or something, and you gather it in and focus it, make it do what you want. I can't tell you how.

Once I asked Fanny how she got those baskets off the [ledge]. "I just think them off" is what she said.

She didn't know how, either.

Such power made the *kegeyowor* frightening to some, especially children. While Fanny Flounder was well known for her humor, we have encountered this fear in Florence Shaughnessy's accounts of her childhood experiences with Fanny. Lucy Thompson remembered doctors brushing their hair over their faces to frighten children and secure their own privacy (1916: 41). Ella Norris, in 1976:

> I remember that in 1902 my mother's mother-in-law went up there [to Doctor Rock]—Mary Williams.
>
> She was *kegey*.
>
> How I found out is she always sit with her back turned—so I told my mother, "What's the matter with that old woman?"
>
> She said, "*Shhh!* She's Indian doctor, don't want to be mingled with too many people. She just came back from Doctor Rock."
>
> They don't mingle with everybody because they praying all the time, they clean, make it work for everybody goes to him. . . .
>
> She had her hair pitched, parted in the middle—that's the way Indians fix it. Wear Indian cap—cap made with just roots, bear grass trimming, no black in it.[29] She'd always have her back turned because kids get nosey.
>
> So I told my mother, "What's the matter with that old lady—she always has her back turned?"
>
> She says, "*Shhh!* Just don't bother her. She's a Indian doctor."

However powerful the *kegeyowor* were, their power had its limits—of which the doctors themselves were well aware. Calvin Rube (paraphrased):

> Two young girls stopped eating. They were both about sixteen and they lived in a village near Weitchpec.

Their parents went around the village asking for help until they had enough to offer a doctor, and then they took the girls down the river in a canoe to Murek where there were a lot of doctors, each one with a different specialty. They lived there right through the time when my mother was alive.

They found the right doctor and she accepted their offer and started smoking her pipe and singing. After about half a hour she stopped and cleaned her pipe and handed back the money.

"Yes, they both have a pain in them but I'm not the sort of doctor to remove that sort of pain. But don't worry. In seven months it will come out the same way it got in."

The girls were pregnant.

THE *PEGɪK KEGEY*

A. L. Kroeber insisted that, among the Yuroks, "when a [*kegey*] is spoken of it is always taken for granted that it is a woman" (in Spott and Kroeber 1942: 155). Male doctors seem to have been more common among the Tolowas, and Robert Spott discusses a *"tolowił pegɪk kegey"* ("Tolowa man doctor") in the same volume (164 et seq.). In fact, in an earlier publication (1925: 68), Kroeber himself mentioned a male Yurok shaman who had a rattlesnake for a *telogeł* and who specialized in curing insanity. Again, Fanny Flounder told Robert Spott of being cured by a male doctor, probably Yurok, who she said was a member of the Shaker Church rather than a non-Christian *kegey*. This doctor sucked on her, however, and Shaker doctors putatively do not suck (Spott and Kroeber 1942: 164; compare Valory 1970: 78–79). Kroeber, in short, seems to have disregarded the information that he had at hand in "taking for granted" that the Yurok *kegey-owor* were always women.

We have seen that the *pegahsoy*, "singing" or "wishing doctors," primarily male, were of considerable importance in earlier times. These doctors are remembered by elders today as "men doctors," *pegɪk kegeyowor*, and as training in the mountains. Kroeber and others, however, tended to negate their significance in reconstructing aboriginal Yurok culture. First, Kroeber denied that Yurok men ever got curing powers in the mountains, as did the *kegeyowor* (Spott and Kroeber 1942: 163). Second, he considered the male sucking doctor who had treated Fanny Flounder a cultural "hybrid," doubting that he had mountain training (ibid., 164). Third, Kroeber and other salvage ethnographers, creating a hypothetical mid-nineteenth-century ethnographic present, were uninterested in the emergent, twentieth-century regional culture that they witnessed in fact and in which male doctors had risen to new prominence with the decline of the sucking doctors. Thus they did not ask what the historical precedents for modern male "Indian doctors," like Albert Thomas and Calvin Rube, might have been. Fourth, it may be that Kroeber and others mistook a decline in the *relative* number of male *kegeyowor* after contact (Harrington 1932: 131) for an immemorial pattern. Finally, their understandings of the reference of the Yurok word *kegey* may be limited.

There is sufficient evidence to establish that *kegey*, while denoting a sucking doctor, usually female, also included among its referents any person who drew spiritual power from the upper world and applied it to the well-being of individuals and of communities. Thus the *pegahsoy* were legitimately *pegɅk kegeyowor*, "men doctors," and other men as well were known by this title.

Kroeber, who both reviewed (1921) and cited (in Kroeber and Gifford 1949: 82, 85, 88–89, etc.) Lucy Thompson's 1916 book, largely ignores her frequent references to the "pe-girk-kay-gay" *(pegɅk kegey)*, the "men doctors." Yet Thompson repeatedly refers to these men, including the *pegahsoy* among them, stating that they tended to come from the aristocratic or "high" houses and, finally, that they played important roles in what Kroeber called "the world renewal cult": "These men doctors help to start and to make the settlements for the white Deer-skin dance. . . . [They] get together about the last of July or first of August and have a talk and settle the questions and give out the announcement that they were going to have the Deer-skin Dance (oh-pur-ah-wah)" (Thompson 1916: 42–43).

Kroeber, while quoting Thompson, expressed puzzlement since he had not heard the term *kegey* "used of men who exercise a function or authority in a world renewal" (Kroeber and Gifford 1949: 82.4). He was also stumped by the occurrence of the *cekce?ił*, "prayer seat," in a Karuk renewal ceremonial: "The occurrence of this shamanistic element in a world renewal is remarkable, because world renewal and doctoring occupy entirely separate compartments of the culture, and no other feature shared by them is known" (ibid., 128).

I think that Kroeber was wrong on several counts and that his errors resulted precisely from his conception of cultures in northwestern California as having segregated "compartments" of traits and his consequent failure to appreciate the complex integration of various domains and associational spheres in those cultures (Bean and Blackburn 1976: 9). Kroeber himself noted that certain ceremonial medicine men were called "Doctor" in English, yet did not attach much significance to this vis-à-vis classic Yurok culture (1976: 265.380). Ella Norris, in 1976, seemed to corroborate Thompson's claims, contra Kroeber:

> Four or five medicine men that fast for ten days before they have jump dance. They stay in sweathouse and pray.
> I seen deerskin dance in 1904, Requa. Jump dance in 1905. Each time they fast for ten days. My great uncle, my mother's uncle, was great medicine man and that's how I know. Charlie Williams' dad, old Charlie—last Indian doctor.
> Welkʷew Requa, Pecwan, Cappell, Weitchpec—five places. They take turns.[30]
> They fast and they have five fires because there are five doctors, Indian medicine men. One each village, leaders in each village. They go into the sweathouse. They're the ones go into sweathouse. Men doctors, *pegⱭk kegey*.

Pilling (1969: 10; 1978) reported that each ceremonial district (such as the five mentioned above) had its own council of trained men who organized upcoming ceremonials and sat as judges in unresolved law cases, settling them before the dances. These councils, said Pilling, comprised the medicine man for the dance and the major regalia owners and "dance makers," manager/choreographers. They also seem to have included calendrical specialists. Kroeber knew that the major sweathouse in each dance district was constructed in such a way as to function as both a lunar and solar observatory, light entering through a small hole in the door striking markings incised in slate on the floors, permitting accurate calendrical observation. The last such observatory went out of use in 1910, according to Kroeber (Kroeber Papers, Carton 7; compare Goldschmidt

1940; Kroeber, in Elmendorf 1960: 26). According to Lucy Thompson, there was a *"haʔgelnin"* at each of these sweathouses who was an astronomical specialist and whose role it was to accurately inform the scheduling of the great dances (1916: 707).

This scheduling was regional, rather than local, the councilors from the entire region—Yuroks, Hupas, Karuks, and possibly others—meeting to settle regional disputes and to establish the overall schedule of upwards of fifteen ceremonials occurring in overlapping yearly, bi-yearly, and tri-yearly cycles (Kroeber and Gifford 1949). Clarence E. Pearsall, a timber cruiser and diarist present in the region at the end of the nineteenth century, wrote that before the 1890 Hupa deerskin dance "the chiefs" went to Doctor Rock (in Yurok-Karuk territory) to meet as members of a regional council, settling law cases, bringing the entire region to peace, and setting the date for the dance (Pearsall 1928: 1625). Harry Roberts spoke of these "chiefs" as "high men" and said that they represented each of the dance districts within the territories of each of the dominant groups in the region—Yurok, Karuk, and Hupa.

These regional "chiefs," "high men" or *"pegɅk kegeyowor,"* also met for unscheduled and private "emergency" jump dances in the high mountains to hold back epidemic disease or famine when they threatened in the later nineteenth century (Kroeber 1976: 186; Waterman 1920: 264). Finally, according to the contemporary anthropologist Lee Davis (personal communications, 1990), the regional council performed highly esoteric work, psychically "retying the knots" of the world sky-net, symbolized by the sacred seats and mountain peaks that defined "the world" in terms of a regional grid, mapped by the roof timbers of the primary sweathouses.

While these most esoteric of the regional council's functions seem to have ceased by approximately 1910, Yurok district councils continued to meet at Requa and at Cappell through the 1930s (Pilling 1978) and began to meet once again, although with altered membership, at Hupa in the 1960s and at Pecwan in the 1980s. There was, moreover, a regional emergency jump dance in Elk Valley, in the high mountains, in 1988, to counteract the ill effects of a negative Supreme Court decision bearing on Indian access to the old "High Country"—the first such dance, in all likelihood, in this century (chapter 7). Hupa, Karuk, and Yurok dancers participated.

It was the men in these regional councils that Lucy Thompson described as *pegɪk kegeyowor*, identifying them with the *pegahsoy*, or "wishing doctors." It is not certain that all of these councilors once had the specific training and visionary experience of the *pegahsoy*, although the capacity to heal in certain cases was undoubtedly attributed to many of them. Again, according to Harry Roberts, all "high medicine" training naturally brings some curative ability as a side effect, although it is up to the individual to develop it or not. This may, however, be slightly beside the point. There is also some evidence, again contra Kroeber, that since the "world renewals," and particularly the jump dances, are thought to heal the world as a doctor heals a human individual, the men integrally associated with these ceremonials are comparable to doctors and are thus included in the associational sphere for which the *kegey* is the prototype. As a contemporary Yurok ceremonial dancer said, in 1990, the jump dance is "a healing" of the world.

George Meldon (d. 1950) was the last medicine man for the fish dam at Kepel. He lost his power, said Florence Shaughnessy, when he did the two things forbidden him: he shed tears (over a lost daughter) and he saw the ocean (when he came downriver to marry Fanny Flounder in the 1930s). His formal title had been "*wi lo hego,* that one dam he makes" (Waterman and Kroeber 1938: 52), although this was customarily shortened to *lo?*.[31] Yet Meldon identified himself, in English, as a "Doctor of the world," instructing Erik Erikson to tell his readers that "he [Meldon] is the world's doctor" and that his prayers, as *lo?*, were "to cure the world" (Erikson 1943: 277, 280). According to Harry Roberts, who knew him well, George Meldon was a *pegahsoy;* but Meldon doesn't seem to be referring to this in speaking with Erikson. The fish dam and its associated deerskin dance were indeed put up in part to prevent sickness (Waterman and Kroeber 1938: 74), as have been all of the so-called world renewals (Kroeber and Gifford 1949). Yet none of the seemingly official titles for the various dances' medicine men overtly designate them *kegeyowor*. Most are idiomatic, like *lo?*, or descriptive in ways that do not refer to doctoring: for instance, at Pecwan, *?wer?ɪ?ge·tegerum*, "talking in his sweathouse," or *wes?onah tegrum*, "talking to the sky" (or "to the world").[32] This talking with (or praying to) the sky (or world) offers access to the associational field focused by the word *kegey*.

When the female *kegey* and the male *pegɹk kegey* went into the mountains they went *heɬkew*, "inland" and, in trance, *wonoyekʷ*, "up in the middle of the sky," to heaven, *wesʔonah hiwonek*. As we've seen, the high mountains and the middle of the sky are metonymic to an extent in Yurok cosmology. Thus, at death, both *kegey* and medicine men go inland to the mountains and from there to dance in the spirit world above, where the most wonderful wealth objects—like albino deer half-covered with the scalps of pileated wood-peckers—live. According to Ella Norris, clairvoyant and prophetic doctors go to "heaven" in trance and see this wealth: "They go into that where they get their 'power,' they call it. When they get their power then they can see things, and they can explain it to you. Biggest part of it always come out just about right. That was same way with that *wonoyekʷ*."

Metaphorically, then, when the *kegey* established her trail into the mountains she established her connection with the world above, the "sky," *wesʔonah*, which is also "the world," *ḱi ʔwesʔonah*, "that which exists," "creation." We have seen that the most advanced men enter trance in the mountains and ascend to the sky, where they are taught by spirit beings. The most powerful men, according to Harry Roberts, enter trance in a seat on what is today called Peak 8, a serpentine dome near Doctor Rock, and from there rise, spiritually, through an aperture in the sky. Thus Peak 8 was both below and *was* "the center of the spiritual world" for Harry.

The *kegeyowor* and *pegɹk kegeyowor*, then, are those who draw power from "the world" or "the sky" to cure both people and the world itself. We have engaged a paradox.

A prayer from the Wečpus deerskin dance says,

kipegahsoy ḱi ʔwesʔonah tuʔ
kowico koʔmi weʔ no·minahpiʔmoʔw
heɬ—toʔ ki skuyeʔn wero·kʷsel
ki pegahsoyetek ḱi ʔwesʔonah

Soon Creation will *pegahsoy*
don't be too afraid of this!
Hey! Then good will blow-off here
creation will *pegahsoy* here.[33]

Doctors get their power to heal from "the sky," metonymic with "creation." Some "men doctors," identified with the *pegahsoy*, doctor creation or "the sky" itself. Yet, creation is also a doctor, a *pegahsoy*, that doctors itself and the people within it through the "world renewal" ceremonials directed by the human "man doctors."

DOCTORS AND THAT WHICH EXISTS

Yurok Indian doctors (*kegeyowor*) once arose along a continuum of human practitioners and powers and spiritual presences. Often they had multiple skills or techniques at their disposal: prayer and herbal treatments, trance and clairvoyance, the power to perceive and to suck out "pains." They were partially ranked in terms of the number and power of these techniques that they owned or controlled but they were also related one to another in terms of two dimensions—vectors of power or associations of spirits, "high" and "low." This system remains partially intact today.

The first vector moves upwards from the "lay" use of constructive or benign prayers and herbs, to "praying doctors," to clairvoyant, mountain-trained "wishing" or "confession doctors," to, once, "sucking doctors." Certain communal leaders and ceremonial participants are associated with this dimension, which includes, at its higher reaches, the *kegey* and *pegʌk kegey*. These are people associated with the high mountains, with summer, and with the sky. It is noteworthy that the full meaning of this association is realized in service to the community, as one or another sort of "doctor."

On the second, low dimension, the continuum once ran from those who command curses to "Indian devils" to "bad doctors." Their powers are those of the below, of water, and of winter. The warrior, as a "mean" person (chapter 4), partakes of this continuum, the obsidian that symbolizes his powers sharing subterranean mythic origins with the devils' fire. Though he may act in defense of the community, the trained warrior's power is essentially selfish, and he could act as a hired killer, as could the *ʔumaʔah*, Indian devil, and the "bad doctors." As such, the warrior's social status was not high, classically, as was that of doctors, although it was not as low as that of devils. Status reflected, at least in elite ideology, service to the community, local (*kegey*), district-wide (*pegahsoy*), and regional (*pegɅk kegey*).

It is for this reason that wealth acquired as a killer or curser, or wealth exchanged as blood-money, could not be used in the great dances, whose purpose is to "cure" or "fix the world." By the same token, wealth that eventually comes to men as a result of their "clean" training (and, today, because of their being "good") or that is exchanged in payment for doctoring and as bride wealth is the most suitable to dance in these ceremonies. This wealth was once thought to "come from the sky," and is "clean." The wealth itself, then, for all that it "symbolizes" nothing beyond itself and is valued simply for its own "beauty" and life, as "people," is not at all "profane," as Kroeber understood it to be (chapter 8). It is, as local people continue to attest today, "sacred": nonsymbolic in Kroeber's terms, but nonetheless abundant with spiritual significance.

If we approach the matter this way, we can understand why *pegɅk*, "man," can also mean, depending on use-context, "real man"—that is, "trained man"—and "rich man," and that is also why a female *kegey* was traditionally a sociological male, *numi pegɅk*—very much a (real or rich) man (Valory 1970).

The Yurok language distinguishes between people who are "just rich," *syałew*, and those whose wealth reflects their spiritual ascendancy, who are *numi pegɅk*. It was the latter who once made up the various levels of councilmen described above, forming local, district, and regional conduits of organization and regulation. This is why we cannot separate individual spirituality from social organization in aboriginal northwestern California: they do not form separate "compartments." It is also why many Yuroks resisted a bureaucratic tribal organization when it was being forced upon them by the federal government in the late 1980s. "We know who to go to when we need to settle things," Calvin Rube said, "and we don't need the government to tell us, or to hold an election, or anything like that." But the traditional regional organization, and the significance of families and individuals who held considerable wealth in the form of dance regalia, was as lost on the federal government as it had been on Kroeber the better part of a century earlier.

6 The GO-Road

If I were a visitor from another planet, radioing home about earth, I wouldn't call Americans Americans. I would give them a name that told a lot about them immediately: I would call them Realtors.

Kurt Vonnegut, Jr., *Breakfast of Champions*

In 1958 A. L. Kroeber told Claude Lévi-Strauss that, several years earlier when he had last traveled to the Klamath River to see Yurok Indians, he visited "one lone person who still speaks the native tongue, and who remembers the myths and legends" (in Valory 1966b: 42). Lévi-Strauss and Kroeber both overstated the case. In 1976, eighteen years later, Ella Norris, together with several other native people in full command of the Yurok language, was teaching a lively and popular Yurok language class at an Indian center in the town of Klamath, California. She told me this story first in Yurok, then in English:

This is a story I told at Klamath the other day about Redding Rock. It's a beautiful story, too, part Tolowa and part Yurok. It starts from Point St. George—about the Point St. George girl and her grandma.

The girl always wanted to go dig potatoes, those that have blue flowers [brodiaea bulbs]. So anyhow, every morning she is gone.

So, old lady begin to suspicion: "I wonder what she does?"

So, she told her grand daughter, she says, "Now don't pick them two pronged ones, two together you know [like a mandrake]." You know, they always got one prong, like those daffodils. "Don't ever get two on," she says.

"Well, why?" she says.

She says, "well, just don't do it," she says.

One morning she went. She wondered, "why does she always tell me 'Don't dig that'? I'm goin' to dig."

She did.

A little boy jumped out: "Oh, Mother!"

Oh, she threw her stuff down. She run home, that little boy right behind.

That old lady said to her, "I told you don't ever dig that. Now you will have to claim . . ."

"Oh no I won't," she said. "I'm not going to claim him because he's an out-of-wedlock child, ka·mu·ks [bastard]. I ain't going to claim him."

So, the little boy felt bad because the grandma was so nice to him, you know, felt sorry for him, and then every morning she [his mother], you know, would go somewhere else—everyday, that potato thing. She's gone every morning.

That boy began to wonder, "where does Mother go?" She goes there but she wouldn't even look at him. Only the grandmother took care of him, you know.

So, the old lady asked her, "Why don't you claim him? After all, you dug him up—now it's your son. You better claim him."

"No," she says, "I'll tell you what," she told her grandmother, she says "if he comes home with the [white] deer, red [woodpecker scalps down] this far [on his chest]—red this far! so beautiful!—then I'll claim him." (She knew he can't do it, see?) "Because where I go," she says, "I see him where I go every morning," she says, "because I am so way up."

And she says, "there's a lot of people up there where I go," she is telling her grandmother.

And she says, "there's deer, a bunch of deer come in and their leader is red this far." She says, "nobody has ever killed it, ever got him." She says, "if he can get that one I'll claim him."

So, the old lady told the boy.

So, the boy says, "I'm going to watch"—tells the old lady—"I'm going to watch."

So, he's watching her—follow her every morning, but he never see where she go.

So, one morning he got up real early and he follow her, just stayed so far, and I guess the Good Lord begin to feel sorry for him. He saw where there's a bush there. She grabbed something out of that bush, stretched it, filled it up—just like that rope ladder, you know. Started climbing.

So, that boy got right [there]. [She] pulled it up, he was right there—jumped one side while she was folding. He followed her up there.

There was a great big beautiful field—I could just see it!—and there was a great big acorn tree right in the middle of it, and people got their baskets set around it. And that mother-to-be put her basket there and the acorns dropped in.

Here was a big bunch of people, said, "now get ready. *Get your bows and arrows because the deers are coming out!*"

Everybody ready.

That boy had his bow and arrow.

Red this far! Beautiful horns.

He thought to himself, "I'm going to get that if it the last thing I do." He shoot his bow and arrow. Down that deer went. He grabbed it.

"Oh, that's my son! That's my son! Oh, my son!"

He never look back. He took it to his grandmother's, drug it in the house (down the ladder because he knew where it was, see?), down the ladder into the house.

That old lady had beautiful pans [baskets]—you know, Indian pans [regalia storage baskets] that have a special name—put it in there.

[Mother] coming. He told his grandma, "I'm leaving."

"Oh, no," she says to her grandson, "you better stay."

"No," he says, "because I was disgrace to my mother. She didn't like me. Now I got what she says she wanted, so I am going. I'm leaving."

So, he started off—and here she come behind. "My son, come back." She started off.

You know Pebble Beach, those rocks go out that way? If you lucky you find abalone shells, because she dropped her tears there. She was following him.

He was going in a canoe. He started to paddle. He was going, kept going, never looked back.

She was right behind him hollering, "My son look back! Come on, come on! She says, "I forgive you" and everything else.

Kept on going until he got to that rock there—I don't know how many miles out that Redding Rock is.

So, she couldn't follow no more.

So, she just throw that acorn [pounding pestle], $?ek^wom$. That's what it is, that's what they call it, $?ek^wom$, an Indian name, because that is what that rock is.

Then he end up in Shelter Cove. That woman was Abalone.

FOR LOVE AND MONEY

The story about Redding Rock was a variant on a mythic theme that was far older than Mrs. Norris (Kroeber 1976: narrative A7). She told me the story after I'd asked her if she knew another old Yurok myth called, in English, "The Inland Whale." "About unwedlock child? No," she said, "but I got almost the same one." Her "Redding Rock" is indeed comparable with "The Inland Whale," another tale of a ka·mu·ks blessed by a pitying spirit. The spirit, in that case, was in the mountains north of the Klamath, not in the sky (Spott and Kroeber 1942; T. Kroeber 1959). As in "Redding Rock," the boy becomes wealthy because of this blessing by a spiritual whale, however, rather than by Mrs. Norris's Good Lord.

It may not be obvious that acquisition of wealth is at the heart of Ella Norris's "Redding Rock." A white deerskin covered with pileated woodpecker scalps from the ears to the sternum would, however, be the very ultimate in dance regalia, although it is important to note that it is not a deerskin—an object—that is described, but a deer, a living being, for all that he is stored, in the end, in a special basket.

Ideally, wealth comes to native northwestern Californians through spiritual practice in the mountains. "Clean" men and women sometimes go, in trance, from the prayer seats in the mountains to the Sky World to learn from the spirit-people there, and spirits may also come from "the spiritual" into "the physical" world, in the mountains, to aid the human beings who are making medicine. As spiritual route to and/or as metaphor of the Sky World, the source of wealth and knowledge, the mountains are of great, esoteric importance in the cosmology of Yurok spiritual training. Harry Roberts, for instance, considered Peak 8, in the Southern Siskiyous, "the center of the spiritual world," as he considered the village of Kenek, in the Klamath River canyon far below, the center of the physical world.[1]

The physical mountains where the various medicine rocks and peaks mentioned in previous chapters (Doctor Rock, Chimney Rock, the "men's rock," Peak 8, Fish Lake—"the whale place"—and the rest) are located are the Southern Siskiyous, the most powerful of them clustered in a defined (relatively) high-altitude area north of the great bend of the lower Klamath River, once referred to simply as *hełkew*, "inland," and now called "the High Country," because of both its altitude and its spirituality: it is where "high medicine" is made. Summit Valley, above the Smith River drainage, serves the same purposes for Tolowas and is in the same region, a scant few miles from Doctor Rock, and Chimney Rock and Elk Valley are used by Karuks as well as Yuroks and, possibly, Tolowas. (The Hupas have their own sacred places, in the Trinity Alps.) Only qualified people who are "clean"—ritually pure—should go into the High Country for spiritual purposes.

In "Redding Rock," as in "The Inland Whale," purity of heart is seen as the key to bringing this wealth down from the sky. It is the boy's "goodness," in contemporary terms, his lack of greed (he wants love, not money), that leads the Good Lord to take pity on him and give him success, despite the fact that he is *ka·mu·ks*, a sociological bastard, one for whose birth no bride wealth has been exchanged. (The boy in "The Inland Whale" is a bastard, too.) In both tales, the boys are polluted from birth and both break the law badly by going up to the most pure places. However, the purity of these boys' yearning is even more powerful than the law.

In Ella Norris's narrative, Abalone Woman's greed, not her shame in producing a bastard, is the root of her suffering and loss—a solidly native northwestern Californian lesson. But she cannot be helped. The boy has become a "real man" (*pegʌk*) through his exploit "so way up," and is now independent. He gives the grandmother the treasure and turns his back on his mother, leaving her angry and weeping, paying the price for her greed and lovelessness. Plenty more wealth will come to the young man now, anyway.[2]

All of this problematizes an understanding of native northwestern Californian dance regalia as simply "objects that possess a high property value—wealth that impresses, but nevertheless profane and negotiable wealth" (Kroeber 1925: 4). From this point of view, "The observing white

man . . . who is at first repulsed by the Yurok moneymindedness and suspicious compulsiveness cannot escape the final insight that his relations
with the Yurok lack alleviating romanticism because Yurok and white man
each understands too well what the other wants, namely possessions"
(Erikson 1943: 258). But the view is mistaken in its very foundations.
Dance regalia are not objects but "people," sentient beings (like deer) that
have *wewecek̕*, "spirit" or "life," and that "cry to dance." As people, their
"purpose in life" is to get out of the baskets and boxes in which they're
stored and dance to "fix the world," make the physical plane once again
like the pure prairie of the sky, *wes?onah*, from which they come. While
individuals obtain and own them, regalia do not ultimately serve individuals, but "the world," *ki ?wes?onah*. The reduction of Yurok purification through training to "suspicious compulsiveness" and the ownership
of communal dance regalia to individual acquisitiveness is a vast and misleading oversimplification.

The materialism of the salvage ethnographic accounts of classic native
northwestern California is coherent with their pervasive tendency toward
objectification, not only of indigenous wealth, but of indigenous peoples
themselves as static epistemic objects, such as "the Yurok." Yet as materialistic interpretations of dance regalia are contradicted by native understandings of what wealth is, so the objectification of native peoples is contradicted by their actual, individual histories, as by the stories they tell.

Ella Norris, for instance, was born of intertribal parentage in Tolowa
country just before the turn of the century. She was sent as a foster child
to a Yurok uncle, Johnny Shortman, at Welk ͪwew (Klamath, in modern
times), on the south side of the Klamath River mouth, across from Rekͪ̕w-
oy (Requa). This was the site of the Yurok first salmon ceremony, last performed in the 1860s. The medicine for the ceremony was kept in a sweathouse at Welk ͪwew that, by the end of the nineteenth century, belonged to
the Williams family, to whom Shortman was related. Shortman himself
was the last to have the medicine for the ceremony, and he raised Ella in
the sweathouse as a young girl although she was not training to be a doctor—an unusual but not unprecedented occurrence after "the end of the
world." Ella Norris, a vigorous elder in her eighties when I knew her, and
a Christian, knew many things.

176   TESTIMONY

Mrs. Norris was bilingual as a girl, in Tolowa and Yurok; she acquired English a bit later in her life. The cultural and linguistic fluidity in her performance of the story are notable. "Redding Rock" is set in Tolowa territory. It is about a mythic figure, Abalone Woman, found in both Tolowa and Yurok mythologies. Ella first learned it in Yurok and ends her narrative 120 miles from (Tolowa) Point St. George, south of the coast Yuroks, Wiyots, and Mattoles, in Sinkyone country, where Shelter Cove is located. (Redding Rock itself, a huge sea stack, stands five miles offshore from Point St. George.)

All of this, of course, should make us wary of conceiving of native groups or even individuals in the region, today or in the past, in the objectified terms of discrete tribes or cultures—"the Tolowa," "the Yurok"—about whom we can make summary statements like, "among the Yurok, the only females to use the sweathouse were those in training to become doctors."

PLANNING AND PROTESTING THE GO-ROAD

In the late 1960s, Yurok and Karuk elders became deeply concerned about the United States Department of Agriculture's Forest Service (USDA/FS), which was mobilizing to complete a federal highway across the Southern Siskiyou Mountains. The road would cut through the center of the Yuroks' most sacred aboriginal territory, the High Country—past Peak 8 and Doctor Rock, and just below it, Chimney Rock, an even more powerful peak for *kegeyowor* and *pegʌk kegeyowor* training among both Yuroks and Tolowas, across the glacial cirques above Elk Valley, with their many "prayer seats," and on through Flint Valley, a place of special importance to Karuk medicine people. As the Forest Service was to be informed, "Believers go to the High Country to communicate with the pre-human spirits who ordained world renewal ceremonies, and through the spirits, with the Origin of healing and spiritual power" (Falk 1989: 518). That spiritual powers include a full, balanced range was perhaps best left for more subtle minds: the High Country also includes *a·kah*, "Bad Place," a dome of granite that forms the center of the dark side of the world, where the "bad doctors" get the strongest of their revolting powers.

Although well known throughout Indian communities in northwestern California, the High Country had been virtually unknown outside of these communities. Kroeber and other salvage ethnographers working in the region between 1900 and 1920 wrote infrequently about spiritual activities in the mountains; their interest was scant and their reports sparse, focusing primarily on women doctors. (It is possible that Indian people simply chose not to discuss men's use of the region with A. L. Kroeber, T. T. Waterman, E. W. Gifford, and others, protecting this last corner of their world that had not been violated by the whites.) However they originated, these lacunae in the salvage ethnographic record were to be of some consequence as the century drew toward its end.

The High Country now lies within Six Rivers National Forest, as part of the Blue Creek Planning Unit, a remote area of 67,000 acres containing an estimated 733 million board feet of prime ancient timber, most of it Douglas fir and white cedar. In the 1960s the Blue Creek Unit and the adjacent Eight Mile Planning Unit were slated for logging in management planning, and the Forest Service deemed the new road necessary to make the areas accessible.[3]

The planned highway, when completed, would run from Orleans, on California Route 96, across the High Country to a point on the South Fork of the Smith River, thirty-odd miles to the west. From this remote point on an unstable gravel road, logging trucks could reach U.S. Route 199 near the hamlet of Gasquet, almost twenty miles away. The Forest Service, in an act of wishful thinking perhaps, called the seventy-five mile project "the Gasquet-Orleans Road," an attractive euphemism that was quickly shortened to "the GO-road." What became known as the "GO-road case" would slog along for twenty years after elders first became concerned about it, a long road itself that terminated in the U.S. Supreme Court in 1988.

In 1968, however, the GO-road was bogged down in engineering problems and in growing local resistance. Two sections were nearing completion, the Summit Valley section, running from the South Fork up to a ridge near Peak 8, and the Dillon Flint section, from Orleans to below Flint Valley. By the 1970s these sections of highway, each centered in eighty-foot-wide roadbeds, dead-ended, separated by 6.2 miles of high ridges and deep valleys and connected only by a rough, narrow dirt track. The planned final section of the highway was called the Chimney Rock section. Forest Service engineers were itching to finish what they had started, understandably enough.

Completion of the GO-road would be the prelude to building two hundred miles of new dirt logging roads. Others were waiting as well: the logging companies that banked on clear-cutting the steep slopes and ridges of the Blue Creek Unit, the mill owners at either end of the uncompleted highway, the many people who might once again make an honest living in construction, logging, trucking, and milling in this economically depressed region, and the many others who simply wanted a quicker route across the mountains. Without a completed GO-road, the shortest route between Orleans and Gasquet amounts to approximately 125 miles, yet travelers' convenience was not a central Forest Service concern: As Vine Deloria noted, "The fact is that federal lands are managed for the benefit of private commercial parties" (1992: 280). A U.S. congressman began to play a strong role.

Neither convenience nor commerce nor timber lobbies were of much concern to a vast majority of local Indian people, even those making a living in the woods and in the mills. For the most part they wanted the road-building stopped; it was widely understood as a desecration. Harry Roberts contacted the Forest Service in Eureka in 1968 and drove with a ranger up the completed Summit Valley section, from the South Fork. He told the ranger little—just that all of the great rocks in the High Country were "people" who had turned themselves into stone at the end of the "beforetime," when the Indians had come. The rocks were sacred and should be left alone. Harry did not think men should tell others things that they could not understand. In time, however, it would become necessary to tell a good deal.

I first visited the area in 1971, camping in Elk Valley with Harry and climbing to the top of Chimney Rock with a camera, to document the prayer seat there at Sam Jones's request. Mr. Jones (Yurok) was organizing resistance to the road, and I gave him slides and black-and-white prints but heard little more about the case until 1974, when Six Rivers National Forest issued its draft environmental statement (DES) on plans to log the Eight Mile and Blue Creek Units (USDA/FS 1975). Opposition to completion of the road had begun to grow, however, among both Indians and non-Indian environmentalists. In 1975, Arnold R. Pilling, an anthropologist with many years of experience among the native peoples of the region, contributed a brief to this opposition in which he argued that the High Country should receive federal protection under the religion clause of the First Amendment to the Constitution (USDA/FS 1977). It seemed quixotic at the time.

The Forest Service had brought the Forest Archaeologist, Donald S. Miller, into the planning group. Miller oversaw a few interviews that his assistants conducted with local Indian people, received written comments from others, and researched the Kroeberian literature on the area. The Blue Creek Unit, Miller wrote in his report, might once have been of some slight significance to the Yuroks of the lower Klamath, though there was no hard evidence that they were still using the area. The only people who once did use it, he continued, were the women doctors who went to Doctor Rock. Since, as Kroeber had argued, these doctors were once connected to specific villages, as part of an overall cultural pattern, and most of the villages had long since largely disappeared—along with what Kroeber viewed as genuine Yurok culture—Indians had no further legitimate need for the area (USDA/FS 1975). Native readers were dismayed.

The Forest Service planners soon recognized that they had to take local protests seriously, however. Two years later, in the 1977 draft environmental statement for the Chimney Rock section, they proposed that route alternatives for the road be reviewed for the least aural and visual impact on the sites, and proposed entering the major sites themselves—Doctor Rock, Chimney Rock, Peak 8—into the National Register of Historic Places, protecting each with a half-mile radius cordon on the perimeter—perhaps to be marked by chainlink fences along each of which would be "interpretive displays" for the enjoyment and education of tourists and other travelers.

I was in northwestern California in the summer of 1976. At the urging of various elders I'd gone to Six Rivers National Forest Headquarters in Eureka, hoping that I might find someone willing to take an oral comment, even a deposition, from me. Donald Miller, the former Forest Archaeologist, had moved on and had been temporarily replaced at Six Rivers by another archaeologist, Henry Gerald Wiley, who had the help of a Wailaki Indian woman, Kathy Heffner. Ms. Heffner, determined to do research on the histories of the indigenous peoples of the area, who were her own people, had somehow landed a job as a "social science technician" with the Forest Service. She had gotten the job, she told me later, because she was of fair complexion: Forest headquarters was not a comfortable place for Indians in 1975. However she had come to be employed, she needed the work, and so needed someone else to confront Donald Miller. Wiley and Heffner sat me down immediately and, after a day's oral testimony, contracted with me for a brief, informal report for yet another DES, this time on the Chimney Rock section of the GO-road, that might address matters Miller had ignored. This I supplied, incorporating in it as much direct oral testimony as I could from Harry Roberts, Florence Shaughnessy, Ella Norris, Frank Douglas, Calvin Rube, and Dewey George (Buckley 1976). The Forest Service was unhappy with my report, and Wiley was transferred shortly thereafter.[4]

After I'd left the region I received Donald Miller's response to my short report. I had, of course, argued strongly against completing the Chimney Rock section on the basis of native testimony and documentary evidence that I suggested Miller had overlooked. Miller defended the Forest Service position that the road could be completed without infringing on Yuroks' or other Indians' rights. I wrote a rejoinder. Six Rivers was forced to start over again.

The Forest Service next hired a contract anthropologist, Dorothea Theodoratus, who had so far had nothing to do with the case, as well as contracting for various new archaeological studies. Theodoratus had a free hand to design and execute her study as she saw fit, within Forest Service and National Register parameters, with only one condition: that she not consult either Arnold Pilling or myself. The "Theodoratus Report" (USDA/FS 1979a) finally came in at nearly five hundred pages and cost the government over $200,000. While the report contained an invaluable wealth of information and new native testimony, its conclusions were rather simple: the GO-road should not be completed for precisely the reasons that both Pilling and Buckley had made clear by 1976. (Pilling had worked pro bono. As I recall, I was paid an hourly wage for my own report, a total of about two hundred dollars.)

SACRED SITES AS COMMODITIES

In 1978 I was back on the river again. One day when I was on the coast I went to observe a meeting of environmentalists and Forest Service personnel at the site of a proposed timber sale near the Smith River—far smaller than those proposed for the Blue Creek Unit. The discussion was civil and informed but clearly, after an hour, was not going anywhere. "Look," a ranger finally said to the environmentalists, "you keep talking about the need for wilderness, the rights of trees and so on—but that's just philosophy. We're not talking philosophy, we're talking facts. There are millions of board feet of lumber here—that's a fact."

Of course there was no "wilderness" there, no natural rights, and certainly not millions of board feet of milled Douglas fir lumber.[5] Only trees could be seen, touched, smelled, heard as the breeze rustled them high up, tasted if you had a mind to. Everybody was talking "philosophy," and Forest Service philosophy was government-subsidized capitalism; the business of America is indeed business.

In the spring of 1978 Dorothea Theodoratus had invited me to join a session on the anthropology of native California to present what would be my first paper at a professional meeting. By August it seemed the time had come to begin work for the November meeting. I began to think over my GO-road experiences in terms of the "symbolic anthropology" that I was then engaged in, and sat down to write the paper in a camp on a river bar near Weitchpec. The paper went something like the following, with rhetoric, verb tenses, and dates occasionally changed to reflect the twenty-three years that have passed since I wrote it (Buckley 1978).

In 1978 many people hoped that passage of Public Law 95-341, "American Indian Religious Freedom" (92 STAT. 469i [1978])—commonly known as AIRFA—would ease the task of protecting natural locations claimed by American Indians as sacred to them. Yet, there was not then nor is there today any enabling federal legislation or regulation that fully recognizes the connections between those profound sentiments protected by AIRFA and the physical locations to which, in many, many cases, they attach. Preservation procedures and regulations on the books fail to acknowledge the relationship between certain concrete symbols and the meanings that they carry within American Indian cultures, replacing these meanings with an alternate set based in non-Indian American culture.

American Indian "sacred sites" (as they have come to be called) on federally managed lands, along with a spread of things including Neolithic pottery shards and early twentieth-century railway stations, must be preserved as historic remnants if they are to be reserved for Indian use at all. This is usually inappropriate: most often, one constituent of a site's sacredness is its synchronic or a-historical meaningfulness, on which ongoing use is predicated. While duration-through-time is a part of the semantic constellation "sacred," that constellation itself is disjunct with the non-Indian notion of "history."

A second major disjunction occurs between the dominant society's definition of these sites as things (i.e., "properties") and Indian emphasis on the sites as the nexes of nonmaterial energies. The conflict is a cultural one, if we accept that culture is, in one of its most important aspects at least, a system of presupposed meanings.

My purpose, in Los Angeles in 1978, was to delineate some of the more important semantic components of the term, or symbol, "cultural resource," which was being offered, implicitly, by the federal government as functionally synonymous with the term, or symbol, "sacred site," and to demonstrate the inadequacy of the former term as a proper equivalent for the latter. In doing so I focused on two major components of the "cultural resource" symbol, "history" and "property," although there were, of course, several others involved. Simply, I selected these two because they appeared to be, on the basis of available glosses, the most dominant.

Cultural Resources

Despite the frequency with which the term "cultural resource" appeared in Forest Service reports related to the GO-road, no precise definition of the term was available through the Forest Service in 1978. The closest approximation to such a definition, according to Forest Service personnel, appeared in the then most recent draft of the Forest Service Manual under "Title 2300: Recreation Management," as item 2361, "Cultural History Resources": "The cultural foundation of our Nation includes buildings, sites, areas, architecture, memorials, and other artifacts. These comprise an irreplaceable resource relating to past human life" (USDA/FS 1977: ii.p.). This "cultural foundation" also includes here the "national heritage left by aboriginal Americans." This "heritage" is described as significant insofar as it includes "evidence of early habitation in America" (ibid.: 2361–2361.1).

These passages constituted the sole basis then available in Forest Service literature for the protection of Indian sacred sites on federal lands: that is, as "artifacts" comprising "evidence of early habitation in America," spirituality (and apparently all culture) being subsumed under the classification of "recreation."

A "cultural resource" was, in 1978, an object: a building or "other artifact." The reification of culture in concrete objects could not be attributed simply to Forest Service bureaucrats, however, as the wording of their Title 2300 rested succinctly on a large catalog of federal legislation, reflecting a widely shared cultural system rather than an idiosyncratic propensity. The draft Forest Service Manual cited a variety of federal mandates and laws on which its own policy was based. These included: the Antiquities Act of 1906 (protection of "artifacts"); the Historic Sites Act of 1935 ("preservation of properties"); the National Historic Preservation Act of 1966 ("protection, rehabilitation, restoration of districts, sites, buildings, structures, and objects significant in American history"); Executive Order 11593 ("preservation of . . . sites, structures, and objects"); the National Environmental Policy Act of 1969 (protection of Native American sites as environmental resources); the Archaeological and Historical Conservation Act of 1974 (protection of historical and archaeological data), etc. (ibid.: Title 2300, pp. 3–10). Conceptual and affective components of culture, other than nostalgic attachment to physical remnants and scientific attachment to those remnants as objects of study, seemed to have no place under the rubric of "Cultural History Resource." There was not, for example, the slightest recognition of the religious sentiments and conceptions of Amerian Indians.[6] In regard to American Indian sacred sites there was enabling legislation sufficient only for the protection of things, and of scientific control of Indian things, through archaeology (cf. McGuire 1997).

We might have expected, in 1978, that the term "cultural value," found equally frequently in the GO-road reports as "cultural resource," would refer to the indigenous cultural postulates that make a material resource somehow special. This, however, was not the reference of "cultural value." There was not even a minimal gloss of this term in Forest Service litera-ture. When I asked, at Six Rivers headquarters, I was told that the defi-nition of "cultural resource" cited above sufficed for a definition of "cul-tural value" as well. This seemed substantiated by federal documents other than the 1978 draft Forest Service Manual. The Bureau of Land Man-agement, for example, described the function of the Antiquities Act of 1906 as, "providing penalties for those who excavate or appropriate the values," i.e., "artifacts" (USDI/BLM 1976: 623.1). A "value" was, it would seem, a material "resource."

Thus in the DES on the final, Chimney Rock portion of the GO-Road (USDA/FS 1978: 91–92), Forest Service specialists reported that (in para-phrase), All of the route alternatives have been inspected and proven to be clear of cultural values. In other words: 1. No part of the specific prop-erties will be destroyed or altered in the proposed action. 2. There is no proposed transfer or sale of any property in the proposed action. 3. There is no proposal that will result in the deterioration or destruction of the sites.

A "cultural value" was, then, a "property" or a "site."

"Property" is of interest for it introduces yet another apparent syn-onym. In the full statement from which the above has been excerpted we read that, "Construction of the GO-Road would cause no known direct physical alteration to any recognized or suspected cultural properties" (ibid.: 91). Two disparate points must be raised here. First, the emphasis on "direct physical alteration" is important regarding sacred site protec-tion, for northwestern California Indians argued that in the Siskiyous not only the sites themselves must be protected but the entire aural, visual, and social (i.e., private) context of the sites needs protection as well, if the efficacy of the sites is to be preserved (ibid.: 360–63). Protection as a finite and isolate "property" could not provide the contextual protection held necessary for ensuring the requisite experience of people making medi-cine. Second, "cultural property" is, clearly, a third synonymous term, in-terchangeable with "cultural resource" and "cultural value." Within the culture that uses these terms, a "cultural resource," or "value," is not only an object, a reification of culture, but is also an object that, according to the above quotation, it is possible to transfer or sell. That is, cultural resources, like natural resources, may be converted into commodities—as all land, in the view of the currently dominant culture in North America, is a potential commodity, or "property."

The dispute over the GO-road was a cultural one. It was a conflict between variant systems of meanings. The cultural basis of the conflict and of the communication break that was inherent in it was one of which native Californians, if not the Forest Service, were acutely aware. To paraphrase Calvin Rube, who was responding to a proposal to save the High Country by declaring it a federal Roadless Wilderness Area through the RARE II inventory process: "We want the sacred country preserved in any way possible. But to do this by declaring it a 'wilderness' misses the point, and it would be better if some other means could be found. That country is not 'wild.' It was made perfectly by the Creator exactly as he wanted it to be there for us to use."

Compare, then, the Forest Service's emphasis on sacred sites as isolate objects, properties, with the emphases of Karuk and Yurok Indians at the time. Charlie Thom (Karuk):

> All . . . things are prayed over from the highest medicine mountains. From Chimney Rock . . . Doctor Rock. . . . They're putting through the GO-Road, which conflicts with every thing involved in getting medicine down into the Brush Dance hole [in the lowland villages]. That road goes right past Chimney Rock, Doctor Rock, Little Medicine Mountain, Flint Valley. Those are places where we can shoot medicine right down into the Brush Dance hole . . . just like radar. [Charlie Thom, in Berg 1978: 148–49]

Again, Florence Shaughnessy speaking of the efficacy of the High Country: "We go there because the forces are there." So, "People go into seclusion and seek something when they're troubled and then this happens and you come out a whole person. Because you have had help. Nature has gathered every force to help you. They uplift you."

The "they," here, are spirit-beings. A young man in training in 1978:

Those places, they aren't just rocks and caves; they're the homes of spirits, unseen beings. But if you are pure you can see them. I have seen the doctors [spirits] dancing in the cave under Doctor Rock with their canes, so many of them they could hardly fit in there, dancing and singing. They will talk with you if you are the one—sit down and have a regular conversation with you. That's what "training" is; that's how you learn.

As for the notion of selling or transferring such places, of using them as "properties" in the commodity market, here is what Calvin Rube told me: "It doesn't matter if some Indians accepted money for that land [in claims settlements]; it was illegal because that land is not theirs to sell. It is the Creator's land, and cannot belong to any person."

History

The "history" in "cultural history resource" was really a sort of folk-history that emphasized the point of view characterized by Herbert Butterfield as "presentism": "the study of the past for the sake of the present." At the heart of presentism is "a tendency to emphasize certain principles in the past and to produce a story which is the ratification if not the glorification of the present" (Butterfield, in Stocking 1968: 3). Interest in preserving American Indian sacred sites on the grounds that they "comprise an irreplaceable resource relating to past human life" and that they are significant insofar as they are "evidence of early habitation in America" and so are part of today's "national heritage left by aboriginal Americans" is clearly presentistic, although Butterfield himself used the term in clarifying more sophisticated and complex manifestations of presentism in historical writing. Presentistic history, by focusing on a single line of temporal process (that which, from a highly specified viewpoint, constitutes a direct line to an equally specified present), denies the relevance and even the reality of other temporal processes occurring simultaneously with that one singled out by the historian as the "mainstream" of history.

This sort of history is materialistic, in an abstract sense. It makes of events, actions, emotions, thoughts, people, peculiar sorts of objects. Denied their full organic and processual complexity through conceptual isolation, events and the rest become things, and it is only with such objectification that temporal/spatial process may be linearized as progressive "history." These objects are easily confused with other, concrete objects. Thus, "cultural history resource," a property, may be substituted for "heritage left by aboriginal Americans," an object. "Heritage," here, is not an implicitly held set of preconceptions, understandings, beliefs, fears, yearnings, and so on, but rather a material accumulation. Indeed, the federal government proposed, in 1978, replacing all of the various synonyms that I have been discussing with a single new term: "heritage resource," to be understood as "a signpost of America's past" (USDI 1978).

Such "heritage resources" are, I've pointed out, commodity-like. Marx's notion of the fetishism of commodities is, of course, pertinent (in Dolgin, Kemnitzer, and Schneider 1977: 245–53). The accumulation of "heritage resources," understood as commodities, glorifies and empowers the dominant North American culture. This effect is precisely that attributed by Butterfield to presentistic history, the sort of history that underlies the definition of a "cultural" or "heritage resource."

Please Go Away So We Can Miss You

North American Indians were conceptually rushed to an early grave in order, in part, to be incorporated as a heritage-commodity. Anthropologists have not shared the tendency toward presentism and objectification of the past as a defense against the complexity and flow of the present. Beatrice Medicine (Standing Rock Sioux) pointed out in 1972 that "the direct outgrowth of the culture-area concept which categorized tribal entities into static units bolstered by traits collected by the 'Laundry List' method" was a state of anthropological affairs in which

> Parfleche designs, moccasin types, and medicine bundles assumed more dynamic qualities than the people themselves. Many Indians were seen as living museum pieces. The recording of music and language grossly obscured the dynamics of Indian interaction and laid the foundation for the "apathetic, defeated Indian." The over-riding conviction of the disappearing native hastened the collection of a record that has formed a congealed ethnographic present impervious to change. [Medicine 1972: 25–26]

By the 1940s it was the anthropological fashion to view "the Indian" as a thing of the past, and I think anthropologists must themselves bear part of the blame for the insensitivity of the federal government toward such matters as the ongoing Indian use of indigenous sacred sites, for anthropologists have had more influence in Washington than they care, always, to admit (McNickle 1972). In 1945 Julian Steward wrote, "Anthropologists are in general agreement that it is purely a question of time before all Indians lose their identity" (in ibid.: 34). Returning to northwestern California, we find John Bushnell, in 1968, suggesting that Hupa Indians henceforth be referred to, and presumably dealt with, as "Indian Americans," rather than "American Indians," for, like Italian Americans, Afro-Americans, and the rest, they were really "ethnics" now, fully "acculturated" to the mainstream of American life and thought (Bushnell 1968).

However, as we have seen in the various Indian statements made between 1975 and 1978 about northwestern California sacred sites, Yurok and Karuk people did not always think, or perceive, in the same terms as members of non-Indian American society, nor do they now, nor may they or their sacred sites be easily relegated to the status of "national heritage," "signposts of America's past." There was already, by 1978, a significant renaissance in indigenous cultures and identities in northwestern California. Indian motivation for the protection of the High Country had little to do with preserving a "heritage resource" as this was understood in federal documents. Dewey George, in 1976: "There are a few [men and women] going up into the mountains now, but more will want to use it later. That's why we want to save it." As it turned out, Mr. George was quite right.

"History" is an important component of the "cultural resource" symbol, yet as with the "property" component of this same symbol, there are irreconcilable non-Indian and Indian understandings of it. In conversing with Calvin Rube about the GO-road, I inquired about "the old Indian Law." Mr. Rube responded patiently: "Sir, you are wrong. It is not the 'old' law or the 'new' law or anything like that. We are not talking about old-time Indians or about young men in training today. The law is the Law of the Great Creator; that's all. It's not old or young or middle-aged."

Two understandings of history and of heritage, a spiritualized native one and an objectified non-Indian one, were in conflict in the GO-road case. It is perhaps for this reason that Arnold Pilling sought to circumvent the entire historic preservation endeavor by arguing for the protection of the High Country under the First Amendment (USDA/FS 1978: 304–10). The Forest Service rejected his argument (ibid.: 291–94), proclaiming the National Register of Historic Places as the only viable means of preservation. This was the case, to be as generous as possible, simply because the Historic Preservation Act of 1966, which produced the Register, was then the only extant enabling legislation for the protection of Indian sacred sites: AIRFA failed in this regard. The 1966 Act, of course, seeks only to preserve "districts, sites, buildings, structures, and objects" (Office of the Federal Register 1977: 378). There is nothing in the act that provides for the protection of beliefs or sentiments, nor is there anything that protects ongoing culturally authentic significance and use. I was told at Six Rivers headquarters in 1978, however, that such conditions might be squeezed in under Register Criterion a.4: "That they have yielded, or may be likely to yield, information important in prehistory or history" (p. 384). Finally, the potential value of indigenous North American sacred sites was understood as their value to archaeologists, not to the people who held them sacred.

Objectification

In 1978, my objection to the National Register as the sole avenue for the protection of American Indian sacred sites was that the criteria for inclusion in the Register were culturally biased toward an objectified, or materialistic, interpretation of these sites as properties, rather than as nexes of complex processes, and of history as a single progressive vector excluding simultaneous processual unfoldings along any of a plethora of other possible vectors. In such a view, history itself is objectified, its processual qualities lost.

The end result of these two sorts of objectification, or materialism, inherent in the "cultural resource" symbol is the reduction of sacred sites to commodity-like properties whose "value" is, in essence, a market value, and which must compete with other commodities in the commodity market. Thus, elsewhere in California in 1978, at Coso Hot Springs, a sacred site was in competition with geothermal energy; in the Siskiyous, sacred sites were in competition with saw-logs. The GO-road, necessary for the exploitation of one resource, timber, was viewed by native Californians as obstructing the use of sacred sites by human beings. In the resultant competition, native people were at great disadvantage: standing timber can be converted to capital; sacred sites cannot, at least not so profitably.

The Forest Service, however, following its program of "multiple use," saw the exploitation of "natural resources" as compatible with the exploitation of "cultural resources": these could be protected, as "heritage," by being listed in the Register of Historic Places. Yet this compatibility could be perceived only through the reduction of two disparate constellations of meanings to a single, reified symbol, "property." For the Forest Service, the exploitation of timber was compatible with the preservation of some sites as cultural resources, Historic Places; for the Indians for whom the environment of the same sites is integral to the meanings of the sites themselves, logging could not be compatible with protection of the sites as focuses of spiritual practice.

In 1978 the Department of the Interior proposed, as a unifying therapy for all of the diverse historical and environmental regulation and legislation then on the books, the National Heritage Program. This proposed program was billed as "Partnership in Action" (USDI 1978: 23). It laid heavy stress on cooperation between local, state, and federal governments, and included the "Private Sector—Individuals, Organizations, Business/Industry" in the partnership. It perceived these various influence groups as "concerned with heritage conservation" and dedicated to helping identify heritage resources, constructively managing them, bringing issues concerning threatened heritage resources to the attention of government officials, and so on (ibid.: 7–8). But of course, in the GO-road case, it was precisely local government (seeking tax revenues), business/industry (construction, logging, trucking, milling, etc.), and other organizations in the private sector (e.g., sportsmen's lobbies) that most directly objected to efforts toward the protection of the High Country and that were the most persistent visible obstructionists (e.g., section of letters in USDA/FS 1975).

The Forest Service, with responsibilities toward both logging and historic preservation (through multiple use management) was deeply engaged in a conflict of interest. In the commodity market, it is not "partnership" that is enacted; it is the profit motive. Six Rivers National Forest's operating expenses were putatively covered by income from timber block sales, stumpage fees on felled timber, and so on.

The National Heritage Program was doomed to failure as an effective therapeutic for these sorts of cultural conflicts. Once more, Indian sacred sites would have come under the classificatory umbrella of "recreation" (USDI 1978: 23 ff.); once again, the National Register of Historic Places would constitute the sole avenue of protection (ibid.).

National Register Criteria

The criteria for registry in the National Register of Historic Places (Office of the Federal Register 1977: ch. 1, part 60) were established to empirically determine the qualifications of a variety of objects for preservation as historic remnants. These criteria, forming as they did the sole bases on which sacred sites could be found worthy of preservation (not protection, as I have used this term above), predetermined the type of research that might be applied in the nomination of places for the Register. These objectivist, materialistic criteria determined research in the same positivist vein. Heavy emphasis was placed, in the consideration of sacred sites, on quantitative archaeology, and while, owing to external pressures, the Forest Service recognized the need for extensive ethnographic research, this research itself was predicated on certain positivist assumptions and the methodology that these generated, both theory and method being, in turn, predicated on the Register criteria. Statistical surveys of large population cross-sections regarding specific properties and historical summaries were stressed rather than intensive study through consultation with native specialists in spiritual practice, of the constituents of meanings accruing to the archaeologists' objects, of native concepts of history, and of ongoing use of sacred areas. The acceptable approach was lauded as "scientific," the latter as "intuitive" and "unscientific" (USDA/FS 1978: 92, 375–409, 411–17). Yet "science," here, becomes scientism, as Yurok Indians pointed out in criticizing the ethnographers who worked on the Theodoratus Report for "skimming around all the time and not settling down to learn from people who know something." As a friend remarked,

> There are Indian people who know about the sacred places and about the law, and there are a lot of others who do not know and are not expected to. For anthropologists to spend their time running around talking to those people is like going to find out how a big university works and talking to all the janitors you meet in the halls instead of the professors and the administration. There's nothing wrong with being a janitor, but there are many things that a janitor is not expected to know about a university.

The First Amendment of the United States Constitution was intended to guarantee religious freedom, and the passage of AIRFA in 1978 can only be understood as a sign of weakness in this amendment. The question had already arisen in 1978, however, as to whether AIRFA itself was fully workable. It was soon to be proven that, without further specific enabling legislation for the protection of American Indian sacred sites, it was not.

So I concluded the paper I gave at my first professional meeting.

OFF TO SEE THE WIZARD

As the Forest Service, in the "national interest," overrode the 1979 Theodoratus Report's recommendations, local activism was becoming well organized. The Northwest Coast Indian Cemetery Protective Association (NICPA), initiated in the early 1970s by Milton Marks, a coast Yurok, was joined by four Yurok individuals from upriver (Sam Jones, Jimmie James, Lewana Brantner, and Christopher Peters). Together, NICPA and the four Yuroks filed a series of Forest Service appeals and sought court injunctions against completion of the Chimney Rock section of the GO-road. They were aided by a Yurok attorney, Marilyn Miles, from California Indian Legal Services, and the "NO-GO" movement took solid root in the area. Chris Peters, Julian Lang (who had gained considerable expertise in ethnographic research as an intern in the Theodoratus project), and others worked to organize resistance and to raise funds for a series of lawsuits against the Forest Service. These suits led, in 1983, to trial in 9th U.S. District Court, in San Francisco, Judge Stanley A. Weigel presiding (C-82-4049 SAW). The defendants were R. Max Peterson, Chief, U.S. Forest Service, and John R. Block, Secretary of the Department of Agriculture.

The GO-road plan, quite aside from the threat it posed to native spirituality in the region, posed equally dire threats to the environment. In the High Country, steep slopes, unstable soil, the presence of extremely rare vegetation, and the potential impact on the habitat of spawning Pacific salmon that large scale road-building and the massive clear-cut logging that new roads would enable all seemed to ensure ecological disaster. The case gained national attention (cf. Matthiessen 1984: 165–200 [1979]). By the time it reached federal district court, in 1983, Yurok plaintiffs had been joined by six environmental organizations, ranging from the Sierra Club to the local Northcoast Environmental Center, as well as two individual environmentalists. A second suit, filed by the state of California, was consolidated with the others, and lawyers, including Marilyn Miles, filed briefs bringing a single collective suit. The list of charges against the Forest Service was staggering: violation of the First Amendment, AIRFA, the National Historic Preservation Act, the Federal Water Quality Control Act, the (California) Porter-Cologne Water Quality Control Act, the Wilderness Act, the Administrative Procedure Act, the National Forest Management Act of 1976, the Multiple Use, Sustained Yield Act, and Hupa Indian water and fishing rights (Deloria 1992: 276).

For all its complexity, the trial itself was relatively short. There were, of course, enormous amounts of documentary evidence and a great many witnesses to be called, but the preponderance of the evidence and testimony clearly seemed to favor the plaintiffs' various cases. The probability of irreversible environmental degradation, particularly of aquatic resources, should the Chimney Rock section be completed was especially well established. Forest Service arguments that completion of the GO-road was essential to serve national interests were very weak, if not specious. The Theodoratus report left little reasonable doubt of the High Country's centrality to Yurok, Karuk, and Tolowa spiritual practices.

I flew to San Francisco to appear as an expert witness for the plaintiffs, but, quite rightly, by the second week of March 1983, Judge Weigel had ordered that testimony be restricted to native witnesses—Florence Shaughnessy, Lewana Brantner, Sam Jones, Chris Peters, and others. I never testified.

Lewana Brantner took the stand on March 15, and her testimony was decisive (C-82-4049 SAW, pp. 226–35):

LEWANA BRANTNER: . . . . we use our herbs from the high country where God has left a piece of land dedicated to the use of the [Yurok, Karuk, and Tolowa] tribes, to go there and pray like they say Mecca, or different places through the world where the people go. . . .

We were only allowed to take those that have passed the test and proven, for they come back to the lowlands and then we pray to our people, asking for help and these dances were not performed for the beauty; they were performed asking that we'll have plenty to eat, we would have plenty of game, for conservation was the mainstay of our livelihood and through these canyons—and we always wanted to protect the top of the mountain, because anyone that knows the Klamath, for the first two miles, it's just rock, stray bluffs and cliffs.

So beyond that, God left us a strip about ten miles wide . . .

We had no chief. We had head men and we all got together and anything that come up, we would come together and talk it over and if there was anything that needed help, then we would see that they all got help. . . . These doctors would go there. . . .

Chimney Rock is a man's place to go have—to prove that they can stand anything that comes along and be brave, to face the world. . . .

. . . we lost everything and now we are standing on the last peak, Doctor Rock, Chimney Rock. My neighbors have lost a lot of their ceremonial grounds due to mismanagement of the people, not because they were cruel, but because they didn't understand.

JUDGE WEIGEL: Not because they were what?

LB: They are not cruel.

JUDGE: Cruel?

  LB: Or unkind. They just did not know.

JUDGE: Who is it that didn't understand?

  LB: The new people that came into the Indian country.

JUDGE: By the "new people," who do you mean?

  LB: The white people.

JUDGE: The white people? Well, you are generous in saying they weren't cruel. All right, go ahead.

  LB: . . . . Now, it's not speaking unkind, but when the Six Rivers National Forest destroyed my village and then allowed them to go in there and mine, part of that Bluff Creek, my people, their bones floated down the Klamath River and it's the same now. On the mouth of the river where we used to have the White Deerskin Dance ending, there is a station up there that the soldiers put in. . . .

The mountains have all caved in. Some of the most beautiful streams, we have only concrete left. . . .

JUDGE: Ma'am, I'm very sorry to interrupt you and I am very sympathetic to everything you say. . . . I understood what you are saying, is that due to the deprivations occasioned by the whites, such as the pollution of the streams and the like, and the taking over of more and more land, that the preservation of this particular piece of sacred land has become all the more important.

That's in part what you are communicating to me; is that right?

  LB: Yes.

There followed a very brief cross-examination by the attorney for the defense, and then Judge Weigel excused Lewana Brantner, solicitously warning her about a bad step down from the witness stand as she rose with her cane. The plaintiffs were jubilant after the Yurok elders' testimony on March 15, the defendants visibly discouraged. "Did you see how the judge warned Lewana about that step?" an observer asked. "He was snowed!" "Well," said Lewana Brantner, "Flo [Shaughnessy] and I were up all night in the hotel room making medicine. By this morning we knew we had him."

Judge Weigel handed down his decison on May 24, 1983. He found the defendants in violation of the National Environmental Policy Act, the Federal Water Pollution Control Act, and the First Amendment of the United

States Constitution. The Forest Service appealed the Weigel decision to the court of appeals for the Ninth Circuit (764 F.2d 581, 585 [1985]). While the Forest Service appealed Weigel's decisions on both the water quality and the religious freedom portions in the 1983 trial, clearly, "the real question on appeal was the religious freedom issue" (Deloria 1992: 278). The appeal was denied, although in such ambiguous and uncertain terms that a rehearing by the same court was ordered. The Weigel decision was once again upheld by a majority of two judges, with one dissenting (795 F.2d 688, 695 [1986]). The dissenting opinion, written by Judge Robert Beezer, addressed the "establishment clause" of the First Amendment, arguing that the danger of abridgment of Indian free exercise of religious belief was accompanied by an equal danger of the government's establishment of such a belief through the establishment of a religious shrine in the Siskiyous. A danger to the government itself seems implicit in Judge Beezer's dissent: if the Weigel decision was upheld, "it would mark the first time since the passage of the American Indian Religious Freedom Resolution that Indian religious freedom could be used to enjoin development of the public lands" (Deloria 1992: 282). Beezer's dissent was to give the Supreme Court reason to hear the case yet again, in 1988.

In the meantime, however, the GO-road case had largely been mooted by passage of the federal California Wilderness Act of 1984, which had set aside much of the Blue Creek Planning Unit as a wilderness recreation area, preserving it from logging. Congress had, however, withheld the GO-road corridor from the new wilderness, even though the rationale for completing the road—logging the Blue Creek and Six Mile Units—was now anachronistic. The Forest Service, under a new secretary of agriculture, Richard L. Lyng, in effect was arguing that, even though the road should not be built, they could build it. What was to go to the Supreme Court in 1988 was a purely constitutional, rather than managerial, case.

The Supreme Court of the United States heard arguments on November 30, 1987, handing down their decision on April 19, 1988, Justice Sandra Day O'Connor writing the majority opinion, supported by four other justices against the dissent of three (Justice Anthony Kennedy did not take part in consideration of the case) (*Lyng v. Northwest Coast Cemetery Protec-*

tive Association, 108 S. Ct. 1319 [1988]). The Weigel decision on the First Amendment was reversed on grounds that the Forest Service had done all that it could to mitigate the impact of road construction and logging on religious practices that, after all, directly involved only a minority of Indians in the region and were not, thus, "central" to Indian religious freedom.

Justice William Brennan's dissent, in which he was joined by Justices Thurgood Marshall and Harry Blackmun, was scathing, reflecting tensions within the newly conservative "Reagan Court." "The Court," Brennan wrote,

> does not for a moment suggest that the interests served by the G-O road are in any way compelling, or that they outweigh the destructive effect construction would have on respondents' religious practices. Instead, the Court embraces the Government's contention that its prerogative as landowner should always take precedent over a claim that a particular use of federal property infringes religious practices. . . .
>
> Today, the Court holds that a federal land-use decision that promises to destroy an entire religion does not burden that faith in a manner recognized by the Free Exercise Clause. Having thus stripped respondents and all other Native Americans against perhaps the most serious threat to their age-old religious practices, and indeed their entire way of life, the Court assures us that nothing in its decision "should be read to encourage governmental insensitivity to the religious needs of any citizen." I find it difficult, however, to imagine conduct more insensitive to religious needs than the Government's determination to build a marginally useful road in the face of uncontradicted evidence that the road will render the practice of respondents' religion impossible. Nor do I believe that respondents will derive any solace from the knowledge that although the practice of their religion will become "more difficult" as a result of the Government's actions, they remain free to maintain their religious beliefs. Given today's ruling, that freedom amounts to nothing more than the right to believe that their religion will be destroyed. . . .
>
> I dissent.

It had been twenty years since Harry Roberts had first told the Forest Service that the GO-road was a mistake, as Sam Jones was starting to organize resistance to it. The federal government, having turned back the threat of a First Amendment precedent, would not chance completion of the GO-road in the face of public protest. The GO-road corridor was included in the Smith River Wilderness Area in 1989, in effect protecting indigenous spiritual use of it, along with the privileges of backpackers. It was a hollow victory for Indian people—indeed no victory at all.

LOOKING BACK

With the passage of AIRFA in 1978 native efforts toward the protection of sacred sites increased in both intensity and number throughout the United States, to the point that they rapidly became a trend noticed even by *Time* magazine (Weathers and Huck 1979: 98). Observers noted from the beginning, however, the need for enabling legislation to supplement the law. In 1978 Kurt Blue Dog, a staff attorney for the Native American Rights Fund, said, "The law has few teeth. It merely points out a clear Federal policy—which is a good start" (ibid.). Those teeth, however, have yet to materialize. In the 1990s, Senator Daniel Inouye's (D., Hawaii) efforts to strengthen AIRFA were to be stymied again and again by Senate conservatives from the western states, and in 1990 a Supreme Court decision of considerable importance (Employment Division, Department of Human Resources of Oregon *v.* Smith) found neither AIRFA nor the First Amendment sufficient to protect Native American religious freedom against Oregon's state rights in banning Native American Church members' ingestion of peyote.

In the 1990s, Forest Service conflicts of interest and budgetary excesses also came under close scrutiny among scholars and the public alike. In 1992, for instance, Vine Deloria noted:

> Congress has had to confront [the] propensity of bureaucrats to sidestep policy considerations and the plentitude of other federal acts, which the Forest Service had been accused of violating, requiring that various steps be taken so that the intangible factors of forest preservation, historic preservation, clean water, and other goals be considered in the management of the national forests. However, these requirements are generally viewed as mere stumbling blocks, hurdles to be surmounted in their quest for managerial control over lands and trees they consider to be their own property. [1992: 278]

Regarding the role of logging in the GO-road case, Deloria continues, "it is useful to note that . . . other multiple uses—recreation, various habitats, and wilderness—actually had no more standing or value in [the Forest Service's] perspective than did the Indian religious uses. While the agency was bound to consider all of these other uses . . . the fact is that federal lands are managed for the benefit of private commercial parties" (ibid.: 280). Regarding the formal trust relationship between the federal government and Indian tribes as it bore on (or failed ultimately to bear upon) the GO-road case, Deloria writes:

> When trust appears at the lowest administrative levels, it becomes merely one factor among many to be considered. And since the efficient and generally acceptable way of doing business is the real context within which administrative decisions are made, the trust responsibility is far too abstract a notion to have impact on the decisions made by forest managers. [Ibid.: 278]

Nonetheless, the Forest Service had recognized, by 1979, the necessity for truly cultural input in land-use planning and required thoroughgoing ethnographic and historical overviews as central segments in all cultural resource management evaluations, generating, in Six Rivers National Forest, the Theodoratus Report. While the report concluded, on the basis of these overviews, that the GO-road should not be completed, however, the Forest Service found that the road had to be finished in service of "national interest"—to wit, the logging, trucking, milling, and construction industries (USDA/FS 1979b). Their arguments for state's need eventually turned out to be little more than "a set of excuses rather than compelling interests" (Deloria 1992: 277), with a—by now, familiar—logic.

> The values of Forest Service personnel who rank possible increases in future timber bids and ease of administration against Indian rights, and the welfare of the forest itself, tend to speak for themselves. The courts, once they are allowed into the process, can do little but credit this reasoning and the commercial values represented by the Forest Service and its clients with a higher purpose. [Ibid.: 277]

With the failure of AIRFA, and given the ease with which First Amendment claims may be rejected on the basis of "compelling state's interest," suitability for registry as Historic Places and the suitability of sites to the recreational desires of a general public remain the sole viable means for the protection of American Indian sacred sites. All that really changed, after 1978, was that "Forest planning will now . . . identify and evaluate sites for the National Register of Historic Places; and identify opportunities for interpretation of cultural resources for the education and enjoyment of the public" (American Anthropological Association 1979: 28). It did not widely become public knowledge until almost twenty years later, in 1997, that the Forest Service had all along been meeting compelling national interests by managing the National Forest system at enormous losses, subsidizing the timber industry at a staggering level.

By then, the National Register of Historic Places (Bulletin 38, 1998) had met changes in popular liberal political culture by stressing the central place of the "culture" concept in evaluation of potential properties (p. 1). Grounded in Boasian theories of cultural relativity, the Bulletin points out the danger of "ethnocentrism" and the "vital need to evaluate properties thought to have traditional cultural significance from the standpoint of those who may ascribe such significance to them, whatever one's own perception of them, based on one's own cultural values, may be" (p. 4). In detailing National Register Criteria, the Register makes clear that the word "our" in the phrases "our history" (Criterion a) and "our past" (Criterion b) "may be taken to refer to the group to which the property may have traditional cultural significance."

The rhetoric is "politically correct," and sometimes this new interpretation of the criteria has worked to Indian benefit—for instance in the inclusion of Tahquitz Canyon, in southern California, and of the upper reaches of Mount Shasta, in northern California, in the Register. Yet there is an underlying absurdity in this mode of preservation that is not immediately apparent. In Massachusetts, for instance, in 1998 I found myself arguing for protection of native sacred places in New England, whose use possibly dates back eleven thousand years, through precisely the same bureaucratic means and under the same National Register of Historic Places criteria, as a colleague who was arguing for the protection of a defunct candy factory's pastel-painted concrete sugar silos, built in 1964.

In California, neither Tahquitz Canyon nor portions of Mount Shasta have been set aside from development because they are sacred to living native people and because constitutional guarantees are, thus, at stake. They have been minimally protected, for the time being, only because they are historical—"representations of history [that] objectify the past through processes of . . . 'fetishization' " (Sieber 1990: 116). As in 1978, so today "almost any historical investigation that brings its analysis down to the present, as opposed to cutting it off at some safely distant point in the past, raises the possibility of becoming politically controversial" (M. Wallace 1987: 52).

Meanwhile, history proceeds. Judge Stanley A. Weigel retired shortly after his 1983 decision and was widely celebrated by California Indians for his courage. Marilyn Miles, who had argued the Supreme Court case for the Yurok litigants, is herself a federal judge now. Kathy Heffner succeeded, both as an ethnographer and ethnohistorian and in her contribution to making Six Rivers National Forest Headquarters the far more welcoming and safer place that it is today for Indian people. Jerry Wiley, the last I heard, was doing well as a Forest Service archaeologist in the state of Washington, but that was some time ago. Dorothea Theodoratus has continued doing her good work in researching California Indian land issues, as a consultant, and the late Arnold R. Pilling was publicly honored by Chris Peters (Yurok) at the California Indian Conference in 1988.

Like Julian Lang, Chris Peters and the other central NO-GO people were discouraged by the 1988 Supreme Court decision, but their movement had contributed significantly to building local political confidence and savvy. Perhaps more important, in the long run of things, it also provided a focus for local Indian identity and spiritual activism and thus contributed directly to the resurgence of world renewal ceremonialism in the region. In 1984 the Yurok jump dance at Pecwan revived after fifty years of seeming dormancy.

PART THREE Understandings

7 The One Who Flies All around the World

Wealth, like human lives, comes from *wes?onah*, "the sky": "creation," "the world." People today usually concur that dance regalia, especially, simply "comes" to people who are "good," although traditionally wealth was a principal object of men's sweathouse training, particularly packing sweathouse wood, and of elite women's menstrual austerities (Buckley 1988). What "interrupts" (to use Calvin Rube's term) the flow of such beneficence "from the Creator" is people's greed and selfishness. All wealth, each item of which itself has a "life" or "spirit," *wewecek*, is "a person," attracted by generosity and purity, repelled by stinginess and pollution. (Dance regalia moves around quite a bit, from family to family within the region, as it always has.)

There is a seeming conflict here. Wealth is the "measure" of spiritual acumen, in the ideal model (Harry Roberts), but greed and selfishness drive wealth away. It is on this paradox that Erik Erikson's comparison of Yurok and non-Indian "money-mindedness" and Walter Goldschmidt's more sophisticated ethnological comparison of Calvinist and Yurok world views both founder (Erikson 1943; Goldschmidt 1951). Wealth (again, in an ideal system that contemporary Yuroks evoke in their testimony) comes to individuals and is maintained by kin groups that consistently use their wealth for the good of the community—"the world"—by letting it out to dance. The highest forms of wealth, dance regalia, come to and stay with people who are dedicated to "fixing the world" through, particularly, the great dances. Wealth, then, does not indicate an individual's personal salvation, as in Calvinist Christianity as understood by Max Weber (1958), but his or her fitness, through spiritual discipline, to contribute to the good of creation itself, an ethic quite distinct from the dualistic Protestant one with which it has so often been compared (cf. Bushnell and Bushnell 1977).

When you pray in the hills and mountains, an elder asserts today, "you must pray for everybody, not just yourself; you must pray for the whole world." Knowledgeable people say that what these men have been doing all along has not been comparable to the self-interested action of non-Indian materialists; that all training, not just that done in conjunction with world renewal ceremonials, is for the good of "the world." It is a sociocentric, or even cosmo-centric, system, rather than one that is ego-centric and overwhelmingly secular. By extension, all training, as an expression of "the Creator's purpose," helps the community (which is, in part, why the community supports individuals' training). While individuals undeniably gain prestige and influence through acquiring and maintaining familial wealth, they do so because it is understood that the spiritual purity of their lives, achieved through discipline, is manifested in their wealth, which is, then, manifestly suitable for the spiritual work of fixing the world (again, speaking in terms of an ideal native system).

One might expect this wealth to be richly symbolic in conventional senses. However, apart from his apparent indifference to the intricate spiritual significance of wealth objects, A. L. Kroeber seems to have been on the right track in declaring that ceremonial feather work, baskets, skins, flints and the rest have no "symbolic" significance—that they are "wealth only" (Kroeber and Gifford 1949). Aside from their general spiritual significance, these things do not stand for something else in most contemporary local views. As sacramental objects they are quite different from those most common in Christianity where, for instance, the Eucharist stands for (or in the Roman Catholic view, is) the body and blood of Christ. Whatever psycho-symbolism Erikson and others have attributed to them (chapter 8), for most native northwestern Californians of my acquaintance these objects are simply themselves. In themselves, beautiful and alive (the part that Kroeber seems not to get right), they exemplify the world's beauty and aliveness. Thus they are suited to use in fixing the world, when the messy lives of human beings have polluted and obscured its true nature, which *is* "beauty."

Yet, from the standing ground, from outside of the cultural system, at least (and for a few native intellectuals as well), wealth seems iconic, manifesting ulterior meanings as well as its own and the world's "beauty." Like Yurok doctors, dance regalia is probably best understood as emerging along a continuum. And as the practices of doctors are coherent with and illuminate world renewal, so the continuum of money and wealth illuminates this world itself—*ki ?wes?onah*, "that which exists."

Before minted U.S. currency was introduced in the 1850s, the primary monetary medium in native northwest California was dentalia shells—the hard, phallic, tusk-like shells of *Dentalium indianorum* and *D. hexagonum*. These were classically traded slowly down from Vancouver Island and Puget Sound. The shells gained in value the farther they traveled, distance and scarcity providing reliable hedges against devaluation and inflation until the introduction of coastwise shipping after the gold rush of 1849.

Five sizes of shells were recognized as money (*c·ik*) by the Yuroks, in A. L. Kroeber's reconstruction (1925: 23). The largest and most valuable were about two and a half inches long, or eleven to a (ca. 27.5") string. The next, twelve to a string, were worth about one fifth as much, and so on down to the smallest, fifteen to a string. Shells smaller than that, "women's money," were strung as beads in necklaces but were not used by men in exchange. The longest and best shells were often decorated with soot-blackened, incised lines (like scrimshaw), bits of red woodpecker scalp, or tubes of skin from colorful small snakes, like the striped runner.

Woodpecker scalps themselves were another form of money (*ci·s* in this case). The large, brilliant scarlet scalps of pileated woodpeckers (*Dryocopus pileatus*) were the most valuable, but the scalps of the much smaller acorn woodpecker (*Melanerpes fomicivorus*) also had an established exchange value.

Shells and woodpecker scalps were not, classically, generalized media of exchange, but were part of a far more complex wealth system. There were "men's money" and "women's money" as well as other things, like food, that were themselves forms of wealth. Money from one system was not used to pay for things from another system. Women's money might buy baskets, made by women, and only the most déclassé of people sold food for shells or feathers. Men's money was quintessentially used to pay for human life: for births and deaths. Monetary systems coexisted with less formal systems of barter and gifting.

Despite profound differences between their monetary economies, Indian people in northwestern California understood quite readily what "white man money" *(wo·gey ci·k)* was when they were introduced to it after the invasion of 1849. Minted currency entered the indigenous economy almost immediately, in 1850, and intermonetary equivalents were soon established. In the 1860s a dentalium shell of the largest size was worth five American dollars, a full string of them about fifty dollars. The next-to-largest shells went for a dollar apiece, the same as a pileated woodpecker scalp. (Karuks called these woodpeckers "dollar birds" well into the twentieth century.) A wife of good family and high repute (or, more accurately, the children that she would bear) cost about three hundred dollars. More was required to pay as blood money for the death of a man of substance.

Men once kept their accumulated dentalia in tubular elk horn purses with a narrow slit for putting money in and taking it out again. These were secretly compared to a woman's uterus. Men sought to attract as much wealth as they could through training and, more directly, to accumulate it through shrewd manipulation of the local legal system, bride wealth payments for close female kin, and gambling. When white man money came, usually in the forms of beautiful gold and silver coins, the same practices continued. Yet differences remained and we might better understand these differences through the study of mythology, rather than economics.[1]

One of the classic Yurok creators, Great Money (Pelin ci·k) has the capacity both to make the world and to destroy it. He comes from the north and is the oldest and biggest of five brothers (the five sizes of dentalia money). Together with the next oldest and largest, Tego?o, Great Money once traveled and traveled, directing the work of the other world creators. His wife is Great Abalone, women's money from the south (see Ella Norris, in chapter 6).

Great Money is perhaps the most powerful of all of the creators. He alone can fly around the entire world, seeing all of it and everything that happens here, and he has the frightening ability to swallow the entire cosmos, should he choose to. (Even the smallest money brother can do this, if he is badly enough offended.)

Great Money has beautiful wings that he is loath to soil. When he travels by boat he sits in the middle, doing nothing, like a very rich man who deigns neither to paddle nor to steer. The other creators—Wohpekumew, Pulekukwerek, Sky Maker, and the rest—did all of the actual work, in the beginning, under Great Money's direction. One of them, the trickster Wohpekumew, gave money itself to people. He said, "A woman will be worth money. If a man wants to marry her, he will pay with money. And if a man is killed, they will receive money from [the killer] because he who killed . . . must settle" (Mack of Wečpus, in Kroeber 1976: 289). Money was brought into the world that Great Money helped to create to pay for births and deaths, for human life.

This is how I have come to think of it, not what I have been told: In the old days, money in northwestern California was a many-layered symbol of what we might call "life force" or "spirit." We've seen (chapter 4) that a person's life spirit (wewecek̓) is understood, by some Yuroks at least, as the man's contribution to human existence. His sperm is the channel through which "the Creator" manifests in the mother's womb. Classically, when a man sought legitimate children, he and his family paid for these children's lives with bride wealth, balancing an account with the bride's natal family, which had, in effect, lost her procreative potential. (Fully paid-for children belonged to the husband's family, and unpaid-for children were "bastards," *ka·mu·ks*, who had few rights save those they won for themselves; initially, they were viewed as socially barely alive.) By the same token, one could kill an enemy for one's own satisfaction if one could pay the deceased's family for his life, with blood money, replacing the life taken with what, I am thinking, was more of the same. A person who could not pay his debts became a slave, a "pet." He had no life of his own. "The price of a life is a life," said Harry Roberts.

To better understand money-as-life, as spirit, we need to consider the broader category of "wealth," for there is far more to being rich, among Yuroks, than having a lot of money. What they have always valued is a balanced variety of wealth, not simply an abundance of money. For instance, in the 1860s, while in theory a wife might be worth three hundred American dollars, such a simple payment would have been without honor.[2] Rather, several strings of large dentalia, some good dance regalia, a well-made boat, as well as some gold coins, with a total valuation of three hundred dollars, made a prestigious payment and assured the prestige of the children that followed. (A woman's [perceived] barrenness was grounds for divorce and the return of the bride wealth to the husband's family.) The death of a high-status man might cost the killer fifteen strings of dentalia, but also valuable regalia and, perhaps, a daughter.

Money—dentalia and woodpecker scalps—was once only the beginning of a continuum of wealth that included and perhaps culminated in dance regalia. Today, people following traditional ways still exchange it, as well as cash, in marriages and in paying for offenses against others. These regalia are used today, as in the past, in child-curing brush dances and in the world-fixing jump and deerskin dances. They include dentalia necklaces and head rolls[3] richly decorated with pileated woodpecker scalps—more than fifty on a jump dance head roll. But these regalia also include beautiful feathers of many other kinds, rare hides and pelts, finely wrought, large obsidian points ("flints"), special jump dance baskets, shaped like elk horn purses, and much else. Women own beautifully made buckskin dance dresses (skirts and aprons) worked with haliotis, olivella, and clam shell, pine nuts and juniper berries, with braided bear grass tassels, worn together with loop after loop of shell necklaces. As the girls and women walk and dance, their dresses sing unique and expressive percussive songs. All of this is wealth, continuous with money. Beginning in the nineteenth century, people used whole and halved American silver coins in decorating both men's and women's regalia, attaching the pierced coins in places where dentalia alone had formerly been seen.

Anthropologists have written about ostentatious ceremonial "display" of wealth by the Yuroks and their neighbors. But Indians speak of the things themselves dancing: "this head roll danced last year at Hoopa"; "every dress has its own song"; "these feathers want to dance, so I'm going to let them go to Klamath." The regalia are alive and feeling. Traditionally, people get money, feathers, and other dance things by crying for them—practicing austerities and seeking the "pity" of the *wo·gey*, who send the pure what they cry for (chapter 4). The wealth itself, once in hand, "cries to dance." People say, "Those feathers were crying to dance, so I let them out to go to Katamin," to the brush dance there, in Karuk country. And while people cry for wealth and the wealth cries to dance, the unseen beings who attend human dances themselves "cry to see" the beautiful things dance. "Give them what they cry for!" said a Hupa acquaintance at a dance in the early 1990s. The intricate processes of interdependence in all of this are deep.

The spirit people join the human beings to watch the dances, standing in special places reserved for them alone, happy to see the feathers dance. The big dances, solemn and powerful, fix the world—restore its beauty, ease suffering, fend off disease and hunger, assure more life. Anthropologists have called these dances—particularly, the jump and deerskin dances—"world renewal dances." It makes sense, then, that some local intellectuals and dance participants have come to see the jump dance as a "fertility dance," along with much else.

Jack Norton mused on this at the end of the Pecwan jump dance of 1990. Part of the jump dance choreography, he said (and Jack is a dancer and singer), in which men raise their baskets (*ʔeʔgurʔ*, in Yurok) repeatedly, with every forward step, from their groins to the peaks of the mountains, then back to their groins on the next step, brings down the power of the spiritual to men's bodies, through which they co-create children. It is an interesting comment in itself, and also historically. Weitchpec Susie told A. L. Kroeber, in 1902, that women's wombs are the *ʔeʔgurʔ* of *ḱi ʔwesʔonah*, the jump dance baskets of the world, "the Creator" in modern times (Buckley 1988).

8 The World

The winter moons are bastards. The sun is proud and will not travel with them; therefore he is alone in the daytime. Yet it is the bastard moons that bring the rains which make the growth in a good summer. So when I fasted and gathered sweathouse wood, I cried out to the bastard moons as well as the others and they helped me.

Kerner, in Spott and Kroeber, *Yurok Narratives*

The Klamath River has perennially flooded, sometimes with devastating effects along its margins where villages have always been built. Winter rains loosen slides in the canyons, and tidal waves occasionally rise at sea, running inland. Earthquakes are not uncommon. Because of the massive changes in the land that such events have brought, the archaeological record is shallow and incomplete. We know, however, that the people who were to be known as the Yurok Indians are relative newcomers, probably entering from the north between one and two thousand years ago, settling in the lower forty miles of the river and along the coast, north and south of its mouth (Chartkoff and Chartkoff 1975; Moratto 1971).

This was a bountiful world despite its occasional upheavals. Varieties of spawning salmon once came into the Klamath regularly, several times a year, and there were seasons of lamprey eels, sturgeon, and steelhead

213

trout. Other cycles were reliable as well. The heavy winter rains nurtured abundant growth that fed large deer and elk herds, and acorns, the staple food, covered the sun-warmed oaks on slopes above the fogs of late summer. The rising Pacific tides brought surf fish and whales ashore; falling tides revealed dense beds of mussels, clam flats, gardens of sea lettuce. The people were healthy, by and large, seldom hungry, resourceful and independent. Many grew wealthy on the great bounty of the world.

Today, we can only imagine ourselves into that world, enduring yet so vastly changed. Once we do that, it is a short but perilous step to imagining ourselves into the minds of the human beings who were a part of it—ʔo·lek^{w}eł in high register Yurok, "people/world," a finer tuning than the ʔo·lek^{w}oh, "people," and łkelonah, "earth," of ordinary Yurok usage (Buckley 1984b). I risk that step here (cf. Margolin 1978).

The people thought that the seemingly steady pulse of goodness and beauty in the world was not due to their own merits. It was well within the range of human beings to become greedy in the face of abundance and fall into hubris in light of the independence that it permitted, rather than being careful of the interdependence that underlay this autonomy. Unrestrained, humans broke the law, violated the pure and reliable order of the world, polluting it, bringing floods, starvation, and death. Metaphorically, as violations of the law accumulated, their weight began to tip the earth-disk in the great, surrounding sea. Tides rose higher and higher, and whales came far up the Klamath, out of place—a dire sign of world imbalance. The river flooded, the earth shook, and diseases began to spread.

There was always a struggle to keep the earth balanced upon the waters, in accord with the law and despite human breaches of it. Knowing that this would be so, before they left the wo·gey instructed certain people in what to do to put the world back in balance when the weight of human violations grew too great for it. The instructions were the basis of "the world renewal cult" and of its central ritual and ceremonial occasions, the "great dances," helomey—jump dances and deerskin dances. Like the runs of salmon or the tides and seasons, these dances and a variety of other ritual events were repeated in a regular way and in accord with interlocking cycles in more than a dozen dance districts, each with its paired principal towns—one male and one female—that provided and dressed the

two "sides" of dancers for their district. The districts themselves were centered around ritual grounds in Yurok, Karuk, and Hupa territories. (Although the Tolowas and Wiyots had comparable dances that Yuroks often
attended, these dances seem to have been outside of the lower Klamath
system.) The cycles of dances and rituals were diverse, some events repeated every year, some every two or even three, the cycles overlapping
in intricate, sometimes ad hoc ways throughout the region, guided by
lunar calendars.

Kroeber called the hereditary spiritual experts who were responsible
for the dances' ritual dimensions "priests" or "formulists." Today they
are called "medicine men" but in Yurok they are the ones who "talk with
the world" and also "the doctors of the world"; in Karuk, they are the
ones who "fix the world." They recite mythic narratives about the first
dances, quoting the First People's speeches and, in some dances, performing acts of power that these *wo·gey* had prescribed. When they pray
in this way they used to use a special, ritual register of Yurok, *wo·gey*
speech, in which they spoke from a *wo·gey* perspective (e.g., "we" refers
to these spirit people, "you" refers to human beings, "Indians" [Buckley
1984b].) In effect, the medicine men become the *wo·gey*, uniting their time
and form with those of the First People in the purity of the beginning
through language and asceticism. Doing this, they gain the power to return the world itself to its original condition.

In their classic forms, the major dances are the focus of great festivals
that last for ten days and are attended by hundreds from throughout the
region (thousands in the mid-nineteenth century). The medicine men and
their helpers prepare for the dances through additional long weeks of
training, purification, and private ritual. Those who hope to attend are
expected to prepare themselves as well. The metaphysics of renewal are
accompanied by universal attention to the physics of social interrelationships—the concrete side of returning the world to balance and beauty. All
litigation and debts are to be settled, grudges laid aside, the grief of
mourners assuaged. It is against the law for those still harboring bad
thoughts (or menstruating) to come to a dance, disrupting its beauty.

In jump dances themselves, the regalia gathered by the hereditary
dance makers, through ownership and also through borrowing from rel-

atives and other allies, are displayed or, better, let out of their storage containers to dance. Paired village clusters form two "sides" in the dances, and dancers from these sides take turns in forming lines in the dance pit, a lead singer and as many sidemen as can be mustered and dressed dancing to a center man's left and right. There are always an odd number of dancers in the pit—five, seven, nine and so on, carefully dressed by specialists to create a gorgeous, subtle, and rich symmetry. The regalia themselves are "beautiful," *mɹwɹsɹyɹh*, the fundamental quality of the world as it was in the beginning and is, now, to be again. In the minds and spirits of the medicine men, in the social relations of the spectators, in the choreography and singing and costumes of the dancers, everything is once more as it should be, decay and death reversed, life affirmed.

Lucy Thompson wrote about the Kepel white deerskin dance of 1876: "I counted upwards of three thousand Indians there. . . . There were five different languages spoken among them." Thompson stresses the use of kinship terms among all of these spectators, who addressed each other as "sister" and "brother." The dance singing in such events, she wrote, "is most perfect in time and tune and makes one feel the love of the great Creator of all things." Of a jump dance at Pecwan shortly before the turn of the twentieth century, she writes:

> All Indians are invited to come, rich or poor, from any and all tribes, from far off and near by. Far away tribes are looked after, fed and asked to take part in the dance, even if they cannot speak the language. . . . This is the time that the very poor and slave class of our own [Yurok] people are made jolly and contented. . . . That are here allowed, both men and women, to put in whatever they may possess that is of value, that is used to dance with. The wealthy ones that own lands, hunting territory, fishing places, slaves, flints, white deer skins, fisher skins, otter skins, silver gray fox skins and fine dresses made of dressed deerskins, with fringes of shells knotted and worked in the most beautiful styles, that clink and jingle as they walk and make one have a feeling of respect and admiration for them. The eyes will strain to look on this most pleasing sight, which can never leave one's memory that has seen it in its flowery days.

The "festivals are held," Lucy Thompson concludes, "for the purpose and equality of the whole people together, the rich, the poor and the slave, make themselves come together in peace and harmony as one family and to . . . feel that there is some good to live for" (1991 [1916]: 145–57).

People periodically had to be brought back into harmony with each other and with the world, lest the weight of their infractions against the law, of their selfishness, throw the whole off balance and destroy them. The repeating cycles of salmon and tides and seasons were accompanied by repeating cycles of great dances among human beings (the First People are *always* dancing, in the spirit world). These renewals became, after the coming of "the Indians," as central to the world, as much a part of the law as anything else, and the balance of the world depended upon them. So, repetitions of dances joined other repetitions, interdependent with them. "We and the world, well, we pretty much support each other," say *wo·gey* in a speech quoted by the medicine man in the Wečpus deerskin dance (Buckley 1984b).

In order to keep the law it was necessary that some people learn to support the world, talk to it, and doctor it. Like seasons and dances, knowledge had to be repeated in the minds of individual human beings, generation after generation, through training and making medicine. ("I can't learn *for* you, can I?" Harry Roberts asked me.) The repeated act of recreating knowledge was itself of the essence of the sacred, like salmon runs or dance cycles. The seemingly reliable and automatic repetition of natural cycles was not quite that. In the face of human nature, these cycles were reliable only when they were accompanied by other, human orders of repetition, the return, generation after generation, of a very few gifted and determined individuals, on their own as it were, to knowledge of how the world actually is when people don't interfere with it, and the cyclic enactment of this knowledge in ritual. It was only on the basis of this knowledge that the great dances could be performed and, through them, the violations engendered by people's failings expunged, the world, unbalanced by the weight of these violations, set right again. Cycles enclosed cycles, all necessary. At the end of the Rek̓ʷoy jump dance, the medicine man's benediction was simple: Keep up the old customs, he told the young (Kroeber and Gifford 1949: 97).

Before 1904 the Rek̓ʷoy jump dance had been put up every three years. In alternate performances—every six years—a redwood plank structure in the village was entirely rebuilt. This was *kimolen ʔɹʔgɹ·k*, the "old" or "dirty sweathouse," and also, paradoxically, the "sacred sweathouse." It was the center of the world, and it supported the world. First built by the *wo·gey*, it had a center post that reached to the sky, and its four beams extended to the edges of the world, holding up "the sky" (*wesʔonah* which, we remember, is also "the world"). This structure was constantly getting polluted (*kimoł*), and it had to be ritually swept out every three years and rebuilt every six, as it had been from the beginning.

There were three parties to this reconstruction—the medicine man, who was the leader, his assistant (a less knowledgeable man), and several helpers (*tał*)—the boys, young men, and—sometimes—unmarried women who were under the medicine man's guidance, as was the assistant. While the assistant worked alone, sweeping out the old structure and the paths used in the jump dance rituals, the medicine man and the male helpers crossed the river in a boat to its south side, near the village of Wełkʷew. There the medicine man felled a living redwood tree with elk horn wedges and with the helpers' help, announcing that he would kill the tree: "I will have you for holding up the sky" he told it before making the first cut. The tree fell—uphill, on account of the man's power, according to Dewey George—and the helpers split the post and four beams from it, burying all five in a grave that they had dug, as a human corpse would be buried. Then they exhumed the timbers, which they carried the way that corpses are carried *to* their graves, transporting them back across the river to Reḱʷoy. There they installed them, rebuilding the old sweathouse around the new timbers (Kroeber and Gifford 1949: 92).

In this process every important action was initiated by the medicine man but completed by the helpers. The assistant seems only to have prepared, as in sweeping, and, in a graphic way, to have held the center while the others came and went. For example, when the post was ready the priest touched it and the helpers set it erect. The assistant steadied the post while the helpers put the four beams in place, each first touched by the medicine man. It seems to me that the three ritual positions—medicine man, assistant, helpers—paralleled three human generations—grandfather, father, sons and daughters—as well as three arcs along a continuum of learning. What was being acted out in rebuilding the sacred sweathouse at Rek͗ʷoy, I think, was the history of human, metaphysical knowledge that "went ricocheting down the generations," as Bruce Chatwin wrote of Aboriginal Australia (1981). The medicine man would pass on and probably be replaced by his assistant, one of the helpers becoming the new assistant, new boys and girls becoming helpers. The medicine man's actions bear a double message: the world must be remade lest it die, but death is inevitable in remaking the world and sustaining it. That world is at once unfolding in time and timeless, when seen truly: time and all-time are parts of each other and support each other. The price of timeless life is historical, human death.

Before 1864, in the spring when the first salmon ceremony medicine man speared First Salmon at Welk͗ʷew, a great cry went up from both sides of the river: "He's caught!" Jimmy Gensaw (Yurok) heard this as a boy and told his foster daughter, Florence Shaughnessy, about it. "I looked into the sky where I could hear a tinkling sound, like bells ringing, and the mist that came down was as though the sky [wesʔonah] wept for the beauty of it." Through this ritual, accompanied by a deerskin dance, the psychologist Erik Erikson wrote, a Yurok hoped "to perform the miracle of his existence, namely, to eat his salmon and have it too" (Erikson 1943: 301). "Kill to live," we remember the Tolowa creators saying (chapter 4). "The miracle of existence" performed by the jump dance medicine man at Rek͗ʷoy was, through the deaths of salmon and redwood trees and the succession of learned ritual participants, to reverse human beings' tendencies toward entropy, mastering death and, thus, supporting the world's life.

After "the end of the world" in the white invasion of 1850, the great Yurok dances disappeared one by one, beginning with the first salmon rites at Welk͗ʷew. The Rek͗ʷoy jump dance held out until 1904, the Wečpus deerskin dance until 1912. Efforts to keep the Kepel fish dam rites going faltered in the 1920s, and what seemed, then, to be the last jump dance at Pecwan was held in 1939. A way that had been "good" (that is to say, "successful," skuyen) since the myth-time had been wiped out in less than a century—or so it seemed. "What's the point of dreaming of elk," Harry Roberts remembered a Yurok man asking, in Requa in the 1930s, "when there's no elk left to hunt?

The GO-road fiasco of the 1970s and '80s did not end in the kind of discouragement and demoralization that had overwhelmed the great dances by the 1930s, however. Rather, the long fight strengthened the younger people who had waged it, brought them into new and intensified contact with knowledgeable elders, and heightened their determination to understand and maintain traditional local spirituality. In the early 1980s there were still surviving elders who had danced at Pecwan before 1939, and these men—particularly the late Dewey George and the late Howard Ames—began instructing new students and helped in re-recruiting the hereditary participants in the Pecwan jump dance. People also combed over the salvage ethnographers' works, from the first half of the twentieth century. The first Pecwan jump dance since 1939 was given in 1984. It was difficult.

Some elders asserted that the dances were all lost, that none of them could be brought back correctly and that trying to bring them back incorrectly would do great harm. There were serious frictions with Christians, particularly members of the Indian Shaker Church. Worst of all, an old man died in the midst of the ten-day dance, while dancing. There were heated debates, but in the end (although not necessarily in 1984) people came to agree that the man had had a good death, not a punitive and polluting one, dancing in the spirit. The younger men and women who had worked hard to bring the dance back persevered, and the dance was held again in 1986, 1988, and 1990, well into its classic two-year cycle. By 1998 knowledgeable people were saying that the dance was even better than those in the 1930s, but by that time virtually all of the elders who had been instrumental in bringing back the dance had themselves passed on. An entirely new generation of participants was on its own, grateful that their teachers had been able to hang on so long and so vigorously.

9 Melancholy

Don't you ever
you up in the sky
don't you ever get tired
of having the clouds
between you and us?

Nootka song, John Beirhorst, *The Sacred Path*

Essentialized, integrated cultures, like "the Yurok," hypothesized by the salvage ethnographers, were *sui generis*, "with discrete boundaries, not unlike species" (Biolsi 1997: 136). It was a model of differences. By the 1920s, these sorts of "billiard ball" cultures (Eric Wolf, in ibid.: 139) prevailed among the later Boasians. Books like Ruth Benedict's *Patterns of Culture* (1934) "seemed to carry the doctrine of relativity to its logical conclusion in the ultimate incommensurability of each human mode of life" (Stocking 1992: 162). Cultures that were ethnological objects had come to be "shadowed by coherence, timelessness, and discreteness," as Lila Abu-Lughod writes, and "culture" was thus a "prime anthropological tool for making 'other,' and difference" (Abu-Lughod 1991: 147). These ethnologically constituted cultures asserted theoretically horizontal taxonomic differences between cultures that replaced vertical nineteenth-century racial taxonomy,

221

displaced in American anthropology by antiracialist and antievolutionary Boasian relativism (Appadurai 1991: 205; cf. Hinsley 1981).

In the othering of "the [species-like] Yurok," the female sucking doctor (*kegey*), a "shaman," had particular importance as a diagnostic trait. Maximally incommensurate with familiar, primarily male biomedical practitioners, sucking doctors epitomized the authentically primitive.[1] As psychoanalytic and psychodynamic methods replaced the earlier culture and personality approaches of Benedict, Mead, and Sapir in the later 1930s, Yurok sucking doctors attracted considerable attention at the disciplinary border of anthropology and psychology. Erik Erikson, arriving at Berkeley in 1939, went to Requa with A. L. Kroeber to study Yurok "childhood and world image" in a short period of field work (Erikson 1943). At Kroeber's suggestion, Erikson's principal informant was the Yurok *kegey* Fanny Flounder, and it was largely upon her testimony that he constructed his analysis of "the Yurok" as a pre-genitally arrested people, locked into a "tubular" personality structure, simultaneously "oral" and "anal"—"crying children" who, nonetheless, remained functional rather than "paralyzed by sadness" (Erikson 1943, 1963; cf. Friedman 1999; Elrod 1992).

Erikson's analysis was both highly influential and widely debated through the 1950s (e.g., Roheim 1950; Goldschmidt 1951; Posinsky 1957; Kroeber 1959), and his interest in Fanny Flounder inspired further psychological and psychoanalytic speculation on pre-contact Yurok shamanism into the 1970s (Posinsky 1956; Valory 1970). The suitability of Erikson's methods and theoretical assumptions was largely accepted without serious question in this extended symposium that focused, primarily, on whether or not "the Yurok" were simply "anal," rather than "tubular." Kroeber, for instance, was mildly skeptical about the specifics of Erikson's dual analysis, suggesting that Yuroks were more anal than oral, but agreed with him in general that "the Yurok" were "infantile, at the least puerile" (1959).[2]

As a psychologist, Erik Erikson considered himself a tyro in the study of indigenous peoples and deferred to the anthropologists that sponsored his research, accepting their definitions of who each of these peoples were. He was introduced to Lakota Indians at Pine Ridge by H. Scudder Mekeel (cf. Biolsi 1997), who was interested in problems of acculturation, and thus included historical experience and change in his analysis of "the Sioux" (Erikson found the Lakota personality "centrifugal," dominated by sadistic orality and by guilt [Erikson 1963: 113, 149–56]). Although his interests were comparative, however, Erikson also accepted Kroeber's quite different definition of "the Yurok" as a people who, in fact, no longer existed culturally, although "remnants of their timeless cultures can be found . . . in a few immensely dignified but culturally mummified individuals" (ibid.: 112). These were, in the main, "the oldest members of the tribe" (113) and, at Requa, they included Fanny Flounder and her husband, George Meldon, although Erikson also interviewed Robert Spott, a younger man that, we have seen, Kroeber viewed as culturally old and, thus, suitably typal (112–13). Through these three, Erikson recaptured "a homogenous cultural reality" (183). Mummification, timelessness, and homogeneity were the guarantors of Yurok cultural authenticity and hence of the validity of Erikson's findings regarding *real* Yurok Indians, as, in a contradictory manner, historical perspective guaranteed the validity of his Lakota findings.

Fanny Flounder, of course, was neither timeless nor mummified. She was born around 1860, grew up through the very worst of the calamity of invasion, and was known locally as much for her refined tastes in silks and satins in middle age, and her notable distaste for white tourists in her old age, as she was for her life-long doctoring. Moreover, Yurok doctoring itself was never timeless. Sucking doctors like Fanny Flounder emerged along a continuum of healers and other spiritual experts that embodied considerable historical development, accumulation, and change in its many variations. (Recall, for instance, the addition of the skills of central Californian animal transformers to Yurok Indian devils' repertoire during removals to combined reservations in the 1860s.) In any case, when both Kroeber and Erik Erikson knew her, Fanny Flounder was a twentieth-century Indian doctor and, far from being a depersonalized human illustration of a timeless culture, she was a vivid individual and given to "a dramatic melancholy," according to Erikson (1943: 171).

At approximately the same time, another of Boas's later students, Cora DuBois, was studying doctoring among the Wintu Indians, to the east of the Yuroks. DuBois noted the prevalence of depression among these doctors. However, she understood their being motivated by "sorrow" and becoming doctors through dreaming as indicating the "slovenliness" of then contemporary Wintu spiritual life, when compared to that of pre-contact Wintu culture in which, she held, doctors had acquired their powers primarily through ritual dancing (DuBois 1940: 103).

Traditional Yurok breast-feeding and weaning practices, as described by Kroeber, were the basis of Erikson's diagnosis of "the Yurok" as "oral." He ultimately exoticized Fanny Founder's melancholy as the infantile depression of those abused by the withholding mothers that were, Kroeber and Erikson agreed, typically (that is, timelessly) "Yurok" (1963: 80 ff.). (Yurok anal retentiveness was evident, Erikson argued, in their displays of dance regalia.) Fanny Flounder's apparent melancholy was thus mobilized as further evidence of developmental primitiveness and of otherness in Yurok psychology, rather than a possible indicator of shared humanity and a basis for empathy. Comparable inverted romanticism occurs in DuBois's account as well, although she interprets the doctors' sorrow in an opposite manner, as evidence of cultural disintegration. For DuBois, real pre-contact doctors had to have been motivated by something less familiar, more thoroughly other. In both cases, melancholy was used to differentiate "real" Indians from those who studied them, rather than as a possible indicator of cultural commensurability.

A. L. Kroeber himself suffered a deep depression for at least two years, and his nemesis, the linguist Jaime de Angulo, was lost in spiritual darkness off and on for much of his life (T. Kroeber 1970; G. de Angulo 1995). Angulo himself—neither unobservent nor untutored in psychology—diagnosed Kroeber's protégé T. T. Waterman as a manic-depressive (in G. de Angulo 1995: 259): apparently, Waterman's "impulsiveness," noted by Theodora Kroeber, had another side to it (T. Kroeber 1970: 149). California Indians, lacking in "mental tenseness" for A. L. Kroeber (1976: 466), funny, wise and humane for de Angulo (1950), a bit of each for Waterman (1951), were decidedly *other* for all of them and, I am suggesting, necessarily so. As Gerald Vizenor writes of Waterman and Kroeber, "These men who represented civilization [found] in the other what they had failed to find in themselves or their institutions: the simulations of the other became the antiselves of their melancholy" (Vizenor 1994: 132).

We cannot know, of course, what any particular pre-contact northern California Indian doctor felt or even if most of them felt anything in common. No culture is ever "mummified," and "pre-contact ethnography" is, of course, a contradiction in terms. In trying to understand Indian doctors and the faith that people for millennia have put in their abilities to heal, however, we might start—experimentally, at least—with what we *can* know. The famous Yurok *kegey* Fanny Flounder suffered "a dramatic melancholy" and, by their own testimony, DuBois's Wintu doctors were motivated by "sorrow." We know this much: in their depression, these doctors were more like the people who studied them than not.

SHAMANISM AND MENTAL ILLNESS

Shamans have been a source of unusual fascination for urbane, upper-class Europeans since the sixteenth century (Flaherty 1992). Their usefulness, in the West, as romanticized "antiselves," emphasized at the end of the twentieth century in the New Age movement, is nothing new, nor is its opposite. The pathologization of shamanism as mental illness dates back at least to 1861 and the Russian ethnologist Krivoshapkin's psychological diagnoses of Siberian shamans as psychotics (Eliade 1964).

Following this old tradition, and with reference to his researches in native North America, in 1940 A. L. Kroeber published a functional interpretation of shamanism as prescientific communities' favored means for containing and directing the energies of near-psychotics in their midst (in 1952: 310–19). The reduction of healing to psychosis by Kroeber and many others accompanied the far more narrow debate on Yurok Indian culture sparked by Erikson's work. In its diverse manifestations, the open season on "the" Yurok psyche, signaled by Erikson, continued to focus on Yurok doctors. Various contributions included S. H. Posinsky's reduction of the doctors' internalized tutelary spirits and power objects, *teloget*, to "infantile introject[s]" (1956) and the declaration by a variety of academics that, like all shamans, Yurok doctors were (alternatively, and sometimes in combination) "hysterical," "hysteroid," "epileptoid," "schizoid," "ambulatory schizophrenic," and "psychotic."[3]

Mircea Eliade, among the first scholars to shift the academic discourse on shamanism from the domain of psychology to that of the history of religions, rejected the ethnological tradition of reducing shamanism to psychosis. Shámans could not, Eliade argued, bear the communal responsibilities that they do, or evidence the stability, canny good sense, and mediational abilities that observers have often noted, if they were psychotics, ambulatory schizophrenics, or the like. On the contrary, shamans—when they are not undergoing shamanic "ecstasy"—are quite frequently remarked upon for their wisdom and evident mental health, as Erik Erikson himself noted regarding Fanny Flounder. A psychotic, according to Eliade, simply could not manage such an impression, let alone a shaman's demanding communal responsibilities (1964: 26–27; cf. Erikson 1943).

While Eliade rejected psychopathological models for understanding shamanism, he recognized that the circumpolar shamans he posited were all locally specified, in one way or another, as "wounded healers," although the nature of these wounds remained "mysterious" (1964). More recently, psychiatric anthropologists, most notably Arthur Kleinman and his associates, have moved to resolve the polarities of Western psychology and comparative religion in useful ways (e.g., Kleinman and Good 1985). Kleinman and his colleagues have demonstrated that all psychologies, including Freud's, are to significant extents ethnopsychologies whose truths are culturally relative rather than positively verifiable human universals. This complex matter is obscured by what Kleinman calls the "category fallacy" (Kleinman 1977): the tendency to treat Western diagnostic categories such as "hysteria," "psychosis," or "depression" as objective labels for universal conditions, rather than as culturally constructed, linguistic—and hence culturally and historically relative—frames of signification. It is for this reason that designation of shamans as "psychotic" or as "ambulatory schizophrenics," with the profoundly negative burdens that those terms bear, is suspect.

Given the dangers posed by category fallacies, there is still ample evidence to suggest that something like, at least, some of the "mental diseases" familiar in the modern West are to be found in other times and places as well. Something resembling depression, for example, seems to have been fairly common among the Huron Indians of seventeenth-century Ontario: resulting from grief and humiliation, it frequently led to suicide (Trigger 1969: 77). Hurons may not, however, have called it anything translatable as "depression" or "mental illness," nor necessarily have located it in the mind. Contemporary Flathead Indian people, for example, frequently suffer grievously from what they tend to call, in English, "loneliness," which they take as a sign of spiritual and moral maturation, rather than mental illness (O'Nell 1996).

Even accepting scientific psychology and neuropharmacology as Western ethnopsychology, it seems quite possible that those who have pathologized shamanism as mental illness have not been entirely on the wrong track, and that Western psychology may, in fact, still be relevant to understanding shamans' mysterious wounds and the power of Yurok *kegeyowor* to heal. It seems possible that what we in the West know as depression, as an immediate experience of intense spiritual suffering, provides a heuristically useful analogy (rather than a diagnosis) in the interpretation of Yurok doctoring. My analogy is more poetic than technical, and I offer it as a vehicle of understanding, not as an explanation.

SUCKING DOCTORS AND DEPRESSION

Aspects of the ethnographic record of Yurok life in the past suggest that what we know today and in non-Indian society as major depression is appropriate to understanding the classic Indian sucking doctors. Erikson, we have seen, noted that Fanny Flounder was of "melancholy" disposition, taking upon herself the "gloom of ill omens" (1943: 206), and Dale Valory (1970: 74), commenting upon Erikson's observation, notes that Fanny Flounder "experienc[ed] what could best be termed for Europeans ... *Weltschmerz*, a despairing of and for the universe, of existence itself." Whether or not her despair was directly linked to the destruction of the world that she was born into, in the second half of the nineteenth century, I do not know: in all published accounts she is made to seem timeless.

Theresa O'Nell's study (1996), linking Flathead Indian "depressive-like affect" with the loss of Flathead lands and traditional ways, is certainly suggestive. As Paula Frederick points out (1996), such reactions to recent history in native North America are far from being exclusively Flathead. Frederick, a sociologist, has observed the same connection in contemporary Turtle Mountain Chippewa society, and "depression" is commonly noted as pandemic in other American Indian communities today, a shared "reality" along with "high rates of alcoholism, suicide, disease, drop-out, unemployment" (Mihesuah 1998: 15). Whatever Fanny Flounder's individual experience, she was alive during the most terrible period of Yurok death and dispossession, "the end of Indian Time" when girls and women were particularly at risk (e.g., Lang 1994). Like all of the other putatively "timeless" Indian doctors whose lives are recorded in the ethnographic record, Fanny Flounder was entirely in, and not at all immune to, modern history.

However motivated, her biography is consonant with the stress on grief and anger as "primary effects considered in psychoanalytic theory regarding depression," and supports the hypothesis that these have cross-cultural relevance (Schieffelin 1985: 107). It is also consistent with the prominence of sleep and eating disorders among those diagnosed as "depressed." Fanny's sisters and her mother (who was herself a doctor) chastised her as a young girl, before she trained as a doctor, because "she always sleeps too long, she is so mean," and Robert Spott reported, "She was an angry girl, quick tempered" (in Beyer 1933–34: 1).[4] Grief—or at least profound sadness—is also prominent in her biography. Regarding the third year of Fanny's training, when she was about twenty years old, Spott reported, "All that summer it seems to me that she cried a lot. . . . she was sad all the time, she's pretty near crying all the time. . . . When she came home . . . she didn't eat very much, she wasn't very hungry. It seems to me in her feelings the sad always come to her" (ibid.: 2).

Spott himself linked Fanny Flounder's weeping with grief. According to Louisa Lindgren (Yurok), who talked with Robert Spott about doctoring in the 1950s, "Crying was a customary indication of one's desire to become a doctor. The dead that the woman may have been thinking about will feel sorry for her and try to help her by sending forth a spirit" (Lindgren 1983a). Fanny's mother seems to have been affected by the same emotions, aroused by her daughter's suffering. Spott recalled that the harder Fanny trained, "the more sadness come on to the mother" (in Beyer

1933–34: 13). By the same token, Cora DuBois (1940: 92–103) emphasized the centrality of the spirits of dead relatives to the acquisition of power by Wintu doctors, called to their vocation by "sorrow."

Finally, we recall Ella Norris's recollections of Mary Willams, another Yurok *kegey* (chapter 5). The doctor "had her hair pitched, parted in the middle—that's the way Indians fix it. Wear Indian cap—cap made with just roots, bear grass trimming, no black in it." Mary Williams was groomed and dressed as though in mourning, permanently it would seem. She also seems to have been depressively withdrawn, although more certainly practicing the "meditative isolation" of classic shamans (Eliade 1964): "she always sit with her back turned. [My mother] said, 'Shhh! She's Indian doctor, don't want to be mingled with too many people.' "

How did these women come to be so wounded, and how did their wounding enable them to heal?

MELANCHOLIA AND TRUTH

For Flathead people today, something very much like what we call depression is understood, according to Theresa O'Nell, as a creative means of growth (when it does not end in suicide). By contrast, regnant opinion in non-Indian society in the United States today specifies depression, a mental illness, as both pathological and an agonizing waste of time, best avoided through psychopharmacology: "darkness visible" in which one can see nothing and from which one emerges having learned nothing (Styron 1990). There has been a more recent countertendency, however. Jonathan Lear (1990) and other writers on psychotherapy have critiqued purely psychopharmacological responses to major depression as short-circuiting fundamental learning processes. The possibility that depression may constitute an excruciating mode of education, of truth-seeking, was not foreign to Sigmund Freud.

Freud's general thesis, in "Mourning and Melancholia" (1917–25), has been summarized by the psychologist Carol Gilligan in a way that seems pertinent to understanding Yurok sucking doctors and their ingested *telogeł,* "pains": "Depression is a disease of mourning, a manifestation of swallowed grief."[5] I am not so much concerned with Freud's analysis of depression as internalized and repressed grief, however, as with his startling appraisal of the melancholic's existential situation. The sufferer, Freud writes,

> must surely be right in some way and be describing something that is as it seems to him to be. Indeed, we must at once confirm some of his statements. . . . he has a keener eye for the truth than other people who are not melancholic. . . . he has come pretty near to understanding himself; we can only wonder why a man has to be ill before he can be accessible to truth of this kind. For there can be no doubt that if anyone holds and expresses to others an opinion of himself such as this (an opinion which Hamlet held both of himself and of everyone else), he is ill, whether he is speaking the truth or whether he is being more or less unfair to himself. [Freud 1917–25]

It is, of course, an incomplete truth that the melancholic discovers, a negative truth that omits all other aspects and dimensions of reality (hence his being "more or less unfair to himself" and to the world), but it is a truth, and a profound one, nonetheless. Thus Freud saw melancholia, in certain of its dimensions, as a terrible epistemology of self. His reference to Shakespeare's bitter judgment, "Use every man after his desert and who shall escape whipping?"[6] suggests that he understood the truth apprehended in melancholia to apply, like Fanny Flounder's "gloom," well beyond the self: indeed, like *Weltschmerz*, to the world at large.

Anton Chekov had come to the same conclusion, somewhat earlier than Freud. "The existential underpinnings of depression . . . include a predisposition to melancholia—" writes Daphne Merkin (2001: 37),

> the possibility of being, like Masha in Chekhov's "The Seagull," in mourning for one's life, of being caught up in a sorrow that stems from the very condition of having been born into an imperfect world. "We've biologized depression to the point where the soul is lost," Glen O. Gabbard . . . cautions. "People have reason to be depressed beyond their neurotransmitters."

To return to the problem of category fallacies and to the cultural (and hence, historical) construction of affective disorders, it is noteworthy that tristitia and acedia, distinct conditions that are nonetheless both comparable to what is today called "depression," were once considered forms of spiritual discipline within the Christian church. Initially, rather than being defined as useless suffering best circumvented by whatever means possible, they resembled contemporary Flathead Indian "loneliness" more closely than contemporary "depression." Affective experience of insight into the true nature of self and world, encountered as a form of grievous suffering, according to Julia Kristeva, was deemed to be "essential as a means towards paradoxical knowledge of divine truth and constituted the major touchstone for faith" for certain Christian ascetics (1989: 8.)

Tristitia was deemed "wholesome sorrow" by the church father John Cassian, a fourth-century Rumanian monk influential in bringing the monastic rules of the Eastern church to the West. But this form of melancholia, a route to "knowledge of divine truth," was rejected by the later church and subsumed under the rubric of acedia—a "noontime demon" of enervating "worldly frustration and distress." Finally, tristitia and acedia were both lastingly condemned as the seventh Deadly Sin, sloth (Jackson 1985: 48). The melancholic's truth, like much mystical experience, was ultimately found inimical to church discipline.

Earlier, however, Cassian had understood tristitia and acedia alike as "weariness or distress of heart . . . akin to dejection, and . . . especially trying to solitaries." For Cassian, the truth realized in this condition seems to arise not simply from the penitence for sins accumulated by the penitent himself (although that is certainly included), but also in recognition of the inescapable darkness paradoxically inherent in the perfect world that God created: the darkness that Hamlet, for instance, recognized, according to Freud's interpretation of Shakespeare's melancholic antihero; the other side of Christian joy, as contemporary Anabaptists put it. This paradoxical understanding of depression as offering access to a truth that complements *and thus reveals* the "good news" of the Gospels is in fact an old Christian tradition.

We find the following exchange in the apocryphal Gospel of Bartholomew (Hennecke and Schneemelcher 1959). Jesus is on the mountain Mauria with his apostles after the Resurrection and before the Ascension:

they . . . said to him: Lord, show us the abyss, as you promised us.

5. He answered: It is not good for you to see the abyss. But if you wish it, I will keep my promise. Come, follow me and see.

6. And he led them to a place called Cherubim, that is, place of truth.

7. And he beckoned to the angels of the west. And the earth was rolled up like a papyrus roll, and the abyss was exposed to their eyes.

8. When the apostles saw it, they fell on their faces.

9. But Jesus said to them: Did I not say to you that it was not good for you to see the abyss? And he again beckoned to the angels, and the abyss was covered up. [Hennecke and Schneemelcher 1963: Bartholomew 111:49]

The imagery encountered in this noncanonical Gospel is widespread—certainly as widespread as shamanism, from which we expect exotic otherness. In the *Bhagavad Gita*, for instance, Arjuna, a mortal, suffers "depression" before a great battle (Deutsch 1968: 29). He laments to his charioteer, the god Vishnu in his form as Krishna:

[Arjuna] Filled with the utmost compassion, sorrowfully spoke: Seeing my own kinsmen, O Krishna, arrayed and wishing to fight,

My limbs collapse, my mouth dries up, there is trembling in my body and my hair stands on end;

(The bow) Gandiva slips from my hand and my skin is burning; I am not able to stand still, my mind is whirling. And I see evil portents, O Kashava (Krishna), and I foresee no good in slaying my own kinsmen in the fight.

I do not desire victory, O Krishna, nor kingdom, nor pleasure. Of what use pleasures or life? [Deutsch 1968: 32–33].

Krishna instructs Arjuna in the yogas through which he might understand the illusory nature of the world and of the coming deaths that trouble him, relieving him somewhat, but Arjuna (like Jesus' disciples) wants more: "I desire to see Thy godly form, O Purushottama!" (ibid., 94). Krishna obliges, showing himself first in glory, and then the other side. Arjuna reels at the sight:

. . . the worlds tremble, and so do I.

. . . my inmost self is shaken and I find no strength nor peace, O Vishnu!

Seeing Thy mouths, terrible with tusks, like time's devouring fire, I know not the directions of the sky and I find no security. Have mercy, O Lord of gods, Abode of the world!

And these sons of Dhritarashtra [Arjuna's relatives], all of them, together with the hosts of kings, Bhishma, Drona, and also Kama, together with our chief warriors

Are rushing into Thy mouths, dreadful with terrible tusks. Some are seen with pulverized heads, stuck between Thy teeth.

As the many water currents of rivers race headlong to the ocean, so these heroes of the world of men enter into Thy flaming mouths.

As moths swiftly enter a blazing fire and perish there, so these creatures swiftly enter Thy mouths and perish.

Swallowing all the worlds from every side, Thou lickest them up with Thy flaming mouths; Thy fierce rays fill the whole world with radiance and scorch it, O Vishnu! [Ibid.: 97–98]

Arjuna has understood what another noncanonical Gospel, Philip, tells us of the Christian Lord: "God is a maneater." It seems close to what the ancient Chinese meant when they called the great cosmic beast, *tao tieh*, "the eater of eaters" (Buckley 1984a), and Kwakwaka'wakw (Kwakiutl) Indians when they speak of "the mouth of heaven" (Goldman 1975). We find other resonances in native North America. A Tewa Indian elder commented, in the 1940s, that the truth is "hard to tell and hard to understand . . . unless, unless . . . you have been yourself to the edge of the Deep Canyon and have come back unharmed" (in Laski 1959: 128).[7] Fanny Flounder's doctor's dream, which came to her after a long period of seeming depression, bears imagistic similarity to all of this. According to Robert Spott (Spott and Kroeber 1942: 158–59),

For several summers she danced at Wogeł Otek, on a peak perhaps three miles from Espew north of the creek. It looks out over the ocean. Then at last while she was sleeping here she dreamed she saw the sky rising and blood dripping off its edge. She heard the drops go "ts, ts" as they struck the ocean. She thought it must be Wes?ona Olego, where the sky moves up and down, and the blood was hanging from it like icicles. Then she saw a woman standing in a doctor's maple [bark] dress with her hair tied like a doctor. Fanny did not know her nor whether she was alive or dead, but thought she must be a doctor. The woman reached up as the edge of the sky went higher and picked off one of the icicles of blood, said "Here, take it," and put it into Fanny's mouth. It was icy cold.

Then Fanny knew nothing more. When she came to her senses she found she was in the wash of the breakers on the beach at Espew with several men holding her. They took her back to the sweat house to dance. But she could not: her feet turned under her as if there were no bones in them.

In classic Yurok cosmology, the sky is a great net woven by the creators and shaped like an inverted bowl. The edge of this bowl rises and falls, striking the horizon, creating ocean waves, a manifestation of the same "energy," as Harry Roberts said, that moves through a person's body and that the doctor ultimately controls, sending it out through her finger as a healing blue bolt. It is pure "spirit" in Harry's terms and in itself is neither positive nor negative but potentially both: it is the energy of creation and destruction, equally, of life and of death. Fanny's doctoring song was, "Where the sky moves up and down you are traveling in the air" (in Spott and Kroeber 1942: 159).

Fanny Flounder's initiatory dream that followed upon her summers of sadness, anger, sleeplessness, and loss of appetite was not *sui generis*— not a purely and typically "Yurok" event. It was commensurate with a very widespread mystical symbolism of mouths and deaths, spiritual guides, and falling down. It is also fully commensurate, in its emphases on creation's destructive aspects, with Erikson's sense of Fanny Flounder's despair "of and for the universe, of existence itself."

Valory, in comparing Fanny Flounder's "gloom" to *Weltschmerz*, correctly specified the latter as a European concept, and not a Yurok Indian one. I am using the terms "depression" and "melancholia" as heuristic analogies, not as diagnoses, hoping through this tentativeness to avoid falling into a category fallacy. I know of no precise Yurok language equivalent of the English "melancholia," and Yurok people that I know have spoken of "Indian sickness" or, more simply, "suffering," rather than using the term "depression."

Yet something very like the suffering of depression seems implicated in the Yurok doctor's career as a mode of realization of the sacred. Thus, for example, the Yurok elder Carrie Turner, born before the turn of the twentieth century, said that she had rejected the opportunity to become a doctor because "You have to suffer too much" (Kathy Heffner McClellan, personal communication, 1978). Fanny Flounder herself remembered her own calling to become a doctor with "pity and terror," according to Erikson (1943: 260). I am suggesting as directly as possible, without claiming positive knowledge of the matter, an interpretation of her "pity" as arising from her terrifying vision of the suffering that is the other side of creation and as a pity both for herself and for the world whose suffering she had been called to heal. Her "pity" equates with the "depressed" Arjuna's "utmost compassion," and like Arjuna, she spoke "sorrowfully."

The paradoxical creation of the *Gita* and of Bartholomew would not have been unfamiliar to old-time, elite Yuroks—*kegeyowor* and *pegʌk kegeyowor*, "men doctors." What some today call "the top layer" of reality, *ʔo·loʔlekʷi soʔn*, may indeed be fundamentally pure, new, beautiful—*mʌwʌsʌyʌh*—the condition that human beings can momentarily attain, through training and in dancing, but reality itself, "that which exists," *kiʔwesʔonah*, is necessarily at once new, pure, and beautiful and also old, polluted, and dirty—*kimolen*. "Kill to live," the Tolowa creators instructed. The "sacred sweathouse" for the Reꝁʷoy jump dance is called *kimolen ʔʌʔgʌ·k*, "dirty old sweathouse." Robert Spott concluded that the *wo·gey* name for (sacred) Red Mountain, where the jump dance medicine man goes for his power, Oka·, meant "bastard," *ka·mu·ks*—socially polluted (Spott and Kroeber 1942: 226). You cannot "fix the world," it would seem, without taking the "bastard moons" into consideration (Kerner, epigraph, chapter 8).

REDUCING "THAT AWFUL STRANGENESS"

The late Tewa Indian anthroplogist Alfonso Ortiz "aimed—as he himself said of another Indian intellectual, D'Arcy McNickle—'to reduce that awful strangeness which has for so long separated Indian and White on this hemisphere' " (Strong n.d.). For all of the insight and intellectual stimulation offered by psychoanalytic hypotheses, Freudian and post-Freudian psychoanalyses of Yurok *kegeyowor* seem to augment, rather than to reduce, that strangeness.

In Yurok shamanism, the doctor's initiatory dreaming is called *ka·mił*, "to dream bad," in contrast to nonshamanic dreaming or hallucinating, *so·nił*. As outlined in chapter 5, having this "bad dream" (or, alternatively, inheriting a doctor's proclivities from the mother), the initiate swallows a spiritual object, *telogeł*, a "pain," embodying her doctoring spirit—another woman doctor, probably dead, in Fanny Flounder's case.[8] Having thus "entered the spirit," which has also entered her, and following an established pattern, Fanny Flounder went "crazy," *kełpey*, running unconsciously back to her village. Roused to dance, she ultimately obtained from another spirit ally—a male chicken hawk—a second "pain" and learned to control them both, vomiting them up and reingesting the two pains, one male and one female.

"Balance," or being "in the middle," *wogi* or *wogwu*, is typically expressed in terms of dialogical pairs of opposites in classical Yurok worldview, where this balance—like that ideally existing between men and women—is indicative of power and, potentially, sacrality (Buckley 1980). Thus, balancing her first pain with the necessary second, femaleness with maleness, empowered by her song (which is also her first helping spirit), Fanny Flounder and other doctors returned to sanity, full of the power to see clairvoyantly and to cure. (Another northwestern California Indian doctor once told her granddaughter, "I know everything man and everything woman. That's why I'm a great doctor" [Kathy Heffner McClellan, personal communication, 1976]).

S. H. Posinsky reinterpreted sucking doctors' pains and dentalia (which Erik Erikson had earlier interpreted as retained feces) as "respectively the positive and negative aspects of an infantile introject, the breast and/or penis" and concluded that "the shell money and the material 'pains' refer *unconsciously* to the breast-penis equation" (1956: 598–99). Posinsky's effort to make Yuroks' wealth and their doctors' spirituality meaningful is valid in terms of Freud's individualistic psychology, but not particularly revealing in terms of Yurok communal psychology. For example, this approach obscures the native meanings of both dentalia and the doctor's pains as means of affirming the owner's identity by affirming that others—through use in bride wealth and dance display, on the one hand, and through curing patients who are fellow sufferers, on the other (cf. Buckley 1989). Psychoanalytic explanations of unconscious referents, while lending significance to others' lives in the analyst's own cultural terms, cannot constitute a comprehension of the doctor's significance within *her* culture.

Anthropologically, if not psychoanalytically, we need to consider the full and specific cultural context of the doctor's pains as "introjects."

For example, in Yurok mythology Mole enters the wombs of women at the creation, bringing death to all humankind in enraged grief over the deaths of her own children (Kroeber 1976). Like the doctor's *telogeł*, "pain," Mole's shape is (in non-Yurok terms) phallic. Like the patients' pains, which the doctor extracts through the power of her own pains, Mole brings death if not properly attended to. And like the *telogeł*, Mole is a spirit that lodges itself in women, the source, in classic Yurok worldview, of the fleshy components of human beings—their bodies (chapter 4). Acknowledging that Mole can be explained as an introjected "breast and/or penis," can we also understand her in a more humane way? And might not what we find in such understanding be quite familiar, rather than wholly other? For instance, the poet Anne Sexton (who committed suicide in 1974) writes, in *Live or Die* (1966: 51),

> This time I hunt for death,
> the night I lean toward,
> the night I want.
> Well then—
> speak of it!
> It was in the womb all along.

Perhaps *telogeł* and Mole both are the suffering and death that is within us, always, and implicate the anger and grief that attend this death? Perhaps when the doctor "cooks" and controls this grief through her dance she transmutes it into knowledge and compassion, knowing now of the suffering that rests, however unacknowledged, in the midst of everyone's life, of the death that must reside in women's wombs as the complement to the life that springs from them? Perhaps her compassionate identification with her patients as human beings, like herself fated to grieve and die, allows her to attract, enwrap, and extract the "pains" that make her patients ill? Perhaps this is most importantly an act of mutual affirmation and validation through shared experience, not an act of professional dominance?

Following Freud's aside, in "Mourning and Melancholia," including his reference to Shakespeare's Hamlet, I am asking if, in the Yurok doctor's case as in that of non-Indian depressives, self-knowledge and broader metaphysical insight are intertwined, potentially at least. Is the Yurok Indian's recognition that this knowledge makes the doctor "crazy" similar, in an important way, to Freud's understanding that the mode of truth-finding that he called melancholia is an "illness"? If so, "mental health" represents a sort of ignorance or, at the least, a balancing of negative knowledge with positive knowledge, of despair with hope, of *thanatos* with *eros*, as the doctor is cured of her madness by balancing her first pain with a second.

DOCTORING

In the central curative act, the spiritual power of the classic Yurok doctor's paired "pains" attracted the pains in the patient's body that were making that patient sick, allowing the doctor to remove those pains. This concept of "pains" and of their place in the etiology of illness and in the doctor's ability to cure was once found throughout the American west, and was especially elaborate and strong in native California (e.g., Jorgensen 1980).

Alice Poe, a contemporary Kashaya Pomo Indian doctor from the California coast south of the Yuroks, says that a doctor cannot cure a "pain" in her patient without having felt that pain herself, immediately and personally. Her understanding is resonant with the testimony of Tela Donahue Lake, a contemporary Indian doctor and a Yurok descendant of Fanny Flounder.

> Indian healers are not like White doctors. We don't experiment on animals, birds, and dead or sick people as a means to learn how to cure. We learn everything the hard way, and usually from healing ourselves first. If you can't heal yourself, then you'll never be any good at healing

other people. The experience and suffering are very important, all part
of the spiritual training. [In Lake 1991: 28]

These women's accounts correspond, of course, with Eliade's cross-cultural, comparative definition of a shaman as "a sick man who has been
cured, who has succeeded in curing himself" (1964: 27).

Valory (1970), following other psychoanalytically oriented scholars,
posited that the illnesses cured by Yurok sucking doctors are far more
often psychogenic than physiogenic. While there were once Yurok doctors who specialized in healing physical traumas, such as rattlesnake bites,
broken bones, and arrow wounds, a contemporary Yurok ceremonial participant told me that he thinks it "self-evident" that the "pains" extracted
by the sucking doctor are "emotional" ones, rather than physical illnesses,
and are manifestations of "spiritual" states rather than of physical pathol-
ogy. It is equally "self-evident" to this man that the doctor extracts these
"pains" through "empathy," as suggested in different terms by Alice Poe's
and Tela Lake's testimonies. In terms of my own use of melancholia as an
analogy in interpreting the doctor's power, we would expect that the illnesses that the classic sucking doctors were called upon to cure were most
often themselves understandable through the analogy of melancholia.

This inference is supported by the anthropological finding that depression is most often experienced and expressed in somatic terms in non-
Western cultures (Kleinman 1977; Marsella 1985: 27; Schieffelin 1985: 101).
While Western researchers have frequently discussed the unusual degree
to which non-Western peoples "somatize" depression, a "mental illness,"
recently some thought has been given to the unusual degree to which
these Western peoples locate depression in the minds of sufferers, rather
than in their bodies. The familiar Aristotelian mind/body distinction itself seems anachronistic to many writers today, however, as the interdependent nature of physical "pain" and mental "suffering" is increasingly
recognized in the West (e.g., Morris 1991).

The ethnographic record of classic Yurok doctoring supports this interpretation, although this record is meager. Somatic symptoms are often
explained in terms of the patients' feelings of guilt or fear of sorcery. These
seem relieved by public confessions that allow a doctor to suck out

"pains," on the one hand, and by sorcery accusations that, one presumes, assign human objects to patients' otherwise unfocused anxieties. Yet precisely what the somatic symptoms are is usually unclear in received testimony, which tells instead of vague feelings of being "oppressed" and, interestingly, of sleep disorders—of ill Yuroks "awake at night but sleep[ing] in the daytime" (Spott and Kroeber 1942: 170).

Cross-culturally, the shaman's "wound" or initiatory illness is most usually similarly vague and reminiscent of Western depression, as in the case of the Siberian shaman who said that he "felt ill, my whole body ailed me, I had bad headaches" (in Eliade 1964: 28). Thus Valory (1970: 200) typifies the Yurok doctor's initiatory sickness as a "mysterious illness." The illnesses of the shaman's patients seem equally "mysterious." However, we note that both insomnia and oversleeping are not only recognized as common symptoms of depression in the West, but were also part of Fanny Flounder's preinitiatory pattern and indeed of the cross-cultural shamanic pattern identified by Eliade.

I am suggesting that the Yurok doctor's initiatory illness is typically analogous to what is termed melancholia in the West and that the diseases that he or she cures are also, very often at least, comparable with what is commonly diagnosed as somatized depression. Thus, the doctor empathizes profoundly with her patient, and this empathy has a crucial role in the efficacy of her power. This is evident in the dynamics of the Yurok doctor's "pains" and those of her patient. These objects, having been sucked from the patient's body, are displayed (sometimes only as vomit) to the patient and witnesses, whose participation in the ritual is customary and may, in fact, be demanded by the doctor.

What is most significant to me in all of this is, first, the complementarity between the classic doctor's pains and those of her patients. These processually complex pairs and pairing of pairs manifest the doctor's balance or completeness, her recovery from madness and, hence, her ability to return patients to balance through the power of her own suffering, by which she has acquired the ability to cure. Second, the doctor affirms the patient as someone suffering from something real, visible in the pains removed from him or her, through the communal display of these pains. This affirmation is complementary to the doctor's initiatory communal validation through control and display of her own pains, in the kick dance in which she cures herself. In these ways, the Yurok doctor's practice manifests an ideology of interdependence and reciprocal interrelatedness. It mobilizes the energy of the community in the most extended sense—one that includes male and female, spirits and humans, doctors and patients, patients and residential groups Finally, this "community" must be seen as including death, with its consequent grief, and life, with its attendant human desire to survive despite the integral presence of suffering in human experience. The sucking doctor's world seems to stand in radical contrast to a more familiar world in which individualism, dualism, and materialism serve to isolate us in suffering by foregrounding the "ego," an *I* far more significant than any discernable *we*.

Mircea Eliade, in returning the study of shamanism from abnormal psychology to the study of religion, sought to show that the shaman's life "is not lacking in tragic greatness and in beauty" (1964). I suggest that the Yurok sucking doctor's tragedy has panhuman significance, and that her greatness arises through her willingness to recognize this significance and to know its tragic dimension intimately. Her knowledge is obtained through the wounding journey "to the edge of the Deep Canyon." The journey is a process analagous to absorption in melancholia. It prepares her to cure, not through establishing her ascendancy and domination over her sick patient by means of putatively superior technical acumen and health, but by means of an affirming and communal empathy rooted in the shared human experience of suffering.

STANDING GROUND

The Indian doctor undoubtedly helps her patients—why else would they have kept her in business for so many years? She is successful in treating individual patients, but she leaves an unanswered question. What is *the* cure?

The disease has been diagnosed long since, by Christ in the noncanonical Gospels, by Vishnu in the *Gita*, by Chinese and Kwakwaka'wakw mythologies, by Anne Sexton and countless modern secularists. In light of the end, said Eugène Ionesco in his theater of the absurd, every human motivation is mad. "Life's tough and then you croak," says my wife. Henry David Thoreau took it personally: I am the best man I ever knew, and the worst.

Writers write against despair, and more power to us. Still, Max Weber wrote, at the end of his melancholy life, of the social sciences' "sacrifice of love," and who can deny it (Rabinow 1991: 63)? "I don't think anthropologists will ever understand us," said Julian Lang; "maybe only artists can." Probably so, but with Indian people's help I have at least understood that our best hope lies in compassion (call it *caritas,* or "Indian love," or what you will), in the knowledge that we are all in this together, and that none of us gets out alive.

There are infinite varieties of human suffering, underwritten by the twin guardians consciousness and mortality. Deep depression is only one vehicle for recognition of the suffering intrinsic in sentience. Freud thought that realized grief, for instance, is something quite other than depression, virtually its opposite, and the mental and emotional arena is but one among at least three, if we include physical and moral realms of suffering as well. Whether we call it mental or emotional or spiritual, within this single field of joy and pain there are many varieties of melancholy alone.

Tristitia and acedia are different shadings of experienced despair, emerging in different contexts. Tristitia is paralyzing sorrow over the greed, anger, and stupidity (including our own) that threaten to harm us all. Acedia is a revulsion against organized efforts to control suffering through, for example, an Indian doctor's training or, in the West, monastic orders. The student doctor may be angry all the time, the monks wind down, the abbot appears a silly autocrat, rising at four in the cold morning seems worse than pointless—all hollow and horrifying jokes. In acedia we divest ourselves of faith, order, discipline, wait only for food, for sleep; we become slothful.

When Yuroks call depression, simply, "suffering," they are not necessarily limiting suffering to the many forms of depression but are using depression as a stand-in for all that we would not be. They are naming darkness, rendering it curable.

Despair lurks in the wings of all of our tragic categories—Weltschmerz, tristitia, acedia, melancholy, depression, loneliness, Indian sickness, suffering, swallowed grief, infantile introjects. We do our best to keep it off-stage, the church by condemning it as a mortal sin while validating it through Christ himself, crying out against his father from the cross. Buddhists accommodate it through existential analyses of suffering—its origins, effects, and practical means of release from it. Yuroks fight it through humor, through doctoring, and through dancing to fix the world, the alternatives being only too obvious on the lower Klamath River. I resist its inexorable presence among us by writing this book.

The psychopharmacologist's chemical fix, met with gratitude and suspicion, affords personal relief for a while, and at least individual functionality. The talking cure offers to reveal the causal sources of individuals' rage and sorrow (if only metaphorical ones)—"father," "mother." These are mitigative prescriptions and objects of blame suitable to the culture within which Freudian psychology arose. Through them we can name the root of our pain, keep its tendrils from throttling our lives, maintain our American optimism, our belief in happy endings, avoiding the possibility that suffering is inherent in birth itself. Indian people in northwestern California find this optimism baffling, like the intricate games children invent when left to their own devices. It is not that they don't understand us.

Certainly, some of these people have suffered, too, because of an internalized, withholding mother—from where else could Ella Norris's two tales of empowerment, "Seagull" and "Redding Rock," get such realism and conviction? But Mrs. Norris told *me* those stories, asked me to record them, because she thought that both I and others would understand them, however slowly and, perhaps, differently. Her telling was a sign of her understanding both of herself and of us. "The Yurok" can no more be defined as discrete from all other peoples by dead or lost or loveless parents than can anyone else.

The psychoanalytic mother is as elusive as God or Indian devils or genetic coding, but the white man of 1865 remains as concrete as invasion, genocide, and dispossession. There is no great mystery here, no analytic nut to be cracked, no puzzle in modern Indian doctors' efforts to shield themselves from "the residue of suffering" caused by the whites, to let the light shine through. We do not need experts to explain it, nor do we have to be masters of empathy to understand that Robert Spott risked acedia, outside the window while white Indian agents whispered against his people behind barred doors, at Requa in the 1920s (chapter 1). We can understand well enough why the Reagan Court's decision on the GO-road demoralized so many American Indians. We just have to relinquish our naive optimism, our Horatio Algerism, our sense of entitlement for a moment, and accept what our history has actually done to other people and to ourselves.

In some ways, native northwestern Californians have been more bitterly fortunate than others in having a concrete evil in which to locate the origins of contemporary despair, when they encounter it, rather than having to speculate about the ulterior causes of human pain. Because a concrete causal origin can be assigned, a therapy other than suicide (voluntary or by seeming mischance) can be prescribed. Jack Norton (1979), for instance, could transcribe and publish the names of 120 white men in authority, between 1850 and 1880, from Millard Fillmore (president of the United States, 1850–53) to a flock of California senators and representatives in the U.S. Congress, 1851–67, down to one Thomas Buckley, military commander at Fort Humboldt, February 9 to April 1, 1865.

Jack Norton and Byron Nelson, Jr., were, I've been told, the only surviving male Hupas of their class at Hoopa High School at the time they published their books, still young men, in 1978–79. Norton's and Nelson's individual survival and individual authorial successes may be somewhat misleading, however, for their books were both communally inspired and communally welcomed. Therapies are possible but, it seems to me, are most effective when they are collective. The two authors, I think, were meeting responsibilities to others, felt as concomitants of personal survival, voicing what others no longer could.

The necessity of community in keeping despair at bay must be at the very heart of the emergence of religions—in Christian congregations, in the Buddhist *sangha* and the Bodhisattva's vow to save all sentient beings, in Indian doctors' healing, and in medicine men's world renewals. In isolation, there is little potential for the cure. This is a marvelous and instructive dynamic, but a terrible one as well. In darkness it can lead to exploitation, oppression, and wars of extermination far more easily than, in light, it might lead to a little peace, justice, and Julian Lang's "Indian love." A yearning for union seems necessary and timeless.

10 The Shaker Church

The yearning for a unified community reemerged in a climate of discouragement and anomie on the lower Klamath in 1926, with the coming of the Indian Shaker Church and what seemed, then, to be the failure of world renewal and traditional doctoring alike.

The Indian Shaker Church originated on Puget Sound in 1882 and was brought into native northwestern California in 1926. Early scholars viewed it as a minor crisis cult or revitalization movement, as opposed to a "real"—that is, pre-contact—American Indian religion. While converted elders quietly defended the Church as a "continuation" of traditional ways (in Gould and Furukawa 1964: 59), they seemed, to certain scholars, to be deluding themselves in a struggle to maintain their Indian identities while becoming pseudo-Christians.

245

But the notion that the Shaker Church is a "continuation" of an authentic Indian spirituality—an "evolution" of it, as a Church member said to me in 1978—rings false only so long as we view modern American Indian history in terms of polarities—Indian/Christian, traditionalist/Shaker, this faction/that faction and the rest. Perhaps it helps to view Europeans/Indians as the typal opposition, of which all the others are tokens, and to remember that it was, first, Europeans who insisted on its validity? But this, too, is oversimple: the Indian Shakers themselves have insisted on a rigid us/them, inside/outside dichotomy (Gould and Furukawa 1964: 57–64), whether such oppositional dualism was traditional or the result of acculturation to Euro-American modes of thought (e.g., Buckley 1980, 1984b, 1988).

Something more complex may be going on here, revealed in part by the powerful reemergence of indigenous ceremonialism that occurred in northwestern California as elsewhere in the Americas during the 1980s and '90s. The contemporary emergence of spiritual practices that non-Indian anthropologists and native people alike once viewed as moribund should alert us to the possibility that, yes, innovations like the Shaker Church have indeed been "continuations" of native traditions, and that—perhaps more difficult to see—reemergent practices are themselves "continuations" or "evolutions" of modern innovations like the Shaker Church. That is, theoretically, seemingly diametrically opposed traditions may be better understood as emergent processes coparticipating in a historical and spiritual dialogue.

A friend once remarked about young men on the Hoopa Valley Indian Reservation, "Well, there are two ways for Indian men to save their lives these days, Christianity and the Indian Way, and that's it." I don't think that she was overdramatizing. It is my impression, at least, that without the support and discipline of a spiritual practice, life for these men—and women—tends to be rough and, tragically often, short. Fortunately, if my friend is right, there is a lively and diverse assortment of Christian congregations in the region, and there has also been a renaissance in much older Indian spiritual practices, gathering momentum steadily since the late 1960s.

Not that "the Indian Way" ever disappeared entirely after 1850, but it had indeed "gone underground for awhile," as a Hupa-Yurok brush dance doctor put it in 1976. Most strikingly, the reemergence of the Indian Way has manifested in the regeneration of the complex system—including religious, social, economic, and political dimensions—that A. L. Kroeber called the world renewal cult and that he considered virtually extinct by the 1940s (Kroeber and Gifford 1949).

RESISTANCE TO CHRISTIANITY

Today, the northwestern California Indian Way tends to be construed by participants as exclusive of Christian belief and practice, and individuals following it tend, in many cases, to forcefully reject Christianity as un-Indian. Anti-Christian sentiment can be traced back to the first years of the post-contact white occupation.

Presbyterian missionaries came to the Hoopa Valley in 1873 and had extended their evangelical efforts outwards, up and down the Klamath and along the various forks of the Trinity River, by the 1890s. Conversions were few, however, and seem to have been restricted to mixed-blood Indians who were, at that time, marginal to both Indian and non-Indian societies and thus had little to lose in moving even further from the moral center of elite native society. By contrast, the native elites did not seek parity with the increasingly oppressive whites, who dominated northwestern California after the end of armed Indian resistance in 1867, through conversion to Christianity. Between 1870 and 1890, for instance, Wolf Morris, a Polish-Jewish trader dealing in dentalium shells with Yurok and Tolowa customers, found it advantageous to stress the fact that he, like his high-status potential customers, was *not* a Christian (Pilling 1970: 4; cf. Pilling and Pilling 1970: 103). I know of no full-blood Yurok Indian who converted to Christianity before the end of the First World War.

There were, it should be mentioned, some notable native efforts to secure religious tolerance and respect from non-Indians through apologia cast as comparisons of traditional belief systems with Christianity. Thus, well before 1900, the Yurok trickster-creator Wohpekumew was being called "God," in English, by certain Yuroks in an effort to increase cross-cultural understanding (Kroeber 1976: 420). This mythical equivalence has been reiterated throughout the twentieth century and is still popular today. A contemporary Yurok intellectual and religious activist has suggested that the first Yurok Indian to compare the licentious Wohpekumew to God was perhaps acting in the spirit of a trickster himself (Peters n.d.)! It is not clear why Wohpekumew emerged, from among several creators, as a Yurok "God," but it may have had to do with his efforts to kill his sons, who nevertheless resurrected and departed from the earth for the spirit world.[1]

But while the Wohpekumew/God equivalence may have reflected some Yuroks' perceptions of the darker similarities of the two myths (cf. Bakan 1968: 96–128), the crucifixion of Christ has not, historically, had much resonance for Yurok people inclined toward traditional ways, or for their like-minded neighbors—Hupa, Karuk, and Tolowa Indians. The late Yurok Indian doctor Calvin Rube told me, in 1978,

> Now Christianity. . . . If an Indian had a brand new pair of hundred dollar boots and cut off his foot with his axe, he'd throw those boots away because they had blood in them and weren't any good. We throw away whatever has blood in it because it's spoiled. But Christians have this cross where they killed Jesus, which is covered with blood, and they fool with it and wear it around their necks, and that's no good.

In light of such strongly held views, Indian efforts at rapprochement through creating intercultural equivalences seemed half-hearted. When Lucy Thompson elided Wohpekumew with God and identified the creator-hero Pulekukwerek with Christ, she reserved a "secret name of the Deity," known only to "lodge" initiates, for truly ultimate reality (Thompson 1991 [1916] and chapter 3, above).

Despite all such resistance, be it softly apologetic or harshly anti-Christian, Christianity has indeed made inroads into the staunch religious conservatism of the region. The Presbyterian Church is a central feature of Indian religious life at Hoopa today, a hundred and seventeen years after it was established. Other churches came much later, but remained in the area as well. By 1928 the Four Square Gospel Church at Klamath was attracting Yurok members, the Baptists were active in Requa, and at least one Yurok woman had become a Pentecostal Christian (Pilling 1970: 5). By 1990 there were Assembly of God churches in Hoopa, on the Yurok Reservation at Weitchpec, and at Pecwan, in Karuk country at Orleans, and so on; Mormon, Seventh Day Adventist, various smaller evangelical Protestant churches, as well as Roman Catholic missions—including the Mission of Blessed Kateri Tekakwitha (the Algonkian-Mohawk saint) at Hoopa—all attracted significant Indian congregations. Traveling revivalists, especially those offering to heal, did a lively business in the area as well.

Still, the rise of these congregations during the past seventy years should not obscure the continuing tensions and occasional conflicts between Christian and traditional ways. Christian preachers and parishioners alike have often castigated indigenous beliefs and practices as heathen delusion, going so far as to urge the burning of traditional dance regalia and accusing medicine people of deviltry. Younger people following the Indian Way, on the other hand, have accused Christians of being "superstitious" in their rejection of "spiritualism":

> Non-tribal religious ideologies condition the conscious mind to instinctively reject or repress the very existence of . . . spiritual energy. . . . spiritualism is feared as being satanic and morally wicked. In recent years, many [Yurok] people, as well as tribal people throughout the U.S., because of acculturation restrict their very own spiritualism due to such superstitious conditioning. [Peters n.d.]

The Indian Shaker Church, a syncretic sect perceived by its members as a special religious dispensation intended by God for Indians alone, has sought since 1926 to mediate this rift that dates back to the earliest years of contact in northwestern California, precisely by incorporating indigenous spiritual practices.

SHAKER SYNCRETISM

In 1882, John Slocum, a Nisqually Indian from Puget Sound, "died." He revived, and then once again died, his spirit ascending to Heaven where he was instructed by "an angel of God." He came back into his body at last, awoke, and instructed those about him in the new religion that God had revealed to him through His angel.

Slocum's experience was coherent with the prophet dance pattern of coastal Washington and the Plateau, and it also showed the considerable influence of both Protestant and Catholic missions in the Puget Sound area. In brief, as God's agent, John Slocum taught that there are

> good things in Heaven. God is kind to us. If you all try hard and help me, we will be better men on earth. . . . They know in Heaven what we think. When people are sick we pray to God to cure us. We pray that he takes the evil away and leaves the good. [This is the] good road for us to travel. . . . do good and sing good songs . . . Christ said he sends power to every believing soul on earth. [Slocum, in Slagle 1985: 354]

This teaching was augmented by John Slocum's wife, Mary, who discovered that the power of the "Spirit of Christ" (Smith 1954: 121) manifested itself in her own body as light trancing and physical trembling—"the Shake" through which she could heal. "The Shake" has been viewed widely by anthropologists as a reembodiment of the indigenous Salishan concept of "power," particularly as it once pertained to "shamans." The recent history of Yurok Indian doctors has been richly intertwined with that of the Shaker Church.

John Slocum incorporated his wife Mary's innovation of the Shake into his own teaching and instructed his followers to build him a church at Mud Bay, Washington, where their joint revelations might be put into formal practice by a congregation. The Indian Shaker Church was organized as an association in 1892 and incorporated in 1910 (Slagel 1985: 353). The wooden church itself was illuminated by copious candles. Services focused on Christian worship as well as singing and dancing to the accompaniment of handbells, which supported the converted in trancing. Preaching stressed the importance of "like-mindedness" among the congregants, and a famous song instructs:

> Make all one mind
> and Jesus will help you. [In Valory 1966a: 76]

The unity of the congregation against the forces of evil outside the church was paramount, and this like-mindedness reinforced "the Shake," which empowered congregants to heal, prophesy, trace lost objects, and cast out evil. "Healing" focused both on individuals and on the world at large. Shakers prayed for the end of war and a return to world balance and harmony, when the necessary and rigid inside/outside dichotomy would be outmoded.

The new syncretic church spread widely in the Pacific Northwest. In 1926 Jimmy Jack, a Yurok Indian, brought the Shaker dispensation to the lower Klamath River. There was a barn there that was being used by Florence Shaughnessy as a dance hall. Jimmy Jack borrowed this barn at the beginning of September for the first Shaker meeting in California. Fifty years later, in 1976, Mrs. Shaughnessy gave this account:

> Jimmy Jack from the old Klamath [Welk^{w}ew went up to Siletz in Oregon, and he married a Siletz woman. The Shakers were there, and they wanted to come down here, so Jimmy Jack brought them. They asked me if they could use the big barn where I used to have my dances, so I let them. They had the whole place full of white candles, and it was quite beautiful. They all started dancing in there and ringing their bells. People kept pouring in until the hall was full, and people kept coming and crowded all around the place in front of the door. It was packed. There were commercial fishermen on the river and they heard bells ringing and they all came in too, because they'd never heard anything like those bells at Requa.
>
> I went with my mother. She asked me to take her and we stood in that crowd outside. But this woman who was dancing inside saw us and she came out, and she touched my mother and said, "You are in terrible trouble; come inside." But my mother said, "Flo, take me home. I feel so weak." So I walked her back, and she was trembling and shaking and she could hardly stand and walk. And that woman was right: two or three days later my mother was found, drowned. Strange things happen. Perhaps she should have listened.

At first, Shakers, like the Presbyterians before them, mainly converted people marginal to respectable Yurok society: half-bloods, the illegitimate, and the very poor. For instance, despite his strong efforts Jimmy Jack was unable to convert Robert Spott, by 1926 one of Requa's most influential residents. Spott attended Shaker meetings out of politeness, as he did Baptist services as well. At one point, Jimmy Jack touched him, transmitting the Shake to him as the Siletz woman had done to Florence Shaughnessy's mother. But Spott refused to convert, even after this experience, on the grounds that the Shakers were Christians and thus un-Indian (Barnett 1957: 76–77, 272–74).

Jack continued to seek such conversions, however, knowing that the Church could gain a solid foothold in the region only with the support of spiritual leaders like Spott. While Robert Spott's sister, Alice, was helpful but ambivalent, other Yurok women of high repute did eventually convert wholeheartedly.

Since the 1880s and '90s, Yurok candidates for the classic doctoring vocation of *kegey* had increasingly failed to gain their powers in the mountain sacred sites or were unable to demonstrate these powers in the requisite *remoh*, doctor dance, put up in the riverine village sweathouses. Nonetheless a number of women who had been spiritually called, while failing to gain full standing as *kegeyowor*, achieved recognition as clairvoyants and healers. Several of these women lived on the lower Klamath in the villages near Johnson's Landing ("Johnsons"), close to Pecwan. They began, by 1930, to find a new context for legitimacy as Indian Doctors in the Shaker Church, whose dancing they claimed as a substitute for the older, non-Christian *remoh*. Although some of the very few old-time *kegeyowor* who survived referred to these new healers disparagingly, as "half doctors,"[2] the younger Yurok "Indian doctors" soon virtually controlled the Shaker Church established at Smith River, twenty-five miles north of Requa, in Tolowa territory. The participation of these powerful Yurok women inspired the conversion of highly respected Tolowa religious people, including the influential Sam Lopez. With this impetus, other important conversions were achieved, including that of Woodruff Hostler, a Hupa Indian. In 1932 Jimmy Jack cured another Hupa, John Charlie, who, giving up all traditional ways and selling all of his family's dance regalia, established a church at Hoopa. Other churches were eventually built at Johnsons and at Jimmy Jack's hometown of Klamath, both in Yurok territory.

Despite its increasing strength, the Shaker Church in California was rife with dissension and controversy almost from its inception, and this conflict centered, generally, on issues of Indian identity. In 1933, the church in northwestern California was divided by the "Bible controversy," "book" congregations arguing for the use of the Bible in services, "shake" advocates insisting that God intended the Bible for white people only, and not for Indians, who received the Holy Spirit directly through the Shake.

A second focus of controversy was ownership of traditional dance regalia and participation in pre-Christian dances, such as brush dances. Some Shakers argued that traditional dancing was of the devil and that all regalia must be destroyed if individuals were to be healed, wars ended, and the world saved. Others declared that this was an individual matter and that the church could not dictate individuals' religious lives. Nonetheless, those like "John," the nephew of a Yurok Indian doctor and Shaker convert, were accused of "backsliding" when they insisted on their right to participate both in Shaker meetings and in brush dances: taking part in "outside" activities, they weakened "like-mindedness" and threatened the "inside," the church.

From one point of view, particularly strong among Smith River Shakers, the Shake was a "continuation" of the old Indian Way, completely Indian but also obviating earlier traditional practices. It was on the strength of this sentiment that the anthropologists Richard Gould and Theodore Furukawa wrote, in 1964, that "it is our tentative prediction . . . that the Indian Shaker Church will provide the most tangible focus for the identity of the 'Indian' in the face of white American culture in this area of northwestern California" (Gould and Furukawa 1964: 67).

However, many Indian people continued to agree with, for instance, the Hupa traditionalists who hold that dancing in the traditional brush, deerskin, and jump dances makes people more Indian, more "real," or *xoche*. The notion was reiterated in 1988 by a Karuk ceremonial singer and dancer, Julian Lang, who said of wearing regalia to dance in ceremonies,

> The whole idea of displaying that stuff is to spark people inside so. . . . if that power is in there sleeping inside them. . . . in the ceremony you're waking up those people, that power inside the people, so when that wakes up and looks at that stuff and it sees all that kinship, pretty soon it wants to go into that stuff again and it wants to participate in that stuff, and it turns the people back into Indians.

By 1965, with the passing of the first generation of converts including, pertinently, most of the Shaker doctors, the Shaker Church was already los-ing significant membership. Sam Lopez, the Tolowa spiritual leader, was drifting away, moving towards the Bible-oriented Four Square Gospel Church. Others, like "John," were attempting to keep a foot in both camps, Shaker and traditional. Most church members, however, while accepting Shakers' attendance at other Christian church services, firmly rejected Shaker participation in traditional dances or the participation of those committed to the older Indian Way in Shaker meetings. Complex negotiations of membership and identity occurred, as when Ella Norris moved to the Four Square Gospel Church both as an adherent of biblical teaching and because church members did not object to her participating in brush dances.

Thus, while Gould and Furukawa wrote in 1964 of the Shaker Church as the probable focus of Indian identity in northwestern California in the future, in 1966 Dale Valory confidently described the Shaker Church as having already reached its peak and beginning to ebb (Valory 1966a: 67). In fact none of the three, all graduate students in anthropology at Berkeley in the mid-1960s, was entirely correct. In 1990, twenty-six years after Gould and Furukawa wrote, the Shaker Church had neither ebbed to insignificance nor did it form a primary religious focus for Indian identity—not, at least, for the most visible and influential practitioners of what I am calling "the Indian Way" in northwestern California.

RESURGENCE OF THE INDIAN WAY

Among these people, often the modern descendants of the old "high families," another option had all along been open, that of denouncing Christianity altogether, as had their lineal ancestors in the nineteenth century and before the 1920s. This option became more attractive as the 1960s wore on and became the 1970s, a time that saw, in northwestern California as elsewhere, a concerted effort among many to selectively renounce ways of the dominant society and return to older traditions. This renaissance was most evident among younger native people, but was certainly not limited to them.

Along with a burst of new enthusiasm for brush dances, the 1960s also saw a profound regeneration of interest in more portentous jump and deerskin dances at Hoopa, under the leadership of the elder Rudolph Soctish. In the 1970s Karuk Indians, led by another elder, Shan Davis, revived their equally solemn new year's "world making," *pikiawish*, at Katimin, on the Klamath River. By the 1980s, Yuroks, under the guidance of the elders Dewey George and Howard Ames, both of whom trained in the sweathouse at Pecwan in the 1930s, restored the jump dance at Pecwan. Slightly later in that decade, Tolowa Indians led by an ex-Shaker protégé of Sam Lopez were beginning to revive their own world renewal dance at Smith River.

In the 1980s, as younger men took over from elders who were rapidly passing away, almost as a group, the anti-Christian sentiment that had long been a feature of "high" or elite thought came increasingly into prominence among, especially, Indian religious activists in their thirties and forties and now responsible for most of the formal traditional leadership positions in the region: the dance makers, medicine men, singers and dancers, feasting camp owners, and so on. Such sentiment extended to the Shakers, who tended to be seen more simply as Christians.

By 1989, however, Loren Bommelyn, a charismatic and respected craftsman, teacher, and linguist, who is an excellent singer as well, had come to regard anti-Shaker sentiment as counterproductive. At a large intertribal gathering in Arcata in the fall of 1989 he introduced an evening of singing by a dozen of the most noted Yurok, Karuk, Hupa, and Tolowa Indian singers, old and young, with an impassioned plea for religious tolerance of the Shakers by those following both Christian and Indian ways. He said that he himself was no longer a Shaker but that he fully respected the church as an authentic *Indian* religious expression and urged others to do the same, opening the evening's singing with a solo Shaker invocation of remarkable beauty and power. It was a brave, virtuoso move on his part, before an audience of three hundred or so people, many well known for their anti-Christian sentiments.

Despite Valory's pessimism in 1966, Shakers remained a strong presence in the religious life of the region in 1990, even then attracting younger men and women who, for whatever reason, did not find the Indian Way satisfying. To an extent, perhaps, the continuing vitality of the church was due to the resolution of the Bible controversy. This long-standing dispute, which had caused schism among the various churches in the region, was not fully resolved until 1984 when Harris Teo, the bishop of the Indian Shaker Church in California, stated categorically that "Bibles were not to be used or directly quoted in any Shaker church" (in Slagle 1985: 354). Shakers have also survived through becoming less rigidly opposed to members' participation in brush dances and other Indian events, or to members' ownership of dance regalia. The once heretical participation in Indian dances by prominent Shakers like "John" came slowly and however reluctantly to be accepted by many. Most, by 1990, were willing to grant the membership far more personal autonomy and discretion than was once the case. People tended to work out their own solutions to the cultural conflicts posed by Shaker and traditional involvements. For example, as late as 1990 a Hupa-Yurok artist, widely recognized as among the finest living makers of traditional dance regalia, an inspired and proselytizing Shaker, would not himself dance in any of the dances for which he made such fine regalia.

If the Shakers had become more tolerant of multiple religious commitments among their members, the same could not, I think, be said of the traditionalists, particularly the younger ones then ascendant in the great dances. Observation suggested that those coming into leadership positions in the great dances were increasingly clear—as their efforts became increasingly successful—in their rejection of the Shakers as spiritually un-Indian.

On the last day of the ten-day jump dance at Pecwan in 1986, for instance, a dance maker staunchly refused to permit "John" to lead a Shaker prayer in the dance pit, as would ordinarily have been "John's" prerogative as a respected elder and a spiritual practitioner—and one with strong inherited connections to the Pecwan dance. But "John" had announced specifically that he wanted to make a Shaker prayer, in the company of other Shakers, and the dance maker refused him on these grounds, saying that the dance was an Indian, not a Christian, occasion.

The dispute elevated to a formal level of traditional legal adjudication in which, while the dance maker did not permit the Shakers to pray, he gave "John" payment for having insulted him, as an elder and as one with certain rights at Pecwan. "John" accepted "Indian payment" which, interestingly, included two sea otter quivers made to dance in brush dances.

Three years later "John" was again refused permission by a dance maker to join in prayers on the final day of the deerskin dance at Hoopa, this time on the grounds that he was Yurok, and not Hupa. Hupa-Yurok enmity had been running high, in the wake of a complex and acrimonious land claim settlement, yet "John" had long been married into a Hupa family and was a resident of the Hoopa Valley Reservation. Some people inferred that his Christian involvement was again at issue. Once more, "John" sought purely northwestern Californian—not Christian—remediation, saying that his power was stronger than the dance maker's and that he was going to "devil" the dance itself.

These things are serious matters in riverine northwestern California. They become the source of endless gossip and are often what people talk about for the two years until the next dance, when something new and equally scandalous may come up. I relate such sensitive matters only to support my conclusion that the Indian Shaker Church, while it continues to exist and even to attract new converts, has largely failed as a mediation of mainstream Christianity and the Indian Way. Indeed, the kind of syncretic fusion that it enabled—a revolutionary response to dispossession and white oppression—itself became a new old way, a "traditional" way that younger neotraditionalists, like the dance makers at Pecwan and at Hoopa, putatively returning to the *old* old way, now reject as old-fashioned and reactionary.[3] However, while the Indian Way is on the upsurge once again in native northwestern California, as a Yurok acquaintance said of his peers, "We may be Indians, but we all die Christians." Shaker and other Christian practitioners have become the most widely accepted and appreciated purveyors of funeral rites, whatever the spiritual commitments of the deceased and his family—much as, in Japan, Buddhist priests have come to be known for the mortuary services that they provide bereaved families that are, at best, only nominally Buddhist (Chadwick 1994).

Despite the broad acceptance of Christian burial services, the broader pattern that I have been describing reflects a widespread national movement toward retribalization and the reclamation of purely local cultural and spiritual traditions in lieu of continuing in the development of pan-Indianism, as offered by the Shaker and the Native American Churches. The dialectic between two sets of oppositions—being "Indian" as opposed to "non-Indian," and being Yurok or Hupa, say, as contrasted with "Native American"—is a newly dynamic one. The new traditionalists reject the Shakers not simply in continuance of perennial anti-Christian sentiment among the religious elite, but also in defense of purely local religious knowledge and practice, as distinct from pan-Indianism.

"REVITALIZATION"

T. T. Waterman, a Berkeley anthropologist of Kroeber's era, made the astute observation in 1924 that "the shake religion of Puget Sound," with its heavy "shamanistic" content, was most appealing to Indians whose indigenous religious practices were still strong; that is, where traditional doctoring was still practiced. Waterman further observed that it was this purely indigenous component of the new Christian sect that attracted influential traditionalists—like, slightly later, the Yurok Indian doctors (Waterman 1924).

There is a mild irony here. The Shaker Church was most successful in converting those who were most *confident* in traditional spiritual practices and who were most resistant to mainstream forms of Christianity, such as Presbyterianism in the Hoopa Valley. It offered an acceptable compromise at a time when, despite strong commitment to the Indian Way, that Way seemed to be in need of updating, in keeping with the radically changed circumstances of post-invasion northwestern California that, for example, mitigated against the Yurok Indian doctors gaining the classic sucking doctors' full powers. The adaptation of Christian belief to Indian purpose among the California Shakers provided a means of "vitalization," in Marian Smith's insightful term (Smith 1954: 122): of adapting still strong cultures to current circumstances, rather than of "revitalizing" moribund cultures (cf. A. F. C. Wallace 1956).

The Shaker Church served as a powerful vehicle of acculturation to non-Indian beliefs—especially to hierarchical, oppositional dualism as found in mainstream Christianity and in such Shaker polarities as inside/outside, Heaven/earth, Shake/Devil, and other dichotomies. And it is such acculturation that has been resisted by the newer generation of traditional practitioners, with their more self-consciously holistic world views. The process amounts to a dialogue with a by-now familiar structure.

Edward Bruner examined the nature of ethnographies of North American Indians and found them to be "narratives" that we anthropologists share with the putative objects of our studies. Bruner claims not only that non-Indian anthropologists and nonanthropologist Indians tell each other stories, but that we coauthor the stories that we each tell: stories that emerge dialogically from our interactions (Bruner 1986).

Bruner argues that, up until the 1960s, Indians and anthropologists shared a narrative of Indian history that was structured by a scenario of *past glory, tragic defeat, current cultural fragmentation, and eventual assimilation*. Our coauthored story changed, he says, in the 1960s to follow a different scenario: *past glory, oppression, current resistance, eventual resurgence*. In fact, Bruner concludes, both stories are true and both are oversimplifications. Our histories are codeterminous and dialectical, rather than mono-causal and linear. A degree of assimilation, he argues, gave Indian people both the means of physical survival and, eventually, a profound commitment to resisting further assimilation. This resistance both ensures cultural survival and brings the self-confidence and firmness of identity that allow communities to accept further moderate degrees of change. So the two varieties of narrative both witness, Bruner concludes, codetermined processes in post-contact American Indian history.

From this perspective the Shaker Church has afforded the Indian people of northwestern California a holding action. That is, its voicing of biblical Christianity was, of course, a (contested) means of assimilation to non-Indian intellectual and spiritual culture, but the church also served as a vehicle for the preservation and transmission of indigenous doctoring traditions in changing circumstances, as its pan-Indianism was a source of both cultural loss, through amalgamation, and of preservation of Indianness, through the church's insistence on the "like-mindedness" of congregants and its inside/outside, us/them dualism.

Ironically, the success of the Indian Shaker Church in northwestern California in these particular directions has ultimately led to its own seeming decline. It has preserved an Indian focus that ultimately emerged in resistance to the Christian context within which it was preserved, in a new expression of old anti-Christian feeling, and in a return from pan-Indian engagement to localized, non-Christian spiritual practice. If the Shake was a "continuation" of the Indian Way, as the most respected members of the church have always claimed, then, too, the resurgent local Indian Way must be viewed as a "continuation" of the Shake.

"And so it goes," as the anthropologically trained fabulist Kurt Vonnegut, Jr., is fond of writing. In the past, anthropologists have written confidently about the imminent demise of Yurok Indian culture (A. L. Kroeber and Claude Lévi-Strauss, in Valory 1966b), about the disappearance of "American Indians" and their replacement by "Indian Americans" in native northwestern California (Bushnell 1968) and, as we have seen, about replacement of earlier native spiritual identities with that of the Shakers. All of these predictions have been wrong and now, for my own part, I would not hazard a guess as to just where the process I have examined leads next. In 1990, mainstream Christianity, the Indian Shaker Church, and the Indian Way all continued to coexist in native northwestern California, however contentious such pluralism occasionally was.

11 Jump Dance

At Pecwan, in the ten days following September's full moon, every other year men dance with beautiful regalia from morning to evening in the pit of a dismantled semi-subterranean plank house. The dancers represent two complementary and competing "sides," taking turns in the pit, and as each side dances, the deeply felt songs of the two lead singers who dance on either side of a center man interweave, bound together by a rock-steady chorus of men ranged symmetrically beside the singers, forming a line. The two lead singers sing two different songs, and their singing is more dialogue than duet.

Through the final days of the ten-day dance, the beauty and antiquity of the regalia deepen and the numbers of dancers and spectators grow. On the last day young women join the men in the pit, at either end of the dance line, but do not sing. Finally all of the dancers, male and female,

261

from both sides join together, momentarily resolving all differences, achieving wholeness and balance: "fixing the world" (to use the Karuk description that is now widely invoked). This long process is called "the jump dance." It is intended to cure the world's ills, and to stave off evil.

During a dance, the two sides (which represent two ancient village alliances) and their guests camp on either side of the small road that runs down to Pecwan from the junction of the Klamath with the Trinity River at Weitchpec, each camp equidistant from the pit and the sacred fire at its center. These camps are run by the senior women in the groups, who haul water and chop wood and prepare hundreds of servings of acorn soup, salmon, venison, and smoked eels, as well as more modern fare. These women oversee the feasting and enjoyment that they share with many visitors, keeping the camp "clean"—ritually pure and harmonious. The women in the opposing camps also compete with each other in hospitality and correctness, in an understated way. It is hard work, and this hard work is the women's prayer. The men from the two sides dance and sing all day, by turns, in considerable heat and dust and the smoke that rises from the sacred fire and the angelica root burning in it. Many younger men fast and thirst for the full ten days and stay up most nights singing ancient men's songs in the jump dance sweathouse, which has existed at Pecwan seemingly forever. The cumulative experience that these men attain is not easily gained.

Julian Lang said, after the 1988 dance at Pecwan, "As Indians we don't have many responsibilities, but one of them is to fix the world." And later, "It's hard to be an Indian."

In light of this hard work and the deep experience earned by it, writing about "fixing the world" is awkward. "World renewal," as most anthropologists refer to it, is something that people *do,* and its meaning is not separable from experience and the ways in which the experience transforms people. This much becomes clear through participation, even as a spectator, but it is also apparent in some written native accounts of the dances, as well as in people's oral testimony today.

As we've seen (chapter 3), Lucy Thompson (1991 [1916]) centers her book around the great dances that she took part in as a young woman, in the 1870s, stressing transformative experience at both personal and communal levels. Like Mrs. Thompson, Kathy Heffner McClellan, the contemporary Wailaki Indian researcher, recognizes the significance of the spectator's experience as well as that of the more active participants (1988: 10): "Attending these ceremonies and directing their prayers to the spiritual world held the people together at the base of their belief system; for they were attending and participating for the same reasons—lifting their prayers for continued proper existence." The witness of spectators seeing the dances is itself a form of prayer, their own contribution to fixing the world.

Spectators and participants, men and women, the two sides in the dance, humans and the spiritual beings who "cry to see the feathers dance," invisible on the edge of the dance ground reserved for them ("Give them what they cry for!" a Hupa Indian participant exulted), even numbers of dancers arranged on each side of the "center man" in the pit (dressed in regalia that "cries to dance"): everything and everyone seems to come in pairs. These pairs complement and oppose each other, and pairs complement and oppose other pairs. In one sense, the purpose of the dance is to bring all of these oppositions together in wholeness, always present as a possibility—in the pit, the fire, the center men—fixing the world. The competition between sides and camps, usually constrained by common purpose, is transcendent, itself becoming an expression of wholeness during the course of the dance.

During the final round of dancing at Pecwan in 1990, on the tenth day, the heat finally broke as both sides danced together, raising in unison the medicine baskets that each male dancer held in his right hand. As they did so, spectators said later, a great spiritual force rose from the pit to hang in the sky above. People were happy (and perhaps relieved) as they went off to feast and talk in the two camps. "If we can get through the dance we can get through the next two years," they said.

These dances manifest primary communal concerns with and commitments to balance. While most native people today call this balance or wholeness "unity," world renewal is negotiated in terms dictated by the tensions between people, rather than by an abstract "unity" that remains largely a yearning: "the joy of man's desiring," as Katherine Clarke nicely translated the novelist Jean Giono's *Que ma joie demeure* (1940).

THE ETHNOLOGY OF WORLD RENEWAL

There is another opposition to be remarked upon here, apparent throughout these chapters, that between myself and my esteemed anthropological predecessor A. L. Kroeber. Together with his student and colleague
Edward W. Gifford, Kroeber wrote the standard work on these dances,
"World Renewal: A Cult System of Native Northwest California" (1949).
The jump dance at Pecwan, they wrote, is part of a "closed system" they
dubbed "the world renewal cult."

The two anthropologists included, in their world renewal "cult system," the Pecwan jump dance as well as dances and rituals once held at
twelve other ceremonial centers in northwestern California. While acknowledging that this system was not a native construct, they held that
it was indeed a reality, an ethnographic "pattern" established through the
trained ethnologist's "apperception" and by "natural analysis" (Kroeber
and Gifford 1949: 1). The Yurok, Hupa, and Karuk Indians who once participated in the "cult," the coauthors said, recognized only "dances," although the Karuk language has a single term designating "world making" or "world fixing" dances. Kroeber (and presumably Gifford) viewed
the cult as "one of the closed systems of native American religion," comparable with the Plains Sun Dance, the Kachina Cult of the Southwest, or
the Hamatsa Cult of the Northwest Coast (ibid.).

For Kroeber the world renewal cult in northwestern California once
presented an organized variety of diagnostic elements. Each of the thir-
teen events manifested different combinations of these elements, which
may be briefly summarized following Kroeber and Gifford (1–3):

1. The rituals that accompanied the dances themselves focused on
   the reestablishment or firming of the earth, and thus
2. the prevention of disease and calamity for another cycle.
3. Rituals might include first fruits rites or
4. building a new fire, and often
5. rebuilding a sacred structure.
6. The entire scenario for each dance was introduced by the
   pre-human *wo·gey* whose words, preserved in narratives,
   provided the bases for

7. "formulas" recited by "priests" who
8. followed set itineraries for visits to specific places near the dance site, manifesting the
9. intense localization typical of the cult.
10. All events associated with a given dance had to be completed within one lunation.

In the midst of this esoterica, one of two dances—called, in English, the jump dance and the deerskin dance—was given for a period that varied from ten to sixteen days with up to forty-eight repetitions of the dance per day. In these dances, teams displayed elaborate regalia belonging to families who owned rights to outfit the dancers with what amounted to items of wealth that danced to the accompaniment of trained singers. Camps were set up by the two sponsoring villages at each dance, and all visitors were freely fed. (Kroeber estimated that the entire cult had had approximately ten thousand adherents before massive contact, in 1850, with crowds of three to five thousand sometimes gathering for a single dance in the late summers and early autumns of the nineteenth century.)

Kroeber and Gifford's accounts were for the most part reconstructions of dances apparently long extinct when they published their monograph in 1949. In that monograph, as in all of Kroeber's comparable work, "the present tense must be construed as a narrative one, referring to a century or more ago," when "the undisturbed, pre-1850 native culture seems to have been largely in static balance" (Kroeber 1959: 236), and before this "primitive culture . . . went all to pieces" (Kroeber 1948: 427). Kroeber and Gifford valued the "native opinion" of their informants in establishing what "does and does not belong together in the native culture, as to organization or systematization" (1949: 1). However, Kroeber's ethnology stressed the "deliberate suppression of individuals as individuals" (1952: 7–8). While individual variation and idiosyncrasy undeniably existed in societies, a valid cultural anthropology, for Kroeber, had to be based in the abstraction of the concrete "products" of human thought and behavior from the matrix of individuality. This Kroeber called "realism" and found necessary in the—ideally, statistical—effort to establish the elements and traits composing a cultural pattern as a "closed system" in a culture held in "static balance," as an integrated and unified "organi-

zation." "Apperception" of such a system thus demanded that the ethnologist disregard any disagreements among individuals in the creation
of a normative, putatively consensual, homogeneous cultural whole (cf.
Buckley 1996).

For example, in the "World Renewal" monograph, Kroeber and Gif-
ford cite Lucy Thompson's *To the American Indian* because of its detailed,
catalog-like descriptions of the Yurok renewal rites at Kepel and at
Pecwan. They do not directly quote the author, however, finding her writ-
ing "sometimes prolix or ethnographically irrelevant." Nonetheless,
Thompson's book "contains some new items," writes Kroeber, and
"Therefore I put it on record here in condensed and reworded form"
(Kroeber and Gifford 1949: 82).

By way of historical comparison, we might note that Kroeber's position in "apperceiving" world renewal as a "closed system" is comparable with Durkheim's method for perceiving "social facts" discernable only
by trained scientific observers (Durkheim 1938 [1895]), especially as this
method was developed into the theory of the "total social phenomenon"
by Durkheim's student Marcel Mauss (1954). For Mauss, such phenom-
ena (the Northwest Coast Indian "potlatch" provided an ideal example)
simultaneously included religious, mythological, economic, jural, and so-
cial-structural elements in a normative unity apparent only to the objective social scientist observing from without. Today, two problems are apparent in these totalizing approaches.

First, this order of objectification must exclude, as important analytic
concerns, individuals and history alike. The erasure of both individuality
and time in ethnology, which various postmodernists have more recently
sought to rectify, in fact was challenged far earlier by the importance placed
by fieldworkers like James Owen Dorsey on the notable lack of consensus
among American Indian informants regarding social organization (Barnes
1984). It was an objection largely disregarded by Kroeber, "the Dean" of
American anthropologists during his lifetime (Steward 1961).

Second, in creating systems closed to individual and subgroup creativity and conflict, focused on the "millennial sweep and grand contours" of a virtually metaphysical history (or History), transmuting time
into place in the form of "culture areas," Kroeber omitted from the ethno-

graphic record the "pitiful history of little events" that recounts the daily lives of individuals like Lucy Thompson and Dorsey's Omaha informant, Two Crows (Buckley 1989, 1996). By doing so he created essentialized cultures and closed systems of spiritual renewal alike, which "could not move easily through time," as Julian Steward noted (1973).

In this book I have joined in complementary opposition with Kroeber, much as dance sides and camps do with each other, hoping that the tensions between our work, separated by almost a century now (from the beginning of his to the end of mine), might tend toward some broader understanding.

For Kroeber, the world renewal cult was a thing of the past. In view of the fact that the jump dance at Pecwan did survive (as did the Weitchpec deerskin dance, revived in 2000), and to make room for individuals like Lucy Thompson and Two Crows, we need a different understanding of culture, of specific cultural productions, and of contextualized spirituality, than those that Kroeber maintained. This is necessary because only through admitting individuality and history into interpretation can we move further toward comprehending how a jump dance, for instance, works to fix the world.

WORLD RENEWAL AS DISCOURSE

The dances continue to contain the elements that Kroeber and Gifford identified and to which they reduced Lucy Thompson's testimony. There could be no great dances without them. But world renewal cannot be reduced purely to these elements or to the structures that they form. Rather, renewal, fixing the world, is also the goal of a discourse into which these elements enter as central motifs or themes and is thus a process, something emergent, rather than a reduced "system," "pattern," or "organization."

Earlier ethnologists sought to reconstruct static systems on the basis of an imagined normative "native opinion." But no "culture," or analytic domain like "religion," or specific religious production like "the jump dance" can be comprehended (rather than explained) as a closed and static system. Stasis, finally, is antithetical to life, and human lives are what we are

trying to comprehend. Rather than an abstract assemblage of structural elements, social life as lived is the ever-emergent result of the "running back
and forth" (the etymological meaning of "discourse") through a community (however defined) of the thoughts and feelings and words and actions
of a plenitude of individuals, both in agreement and in conflict. It is also
a running back and forth between a broadly shared cultural ideology—a
received, ideal structure of yearning—and the inescapable facts of difference and change. This is what the two sides are engaged in at Pecwan.
While discourse *theory* may provide an interpretive mode for understanding what these people do, what they do *is* a mode of discourse, of oppositions simultaneously yearning toward wholeness.

Mikhail Bakhtin's understanding of discourse as "dialogue" may be
particularly helpful here (e.g., 1981). In this understanding, dialogue is
discourse on differences that leads to further ramified differences, not to
synthesis or any other order of lasting resolution. It differs, in this, from
classic dialectics. Dialogue is discourse on the irresolvable, and phenom-
ena like jump dances emerge through time from the differences among
people and between people's experience and their ideals. Paradoxically,
the transformation toward unity that Thompson and Heffner McClellan
write about, "fixing the world," can occur only through the dynamics of
difference between individuals, and between those individuals' experiences and their shared yearning. And it can lead only to reengaging these
dynamics with renewed vigor.

After the dances, for instance, participants often go off with their friends
to relax for a few days. Talk is usually about the dances and their side's successes in being better than the other side, and about dances to come, when
they'll have even more dancers, more and older regalia, and their side's
dance maker will again outdo the other's. Difference reasserts itself almost
immediately, though gently at first. The dance has indeed succeeded, but
only momentarily, as an acrobat on the high bar swings to the top and
comes momentarily to rest, feet straight up in the air in a beautiful but extraordinary posture, before swinging down again to hang by his hands and
swing again. A year and a half or so after a dance, people have lost the joy
and relief of the last dance's final moments. There is trouble, anger, illness,
maybe floods, pollution in the world. It is time to start working toward the
next dance, through careful negotiations with regalia owners and elders

and participants until people can come together again, putting aside bad thoughts, "lifting their prayers for continued proper existence."

The salvage ethnologists held that there was a closed system unknown, or at best dimly perceived, by the social actors themselves. But I am saying that there is no fixed system. Rather, systematicity constantly emerges through dialogic discourse on what does and does not belong in an ideal system that Indian people engaged in spiritual practice are fully capable of—indeed, dedicated to—imagining. In this, the progress of a single year's dance instantiates the immemorial general process.

DIALOGUES

As was every aspect of indigenous life, the world renewal dances were grievously affected by massive contact with whites, fomented by the California gold rush of 1849. One by one the dances were curtailed or extinguished throughout the region, although the Yurok jump dance at Pecwan was made more or less continuously until 1939. The Hupa deerskin dance at Takmilding was never entirely lost and reemerged strongly in the 1960s. In the 1970s the Karuk "world fixing" at Katamin was fully restored. In 1984 the Pecwan dance was once again held, to be repeated biennially through the present. The 2000 deerskin dance at Weitchpec was successful and is also expected to be repeated according to its old schedule. The Tolowa feather dance, comparable to Kroeber's world renewal dances, also has been given regularly again since the 1970s, on the Smith River, north of the Klamath.

All of these dances are, to a greater or lesser degree, interdependent, each depending to some extent on the participation of regalia owners, singers, and dancers from the other tribal groups, and they are also among the strongest expressions of autonomous group identities. Thus Heffner Mc-Clellan writes (1984: 28) that the dances "[reinforce] the bonds of Indian heritage, tribal identity, inter-tribal relations, and most important of all . . . [people's] bond to the spiritual world." To participate in the dances in any way is both to express one's Indianness and to become more Indian. For these reasons, the discourse on fixing the world in northwestern California today at once includes dialogues on being Yurok (or Hupa or Karuk), on being within the small world of native northwestern California, properly, and on being Indian. Indeed, all these dialogues implicate all the others simultaneously. Very often specific dialogues occur as debates.

Kroeber and Gifford's ethnological question was, what really belongs in the closed system of world renewal and what does not, whether or not native people recognize it? This, for instance, was the basis of Kroeber's interest in Mrs. Thompson's book. It is of note that world renewal discourse in northwestern California today is much concerned with the same questions, as might be expected in the midst of ongoing efforts to restore traditional ways correctly. Here is a sampling of debates that were in the air at the time of the Pecwan jump dance in 1988:

- Should dances be given up entirely, rather than doing them incorrectly and possibly causing the world harm?
- Do changes in materials and techniques for making regalia change its meaning and efficacy?
- Should male dancers appear nude under their deerskin wraps, as they did before the 1870s, or should they wear shorts as is currently the custom?
- What is the proper relationship between Christian believers and the dances? Should Christians be invited to pray at the non-Christian dances, in light of the high regard in which some Christians are held as spiritual leaders?
- What is the proper timing of dances? Should unscheduled jump dances be held in the high mountain spiritual precincts as they once were, in world emergency, or has the knowledge of these "calamity dances" been so completely lost that efforts to put them up now can only be destructive?
- What is the relationship between death and world renewal? Is a death during a dance a sign that mistakes are being made, or is it in fact a good time to die?
- And what is the appropriate role, if any, of non-Indians? Should they be permitted to dance? To be there at all?

These are not trivial questions. Rather, they were the organizing topics of some of the most intense spiritual, intellectual, and political dialogues in the region in 1988, and "fix-the-world people" took them very seriously. In part this is because dialogues on world renewal have far broader cultural relevance and purpose. World renewal discourse is a means of manifesting and enhancing regional native culture, and also for exploring its proper nature. The primary locus for these dialogues during the dances themselves is at the camps' tables, and there is a dialogue going on, including these verbal dialogues, between the (women's) camps and the (men's) dance pit. The fruits of discussions in the camps, in a sense, dance along with the regalia. At times discussions within and between the camps grow heated indeed. Not too long ago this dialogical process included terrible arguments between the two camps at a major dance, whose respective leaders were, at the time, vying for wider influence in the community they shared. The sacred fire was put out, regalia owners withdrew their "stuff" from both sides, the county sheriff was called in, and the dance ended with bad feelings all around, one leader going into seclusion in its aftermath. Things didn't settle down for months, and when they did, community life was changed—again.

It might seem that confrontations like this have nothing to do with world renewal per se, but that they are basically political, rather than spiritual, arguments. Such distinctions have to be made very carefully. It may be that "religion" and "politics" are usefully distinguished as analytic domains, but on the ground, so to speak, each is in dialogue with the other and all are subsumed in an overarching social discourse. This has been most easily recognized, by anthropologists, in small, face-to-face, "traditional" societies. It is what Arnold Pilling meant when he wrote that, among Yurok Indians on the Klamath, "law, health, and religion are all one topic" (1969). "Jump dance *is* politics," said an Indian friend. This is nothing new on the Klamath: "Sandy Bar Bob (ca. 1900) was considered a wealthy man because he was a responsible religious person whereas Sawmill Jack had little respect because he was not considered to be a religious person who was concerned for the community" (Heffner 1984: 12).

Again, one might think (as do, in fact, many of the more skeptical native people) that these religio-political-cultural disputes are clear signs that it is too late to restore the dances, whose true spirit has been lost. It is interesting then, to find that bitter acrimony and dispute over the correct way to do the dances seemingly goes back to earliest mythological times among the *wo·gey* and to have been quite common at human dances in the nineteenth century as well. Contention would seem to be in the very nature of the dances.

A Yurok myth, for example, tells of the efforts of Wohpekumew and nameless *wo·gey* to begin a new deerskin dance on the Pacific coast, south of the Klamath:

> At Melekwa, by the trail, on a big rock, they saw two men sitting. He said: "I come because I want to see you also have the [deerskin] dance." But they said to him, "No, I saw you, you tried it. You saw for yourself that you lost the song, because that sort is not good about here. It will be best not to have it." He said, "I thought it would be well." But they said, "No, we do not want it." . . . He looked across [the lagoon] and saw they were beginning at Hoslok. Those about to begin the dance were with Wohpekumew. Now he who had come was angry. As they were commencing, "That dance they shall not have here," he said, and blew out toward them. Thus he did. Then they all remained standing on the hill. One can see them now, those firs, standing like a Deerskin Dance. [Tskɪkɪ of Espeu, in Kroeber 1976: 197–98]

Such myths of the origins of the various dances, upon which the formal dance prayers are based, are accounts of trial and error, of failed attempts made by the *wo·gey* to do the dance correctly, for all time, and of their ultimate success. The Yurok deerskin and jump dances at Wečpus began this way:

> Then that one went to get his deerskin. When he brought it, he said, "This dance will be so. They will not begin in the morning. As long as this world lasts, if my dance is straight, they will begin toward evening. That is how it will be." Then toward evening they began. They began to make the dance from that place. They started down the sand beach. "How will they stand?" his friend asked him. "One will stand in the middle. He will face in the direction which I grew. Some will turn to Hupa. Some will face upriver. So we shall reach all those places with the dance." "Yes," he said. And then they began to dance there.
>
> In the morning his friend came over (from Pekʷtuł) again and said, "That (also) did not go right. I think something bad will happen. Let us try to dance in another place." "Yes. Let us wait until evening." Then they went to where the dance was to start. He said to them, "Try it (fac-

ing) downstream." Then they tried it. When they swayed their deerskins once the sticks broke off where they held them. "I think it will be best if we bring it up to where my house is," he said. Then they went uphill. When they came to where the dance place is (now), one of them said, "Let us try it here. Let the people go uphill; no one is to stand below. We shall stand in a row facing them, and hold the deerskins pointing uphill." Then they tried it so. When they saw it, they were happy. All felt good. Looking about, they saw everyone in the crowd smiling; some were laughing. The Wecpus young man said, "Well, how do you feel about it now?" "This is a good place. When I look away, I think that I see nearly the whole world, the day is so fine." [Lame Billy of Wečpus, in Kroeber 1976: 30–31]

Note how the *wo·gey*, too, set the dances for all time, instantiating an ideal structure, but then had to revise again, through dialogue (see also Spott and Kroeber 1942: 247). Like the founding First People, human beings today ultimately find that doing it right when they do it, seeing that "all feel good" at the end of a given dance, may be the best that they can do. Thus these myths suggest that the constant effort *to* get it right is of equal importance and interest to *getting* it right. If so, then what is going on in the constant debates over what is and what is not appropriate to the dances is not a historical aberration encountered in a culture "going all to pieces," as Kroeber had it; it is central to the process of world renewal, and always has been.[1]

And note that while Kroeber, too, sought a fixed system, valid for all times, he found as well that historical experience has always been at variance with the ideal. For example, while the origins of the Wečpus dances were attributed to the *wo·gey* of the mythical beforetime, Kroeber's informants knew that the dance had been inaugurated when the people of the town had become wealthy and influential enough to do so and held it to be to their political advantage (Kroeber and Gifford 1949: 66). Arnold Pilling (1978), another anthropologist with deep command of Yurok data, speculated that a dance came and went on the upper reaches of Blue Creek, above Pecwan, during relatively recent times, as a deerskin dance had perhaps come and gone, long before contact, at Wełk\ew (Spott and Kroeber 1942: 244). Again, the aboriginal details of scheduling that Kroeber reconstructed suggest that he and Gifford, despite their insistence on a closed system, were quite aware that the dances constitute processes within other, wider processes, rather than being static, ahistorical epistemic objects.

> Throughout our data, and in fact in earlier ones since Goddard [1903–4], there runs a wavering of native statements as to whether dances were made every year or every other year. . . . Many Indians seem to believe that in the good old days rituals were annual, and that the every-second-year schedule is a result of modern breakdown. Kroeber encountered this belief not only recently but more than forty years ago; and Goddard suggested it in 1903. It would therefore seem that indecisiveness in this matter is an old feature of the system, rather than a symptom of its decay. . . . In prosperous periods, there might be year-after-year dancing in a town for a while. But let the acorns or salmon be low, or sickness or death invade the strength of the leading household or two, and respites would be taken. [Kroeber and Gifford 1949: 129]

By the same token, Kroeber and Gifford knew that, despite the systemic ideal of settling or laying aside all outstanding litigation, quarrels, and deviling—all "bad thoughts"—before putting up or attending a dance (ibid.: 82), quarreling broke out at the dances themselves with some regularity, occasionally resulting in the truncation of the event (66, 68, 69–70, 78, 81–82). Heated arguments also resulted in changes in the planned transmission of esoterica for certain dances (97). Like the creator who turned his enemies into fir trees at Hosuluk in the beforetime, the elder who ostentatiously deviled a dance maker during a dance a few years ago was acting in a manner as old as the putatively ideal dance forms that many native people believe existed once, and seek today. Yet we notice that these local people have in the past, as today, declared that deviling is not permitted at the dances (Robert Spott, in Spott and Kroeber 1942).

CULTURAL POLITICS

People do not easily agree upon what the ideal forms once were, on how to seek them out today, or on appropriate ways to communicate about them. Efforts to resolve such issues are as significant and intense as the effort to

renew the dances themselves today and as intense as the First People's efforts to discover the correct forms at Wečpus and at Hosuluk, long ago.

For example, some people today claim that the appropriate epistemology is purely spiritual—that knowledge of the ideal dances can best
be rediscovered through asceticism, solitary vision-seeking, and inspiration by the spirit. Others hold that this charismatic approach is fraudu-
lent and that claims to spiritual inspiration represent political moves
rather than transcendent understandings (separating the two as do most
members of the dominant society and unlike the man who said that "jump
dance is politics" and whose statement may itself embody an ideal rather
than a fully operable conceptual reality). These people argue that the most
reliable route to safe and efficacious restoration of the dances is study with
elders and careful scholarship—largely, out of necessity, in the writings
of A. L. Kroeber who, while "he didn't know what things meant," at least
"got his facts right." The matters being debated here, of course, are not
limited to the dances, but concern the sources of authentic culture and appropriate modes of leadership in native communities as well.

In this debate, or dialogue, language plays a central role. The original
dance prayers, or "formulas" as Kroeber and Gifford had it, were once
couched in a special high register of ritual Yurok. This speech register identified the priests (now, "medicine men") with the *wo·gey*, to whom it was
attributed, and it gained some of its ritual power through the contrast it
formed with ordinary human speech. Use of this variety of speech also
identified any speaker as a member of the elite, the aristocracy whose su-
periority was evident in economic, intellectual, political, and spiritual as-
cendency alike (Buckley 1984b; cf. Sandy Bar Bob, above). As English became the first language along the lower Klamath, "high language" Yurok,
as a coherent register, disappeared. By the 1970s, ordinary Yurok, now fully
commanded only by a few elders, replaced the high register in ritual contexts as English replaced ordinary speech. In the mid-1980s these elders
began to succumb to old age, virtually en masse, and the younger generation of ritually active men and women, who spoke little or no Yurok, were
faced with a dilemma. What was the appropriate register of English to use
in religious contexts? High register English, "the way lawyers [and preach-
ers] talk," might be suitable, but it was identified with whites and with the

Christian churches from which the younger people tried to distance themselves. One solution has been sought in ordinariness itself.

An alternate or accompaniment to both modes of dance leadership—
charismatic and intellectual—has all along been to "just do it"—to act
with heart and head together, without too much show or talk. This, if anything, is seen as the "real" Indian Way by many and itself constitutes a
sort of ideal (as authenticity often does, in the world at large). It is difficult to achieve, resting on complete confidence—hard to acquire as one
feels one's way along in the risky task of dance restoration—and perhaps
especially so for those who are, like their old-time predecessors, among
an educated and cosmopolitan minority. The most active people in restoring the dances, naturally enough, are often intellectuals and artists and
other creative people with some experience in the world beyond the lower
Klamath, with its sophisticated talk.

One solution to the problem of speech that has been tried by some in
this group is "broken English," called "Indian English" by many whites.
This regional dialect connotes membership in a group of Indian people
who do "just do it," surrounded, as they say, by "inlaws and outlaws,"
maintaining the low profile, independence, and, often, the isolation and
poverty that are parts of the price of "living like a real Indian" in the
United States today. But the irony of invoking this speech in a group of
people most of whom have at least graduated from high school and many
of whom have college and graduate degrees is lost on no one. (The hot
reading among Yurok dancers at Pecwan in 1988 was Stephen W. Hawking's *Brief History of Time* [1988].) Again, of course, the issues are simultaneously political, spiritual, and cultural but, here, political in the acutely
modern terms of class conflict. There are other terms as well.

While ideally the dances "reinforce the bonds of inter-tribal relations,"
as Kathy Heffner McClellan wrote and Lucy Thompson witnessed, they
are also used as forums for manifesting the fissures in those regional relationships. This was especially true as regards Yurok and Hupa Indian
relations at the end of the twentieth century, mightily strained as these
were by decades of conflict over reservation lands and resources. Most
Hupa tribal activists, for instance, avoided the 1988 Pecwan jump dance,
because at the time of the dance, in Yurok territory, the Yuroks and Hupas

were embroiled in a particularly bitter altercation over the formal split-
ting of the reservation that they still shared then. It would have been bad
manners indeed for Hupas to bring those bitter feelings into the sacred
space of the dance, so they stayed away. The alternative would have been
to settle the dispute before the dance—as the old-time law required—and
that was out of the question, so tied up was it in dominant society court
and bureaucratic procedures. The issue was an especially painful one for
many who had deep affiliations with both of the somewhat artificially
constructed tribal groups.

DISCOURSE AS WORLD RENEWAL

"I wish the rains would come and wash all the bugs and ticks and spiders
and Yuroks down the river," said a man at the Hoopa Valley shopping
center in the late summer of 1988. "Don't say that," said a second man,
active in the great dances. "You'd wipe out half of your relatives."

I have presented some of the more heated dialogues on the lower Klamath in 1988 in binary terms—Christian *v.* non-Christian, Indian *v.* non-
Indian, Yurok *v.* Hupa, ordinary *v.* elite, life *v.* death, religion *v.* politics—
like the two sides with their separate camps at Pecwan. These dialogues
go on not only between individuals and groups, but—perhaps most important—within the minds of single individuals and in their hearts, where
alone the world may, finally, be renewed. What goes on in these dialogues
is not a zero-sum effort to establish one side as enduringly and isolatedly
superior: the winner. Such victories could only be Pyrrhic, when half of
one's friends and relatives are Hupa, or white, or Christian, or women, or
lawyers, or dance on the other side, or whatever. The real, realistic victory
comes in emulation of the two lead singers in a dance whose voices, when
they are both equally good, harmonize rather than strike a single note.

Nor I think is the effort in these dialogues directed to dialectically resolving differences in synthetic consensus, "unity." Rather, it seems to me
that the point—so entirely lost on those outsiders who have held "factionalism" to be the downfall of Native American communities, rather
than a creative means of social survival—is simply to keep talking, even

arguing. In this creative discourse, albeit occasionally disguised as creation's necessary complement, destruction, is the very renewal of the world that is fervently desired. As the old myths tell us, this discourse on the dances itself realizes the objective of the dances, fixing the world. "Jump dance is politics," yes, but politics is jump dance, too—a point that, like Kroeber's closed system, is perhaps most accessible to disengaged outsiders. Like some outsiders, most native people tend to see these disagreements as destructive "factionalism," far from the idealized unity that they seek through world renewal. But I disagree with them as well as with Kroeber! I see differences and distances from the ideal as crucial to creative action and expression and survival, as the loci of what is most vibrant and vital in the dances, as the very means through which the dances work. And so I enter the discourse on world renewal as on anthropology, too, hoping to offer encouragement rather than a further authoritarian inscription of meaning or proper method.

Of course, what I am representing as creative cultural life, the process through which an ancient regional culture constantly emerges in a tumult and dissonance of dialogues, renewing itself, approximates what Kroeber regarded as that culture's "going all to pieces." Yet it is what he himself witnessed, as regards the dances, and what the oldest myths speak of, too. We have no basis on which to believe that the dances ever manifested for more than a moment an ideal and fixed, or closed, system—and then only when the yearned-for "real Indian Way" had been earned, by doing. The "real" dances attributed by old-time people to the *wo·gey* and by contemporary people, as by Kroeber and Gifford, to the "real old-time Indians" encompass an ideal that people engage in dialogue with their own dissatisfactions, as a form of yearning: this immemorial dialogue is close to the very essence of spiritual practice, rather than evidence of decline.

The discourse on fixing the world includes dialogues on most of the largest-order questions of the day: life and death, language, gender, politics, identity, spirituality, survival, freedom. The marvel of Kroeber's "world renewal cult" is not its standing among the great "closed systems" of native America, but its flourishing anew among the great open processes to be found here. It is a master discourse that encourages dialogues on all of the culture and all of life for those who enter into it. The questions that arise within individuals but become manifest most clearly as differences between groups have no answers, immediate or otherwise. They might better be understood as longing than as argument. They will not be resolved through discussion or feud, either. Their function is to foment negotiation—even in violent forms—creating and recreating, renewing a discourse that is endless and, really, timeless. It has gone on, has been done, in northwestern California ever since the First People took it up in the beforetime.

Finally, what we have grown used to calling "the world renewal cult"—and, for that matter, "Yurok Indian culture"—are not things, epistemic objects, to be explained as systems only; they are open processes that, as long as they survive, defy all totalizing statements. The totality of fixing the world is ever-emergent, a product of subdiscourses, or dialogues. When this dialogue stops, world renewal will become a closed system, and fail.

Notes

INTRODUCTION

1. See Buckley 1987, 1989a, 1989b, 1991, 1996.
2. Among anthropologists, Arnold Pilling (1978) and Alfonso Ortiz (Tewa) (personal communication, 1982) both noted this continuing autonomy and cultural particularity.
3. I recall a wry man at the 1988 Pecwan jump dance who held an insulated plastic coffee mug in his hand, relaxing in one of the camps. With a black marker, he'd written "Two Rock" on the brownish-white, well-used mug. "Yes, I'm two rock," he smiled, "half You-rock and half Kay-rock."

In the 1980s, Puliklah was taken up by some Yuroks both as a more appropriate name for their linguistic, cultural, and historical group and also as a political tag. The Puliklah movement might best be described as politically radical and culturally conservative. To a large extent, its views lost out to those of more "progressive" (that is, politically conservative) interests as the emergent Yurok Tribe moved toward federal acknowledgment. This order of politics, important though it is, lies outside of the immediate concerns of the present book.

4.   *Wo·gey* is most literally translated "ancient" or "holy ones." Yuroks have more recently called these ancient culture-bringers "unseen beings," "First Nation People," "spirituals"; today, *wo·gey* seems to be coming back into usage, although in the 1970s and '80s its dominant meaning was "white men." Hupas today tend to call their equivalent spirits "Immortals." However these spirit people are named in English, most people adhering to old ways today agree that some of them are still in the world with us.

5.   Ideally, I think, readers should read Kroeber's *Handbook of the Indians of California* (1925), or at least pages 1–97 of this very large volume, before reading the present book—both to better appreciate Kroeber's enormous contribution in recording factual information on "the [hypothesized] Yurok" and to better understand the opposition that our work has joined in.

6.   Since 1993, the chronic poverty of the Yuroks has been somewhat alleviated by long-withheld timber payments, two small casinos, and other tribal investments and benefits of tribal organization.

7.   See Bean and Blackburn's now classic critique of Kroeber and other early ethnographers' failure to perceive subtle and intricate systems of social organization in aboriginal California as such (1976).

8.   In fact, native authors in northwestern California had been publishing their own accounts of their life-ways since 1916, and important books continued to appear in 1978 and beyond. See Chapter 3.

9.   As for the history of anthropological theory, from Herodotus or Montaigne or wherever you want to start, to Geertz or Clifford or wherever it is convenient to stop, while it has not led us to any inarguable epistemological conclusions, it makes of itself a good story for those with a taste for such abstruse tales—as George W. Stocking, Jr., another strong influence, was so usefully demonstrating throughout the postmodern hullaballoo.

10.   Some years ago, Kroeber's daughter, Ursula Le Guin, wrote me a thoughtful letter regarding an essay that I had published on Kroeber and on anthropological indifference to human suffering (Buckley 1989), advising me to "be careful." I continue to appreciate and to respect Ms. Le Guin's concern for her father's reputation, and do not suggest that Kroeber—who was generally apolitical—was in any sense personally a fascist or political totalitarian of any sort. The connection I've drawn between social-scientific totalization and political totalitarianism—a connection deeply plumbed in the voluminous works of Foucault—is cultural and historical, not personal.

CHAPTER I. THE YUROK RESERVATION

Epigraph: Verbatim transcription, tape recording, Requa, California, 1978. I made this tape at Mrs. Shaughnessy's request. She said, "I have a poem and I want you to write it down and, you know, make it nice." She was politely disappointed when I showed her the tape-transcript, typed out in prose paragraphs: she'd wanted it to *look* like a poem, with line breaks and stanzas. Here, I remedy my mistake. (Harry Roberts said that spiders and their webs protect camps and houses.)

1.   Robert Spott's address was arranged by Ruth Kellett Roberts. A socialite from Sonoma County and Piedmont, across the Bay from San Francisco, she was Harry Kellett Roberts's mother. Ruth Roberts was "Chairman of Indian Welfare of the Women's Federation for the district embracing the lower Klamath" (Graves 1929: 101). While Spott apologizes for his "broken" English in his 1926 address, the transcription of it hardly merits this description. The late Arnold R. Pilling suggested that Mrs. Roberts herself made the transcription, bringing Spott's "Indian English" into closer alignment with what she perceived to be standard English.

CHAPTER 2. DOUBLE HELIX

1.   A. L. Kroeber put Captain Spott's birth "around 1844" (Spott and Kroeber 1942: 147), while Arnold R. Pilling placed it ca. 1821 (Pilling fieldnotes, 1968): a considerable difference. Pilling gave 1911 as the year of the Captain's death, which is accurate, and people had told Pilling that the Captain was about ninety when he died; certainly he seemed older than sixty-seven and, in terms of cultural change during his lifetime, *was.*

For more on Captain Spott, an outstanding man of his generation, see Spott and Kroeber 1942: 144–52, and Kroeber 1976: 419–20.

2.   Here and below, Captain Spott's story bears striking similarities to the Yurok myth "The Inland Whale." Whether Robert Spott's definitive rendering of the narrative in English (Spott and Kroeber 1942) reflected his adoptive father's life, or whether the various renderings of that life I draw on here reflect the myth, or to what extent both are true, I don't know—but the similarities are obvious (see also T. Kroeber 1959).

3.   "The mysterious thing," *ʔumaʔah,* is putatively a small kit of miniature poison arrows with which a sorcerer (also *ʔumaʔah*) introjects a *teloget,* "pain," into the body of his victim from a distance. These arrows are associated with obsidian, rattlesnakes, and fire. The bundle itself may blaze with mystic heat, is unnaturally heavy, and stinks like rank angelica root. A person who owns one is said to "have a devil." Some say that Captain Spott's adoptive daughter, Alice, threw his *ʔumaʔah* away in disgust, after his death, and that it was enveloped in a fiery ball as she did so.

4.   Same-gender sexual and affectional preferences were certainly known among Yuroks in the past, as they are today, although the English "homosexual"

carries cultural connotations that do not necessarily represent these individuals accurately.

There were largely celibate "priests" some of whom may have had, nonetheless, same-gender sex. (Such men were also known to act as secondary inseminators of pregnant women.) There were certainly transvestite men, *wergern*, who did women's work, like basket weaving. Some but not all *wergern* were "homosexual"; some are known to have married women. Whatever the intricacies of sexual identity in the past, in the twentieth century homosexual men were controversial figures—indeed, they are sometimes referred to as "controversials" today. Robert Spott was caught up in this controversy, the more so because he was knowledgeable about basket weaving—women's work—whether or not he had a same-gender sexual preference.

At the same time, "high men" like Robert were expected to command a considerable amount of women's knowledge, as female doctors and other female sociological "men," *pegɹk*, commanded considerable male acumen. Alice Spott, Robert's sister, who had several husbands and many children, was highly respected as *numi pegɹk*, "very much a gentleman": she was a hunter, canoe-handler, and trained warrior.

A full discussion of Yurok gender would be a large undertaking. In lieu of it, and lacking full knowledge of the matter, I leave Robert Spott's sexuality ambiguous.

5.   The term is the all-purpose third-person inflection of the inalienable noun *hekcum*.

6.   Sgt. La Foret to commanding officer, Ft. Gaston, May 8, 1889; U.S. Army Archives, Carlisle, Pa.; courtesy of Sally McLendon.

7.   Seeing or hearing the *wo·gey* is not always profoundly portentous, but it was in Harry's case a sign that he had a "natural calling" to spiritual experience, the highest calling, more powerful than an inherited calling or one obtained by sheer will, through training.

8.   See Robert Spott's remarks about Sregon Jim in chapter 4, below.

CHAPTER 3. NATIVE AUTHORS

1.   I use the term "classic" to refer to Yurok culture before 1849—Kroeber's salvaged and reconstructed ethnographic present. This term seems preferable to "pre-contact" (which the Yuroks were not in 1849) or "aboriginal," which could imply historical stasis. Above all, "classic" suggests, it seems to me, the place that the earliest Yuroks to be described hold in contemporary Yurok consciousness.

2.   The late Arnold R. Pilling claimed to have collected a Yurok genealogy in the 1970s that reached back into the fifteenth century (personal communication, 1982).

3. Thompson's use of Christian analogies, as well as her motives, might be compared to those of her contemporary "Red Progressive," Dr. Charles Eastman.

4. Critics of *Our Home Forever* have pointed out that a team of non-Indian historical researchers, working for the Hupa tribe, played an important role in its composition. Yet I do not see this as reason to refute its authenticity as native-authored. All published writers receive support and help, from editors if no one else, and research colleagues often receive considerable assistance from other researchers.

Kroeber's role in the published version of Spott's "Yurok Narratives" has been suggested above. Lucy Thompson's *To the American Indian* was undoubtedly vetted by her husband, Jim Thompson, whose florid Victorian prose occasionally overwhelms her own, more straightforward (if poetic) writing. Jack Nelson received considerable support from his mentor and publisher, Rupert Costo (Cahuilla), in writing *When Our Worlds Cried*. The anthropologist Arnold R. Pilling contributed a good deal to Robert G. Lake, Jr.'s, *Chilula*, as the linguist William Bright assisted Julian Lang while Lang was writing *Ararapíkva* (both discussed below). Such collaborations, however, have often seemed to raise more—and different sorts of—questions in the cases of American Indian authors than in those of others, as though "Indians" aren't *supposed* to write. Full exploration of this situation would demand an entire, further chapter in the present book, which would fall outside of its objectives.

For my purposes, it suffices to deal with the named authors of the books under consideration in this chapter as simple indicators of the people who wrote them. However complex the actual circumstances of their composition may have been, what directly concerns me is not what help their authors received, but the degree to which the works attributed to them have been received by the communities that they represent as authentic and desired reflections of those communities' self-understandings.

5. Many other factors contributed to the easing of relationships between native and non-Indian scholars during the 1980s. Non-Indian advocacy anthropologists, like the late Arnold R. Pilling, were useful and supportive in the effort to stop construction of the GO-road—a protracted battle that, though ultimately lost, was of considerable importance in building awareness and solidarity among the new spiritual traditionalists. Others, like Lee Davis, did much to secure native access to the University of California's vast collection of northwestern Californian ethnographic materials—including a great many recordings of dance songs made by Kroeber at the beginning of the twentieth century. The annual California Indian Conference, bringing native and non-Indian experts together, beginning in the mid-1980s, has also been effective in bettering relationships between "anthros," "histos," and Indians. Many other factors and events have made important contributions to the process as well.

CHAPTER 4. SEEING WITH THEIR OWN EYES

1.   There are other aspects of being human as well—"shadows," *sa?awor*. At death the shadow should go away, not remain around as a ghost. A person who had the medicine for sending away ghosts of the recently dead used to say, *ko?l so·k hikok*, "the thing is gone," according to Florence Shaughnessy (lit., "something [gone] across [the river of the dead]"). My teachers didn't like to talk about this "thing," or "stuff," and I can say little more about it.

2.   I am uncertain of my transcription from my own poor tape recording here; the phrase can, however, be translated as "[motion] early [exclamative]," perhaps an idiomatic "move quick, hah!"

3.   Dewey George had a "war song" for the dance at peace settlements that tells of a man running to Hoopa to tell the Indian agent that his son had been killed. He translated this song as,

> Here he come
> running to the agency
> son been wiped out

4.   The transcription is Sylvia Beyer's. Beyer worked with Yuroks under A. L. Kroeber both in Berkeley and in northwestern California, where she stayed with the Lindgren family in Trinidad. While she was seemingly not much of a linguist (the formula given here does not represent identifiable Yurok speech), in 1990 Axel Lindgren (Yurok) remembered Beyer fondly as a welcomed guest, a family friend, and a conscientious field worker deputed by Kroeber to study, especially, Yurok doctors.

5.   The pharmacological effectiveness of *N. biglovii* is perhaps most vividly indicated in its use by doctors (chapter 5).

In northwestern California, use of tobacco has never been restricted to ritual or meditative practice. Older people, particularly, smoked simply for enjoyment, in the past as today. Some elders remember seeing old men sitting on the roofs of sweathouses smoking pipes of strong tobacco, falling over as the effects hit them, then sitting up to smoke again. It would seem that some tobacco was extremely soporific.

While scholars have concentrated on use of the white-flowered, mildly sedative *N. biglovii*, some people say today that there are, or were, also yellow- and blue-flowered varieties of native tobaccos, the former soporific, the latter stimulating. A contemporary Tolowa cultural expert says that there are five kinds of traditional tobacco, "one of which happens to be *Cannabis sativa*." Presumably, the fifth is *N. virginianica*, commercial cigarette tobacco.

It is hard to know if the tradition to which this man refers predates the twentieth century or not. Many people assume that marijuana smoking was first introduced by the Mexican migrant workers that local Indians met in the hops and lily bulb fields of northern California and southern Oregon in the early years of the century. Today many people consider marijuana use, like that of alcohol, antithetical to traditional spiritual practice.

J. P. Harrington's "Tobacco among the Karuk Indians of California" (1932) remains the most authoritative source on tobacco cultivation and use in classical native northwestern California. It is, in my opinion, an ethnographic treasure that has much to offer contemporary readers. In it, along with a great deal more, Harrington points out that *N. biglovii* closely resembles the *N. quadrivalvis* of the Mandan, Arkara, and Hidatsa of the upper Missouri.

On contemporary cultivation of marijuana by non-Indians in northwestern California, see Ray Raphael's *Cash Crop* (1985)—a more modest undertaking than Harrington's but one with its own virtues.

6.   Axel Lindgren, Sr. (b. 1890) recalled, in 1969, that the last two men using the Trinidad (Čurey) sweathouse were Saul (or "Old Čurey") and Mau (A. R. Pilling field notes, September 5, 1969). "Humpback Jim" may be another of Mau's names, or Charlie Morten and Axel Lindgren, Sr., may have had different recollections.

7.   I have argued elsewhere that after women were evicted from the sweathouses in mythic times, menstrual seclusion houses became their gendered equivalent as centers of spiritual training (Buckley 1988).

8.   In addition to abstentions, there are other traditional ways of making oneself pure. Men cut themselves with sharply edged flakes of white quartz, slashing their arms, legs, chest, and belly in different ways associated with different purposes (see Gifford 1958: 254)—a practice referred to as *ki pehpego* (Kroeber 1976: 381.5). (Kroeber's transcription should probably read *ki pehplego[s-].*) Robert Spott noted that *"peihpegos"* is a white rock from the mountains (Spott and Kroeber 1942: 245). The bleeding that results is held to purify a man's "spirit" or "life," *wewolo-cek̓*, as sweating purifies his body.

Harry Roberts, at least, had used purgatives as well, especially cascara bark, a laxative.

Men also once purified themselves after leaving the sweathouse and going to the sacred mountain precincts by sweating in a shallow pit where they built a fire and allowed it to burn down to coals. Then they covered the coals with fir boughs and lay down on top with a robe over them (Count 1934: 1–5). Sometimes this practice was combined with scarification and bleeding. Anafey Obee, in 1976:

> Those fellas—they went out into the mountains for luck or riches. They start with dry wood and take that green fir boughs. It makes a big smoke; it stinks. My father said he tried it. You go out in the mountains and build a fire and you lay on top of that. He had [cuts] across his belly. That smoke gets in and it irritates. You make luck that way. You steam out your impurities, your sins.

9.   Even with medicine for hunting luck, a hunter (ideally) must train to some extent before going out, getting clean and free of (especially) menstrual contam-

ination and "cleaning" his weapon as well, smoking it over a medicine fire and praying over it. Hunting songs and formulas may be sung and recited. (Tskɪkɪ of Espeu gave Kroeber a mythic narrative to be used as a hunting prayer, or "formula" [in Kroeber 1976: 198–200].) These practices were still very much alive in the 1970s, at least.

10.   See, for example, the myth of the Inland Whale (in Spott and Kroeber 1942) that begins by telling of a power place, a lake in the mountains, that may be seen only by those who are pure. Florence Shaughnessy stressed that this was probably the single most important piece of information for understanding this highly esoteric narrative of power acquisition. Theodora Kroeber (1959) popularized this narrative as a love story and proto-novel, writing a lovely tale but obscuring somewhat the Yurok original's mythic and esoteric profundity.

CHAPTER 5. DOCTORS

1.   See Erikson 1943; Beyer 1934–35; Count 1934; Louisa Lindgren (in Lindgren 1983b).

2.   Erikson 1943; Roheim 1950; Posinsky 1956, 1957; Valory 1970; Bushnell and Bushnell 1977.

3.   Valory's doctoral dissertation, "Yurok Doctors and Devils: A Study in Identity, Anxiety, and Deviance" (1970), is, as its title suggests, yet another product of the Eriksonian cottage industry of Yurok cultural psychoanalysis. As such, it is anachronistic. Nonetheless, while Valory's accounts of doctors are mainly drawn from already available sources, he did original fieldwork and extensive interviewing, gathering entirely fresh ethnographic and historical materials on the ʔumaʔah that are both unprecedented in the received literature and very interesting. This important material should be made more widely available in published form.

4.   The Tolowa equivalent of the Yurok ʔumaʔah is called t'Σ'na:gi, "at night travels" (Drucker 1937: 258).

5.   Lit., "What? Here still you tied up"

6.   That is, in return for the wealth the young man must keep the devil's human identity secret.

7.   Recorded by Diana Heberger in 1975. Retranscribed by Carrie Lilly in 1989.

8.   Holt (1946: 326) says that Shasta sorcerers also turned themselves into dogs.

9.   Valory heard something very similar from another Yurok woman, a version that has an annoyed camper shoot the devil in the anus with an arrow (Valory 1970: 128). The most common version has people camping in the mountains. They hear a devil whistling and poking around in the brush and trying to blow out the fire. Someone throws a rock into the night and hits him: "a·gah," etc.

10.   Point St. George, north of modern Crescent City, is in Tolowa country. Again, Ella Norris had both Yurok and Tolowa heritage and spoke both languages.

11.   The cry of the timber owl itself is an ill omen, but the bird may also be a transformed human sorcerer, come to "devil" people. Either way, it's bad news.

12.   These prayers against the power of timber owls' messages are common up and down the Northwest Coast. Edward Sapir transcribed and translated a complete Takelma "formula" from Washington State, used for this purpose, as well as one "for when Hooting-owl talks" (Sapir 1909: 195).

13.   *Teno·* = "to be much"; *wok* = "he/she." Robins (1958: 255) gives "educated person" for the nominal *teno·wok*. Mrs. Shaughnessy did not mention purchasing or inheriting prayers, although it is clear that at least part of the "educated person's" knowledge came by these means.

14.   This would have been on the fourth morning after they had been on Red Mountain, since the dance lasts for three nights and ends after dawn on the fourth day. Usually today dances start on a Thursday evening and end early Sunday morning, with Friday being a "rest day."

15.   See Spott and Kroeber (1942: 157) where a doctor sees a *hegwono·*, a mythical bird, "come to the shadow" of someone who had broken the law, indicating his guilt.

16.   Robins (1958: 205) phonemically transcribes the Yurok word as *kegey*—the rendering I use throughout this book. Kroeber gave it as *kegeior* (1925: 66), as *kegei* (Spott and Kroeber 1942), and as *kigei* (in Elmendorf 1960). The Yurok writer Lucy Thompson gives it as *kay-gay.* Howard Berman (letter, 1990) suggests that *kegeior* is a variant of *kegey* and should be phonemically rendered *kegeyor.* He has given the plural as *kegeyowor* (Berman 1982: 201). All of the Yurok-speaking elders with whom I have worked have referred to these people in English as "doctors" or "Indian doctors."

Gifford (1958: 251) gives *k:ein* as a Karuk equivalent and Drucker (1937: 258) gives *t'i':nun* for Tolowa.

17.   Both Calvin Rube and Georgina Matildon (Hupa) were said to have inherited power from the doctor Nancy Rube at her death (above). In Robert Spott's accounts of Fanny Flounder's career, however, Fanny turns down her mother's offer of help in order to get her power on her own, knowing that her power would then be greater and independent of others' claims (Spott and Kroeber 1942; Robert Spott, in Beyer 1933–34).

18.   There has been a long and inconclusive debate about the place of guardian spirits in Yurok religious thought and in doctors' training (Beyer 1933–34; Spott and Kroeber 1942; Kroeber, in Elmendorf 1960; Valory 1970). Other than the *wesk^weloy* and the *kegeyowor*, Yuroks did not seem to seek guardian spirits as, for instance, people famously do in the Plateau culture area. However, earlier writ-

ers on Yurok culture seem to have largely ignored *ʔekonor* (from *ʔekonem-*, "to hold," "to keep"), personal spirit-guardians, "guardian angels" that protect every individual.

The argument over guardian spirits spun on without reference to these popular guardians and revolved instead around whether or not the doctors' "pains," *telogeł*, were animate manifestations of their guardian spirits. It was an argument determined by now anachronistic typological, comparative concerns and muddled by inconclusive interviews with Yurok experts who neither shared these concerns nor seem to have shared, consistently, the discursive presuppositions of their interlocutors. I do not address this controversy as such in the following. It will become clear that 1) Yurok *kegeyowor* had spirit-helpers that appeared to them in both anthropomorphic and animal forms, and 2) doctors' *telogeł*, shamanic power objects, were enlivened by the life spirits (*wewolocek̓*) of these guardian spirit–like helpers. Systematizing these facts as a theory of guardian spirits and their powers does not seem to have been a traditional Yurok concern, although it once amounted to an anthropological obsession.

19.   Lewana Brantner (Yurok) said that there were once many trails up to Doctor Rock from the villages on the river—from Bluff Creek, Martin's Ferry, Blue Creek, Katimin, and from the Smith River as well. She said that when doctors ran down from the rock toward the mouth of the river they "pulled out" of their trance on Red Mountain, upstream from Requa (USDA/FS 1979a).

20.   The use of a strap—reportedly about twenty feet long—to restrain the novice as she ran in a frenzy (*kełpeyew-*) brings to mind the similar restraint of Hamatsa (Cannibal Society) initiates among the Kwakwa̲ka'wakw and again reminds us of Kroeber's and others' classification of the Yuroks as in part Northwest Coast people.

21.   Harry Roberts spoke often of the importance of keeping trails clean by cutting overhanging brush and removing detritus, especially if the trail was to be used in making medicine. I have heard from others of cleaning the trail from Blue Creek to Doctor Rock that is now called the Golden Stairs. The spiritual significance of these acts is perhaps suggested by the range of meanings incorporated in the *kegey*'s "making her path into the mountains."

22.   Drucker writes (1937: 257), regarding stage 1, above, that "A potential [Tolowa] shaman often received her call in a dream, it is true. These dreams, however, were vague and served only to indicate that her quest for power would be successful. One dreamt 'about the mountains' (since the pains came from the mountains), or 'about the sunrise' (whose colors indicate the color of the pains the dreamer will obtain)."

23.   Compare with Thompson's (1916: 40) depiction of the *kegeyowor* as "seers" and with Eliade's generalization that the shaman sees the soul of his client (1964: 8). Both this technique and the theory of illness that it reflects (that disease is

caused by intruded objects) are common throughout the native North American west (Jorgensen 1980: 296).

24.   Arnold R. Pilling notes, Yurok Book XLVIL 19, 1975.

25.   Although Fanny Flounder was among the last of the "high doctors," her fame today—like that of Robert and Alice Spott—also depends in part upon the fact that she talked with many ethnographers and other visitors. This reflected not only her openness to outsiders but (like the Spotts) her physical accessibility: she lived on the coast within relatively easy reach of San Francisco and Berkeley by automobile. It may well be that her seeming dominance of the ethnographic record reflects this simple fact as much as her—indeed impressive—accomplishments and the rarity of *kegeyowor* in her era. And it may be that this dominance obscures the reputations and accomplishments of other, more physically remote shamans active during her lifetime, however few they may have been.

26.   Mrs. Norris was referring to the GO-road controversy (chapter 6).

27.   The lake in the mountains where the Inland Whale lives. See Spott and Kroeber (1942: 24–27).

28.   Mr. Roberts's account resonates with Aileen Figueroa's childhood memory of her mother, the Shaker doctor Maggie Pilgrim, healing Aileen's sore shoulder with her hand. Mrs. Figueroa said she could feel heat emanating from her mother's hand.

Kroeber (in Spott and Kroeber 1942: 158) wrote that upon occasion the doctor "does no more than touch the patient with her fingertips and blow the cause of illness away from these." Cora DuBois (1940: 91) reported that Albert Thomas sent out bolts of power in a long spark, "like electricity," from the tip of his index finger. Comparable reports on Essie Parish and other Pomo doctors, however, stress that the power is channeled through the middle finger.

When spirit appears as light it is usually reported, by Yuroks, as being blue—as in the blue light seen above Burrill Peak by those who are pure. One of Calvin Rube's students reported that the human body is surrounded by blue light that is dark when the individual's spiritual capacity is strong, growing lighter as he grows spiritually weaker.

29.   It sounds as though the *kegey,* Mary Williams, was in mourning.

30.   The five Yurok "world renewal" dances on the lower Klamath were centered at Wełkʷew, Rekʷoy, Pekʷon, Kepel, and Wečpus. There were once also dances on the coast south of the mouth of the Klamath at ʔolekʷ and ʔoketey (Kroeber and Gifford 1949). Pilling (1978) speculates that there was once a dance high on Blue Creek at the village of O·luʔuk, given up when the village was flooded out and before any record was made of it. Mrs. Norris referred to the five major post-contact downriver dances and to the politico-ceremonial "dance districts" named after their central villages.

31.   "*wi lohego*" should probably be *wi lo?hego?l*, "he goes to make the dam." Robins (1958: 217) gives *lo?* as a noun, "chief builder of the Fish Dam at Kepel." Waterman and Kroeber (1938: 52) give "*lo?ogen*" as the name of the dam itself.
32.   Kroeber (in Kroeber and Gifford 1949: 87) gives "wes'ona tigerem, 'reciting to the sky,' " and "wer-ergerk tigerem, 'reciting in his sweathouse.' "
33.   The prayer is in the Kroeber Papers, Bancroft Library, University of California–Berkeley, Box 7.

CHAPTER 6. THE GO-ROAD

1.   Analytically, the mountains are a segment of the *axis mundi,* symbolized by the center poles of sweathouses in the riverine villages where human beings train and get clean before going up into the mountains. These center poles "hold up the sky" and, in Mrs. Norris's story, terminate in the great oak in the middle of the Sky World.
2.   Abalone Woman is a powerful and problematic figure. Greedy, clinging, she is usually a cautionary presence. But it is interesting that, in this story, her tears became women's wealth—abalone shells. An abalone shell is also central to Tolowa girls' puberty ceremonies.
3.   Blue Creek runs down from Elk Valley to the Klamath, a significant tributary that enters the river near Pecwan. The "Golden Stairs," the doctors' trail leading up to the High Country, takes off from the Blue Creek drainage and leads up to Doctor Rock.
4.   Kathy Heffner McClellan managed to stay on at Six Rivers, where she was to write a series of exemplary reports on a variety of ethnographic and ethnohistorical topics pertinent to Forest Service management of lands claimed as part of regional Indians' aboriginal territories (e.g., Heffner 1983, 1984, 1985, 1986a, 1986b, 1986c).
5.   To some extent, contemporary non-Indian environmental romanticism reflects widespread native views, which have, of course, profoundly influenced it, but in others ways the two views couldn't be more culturally dissimilar. As Vine Deloria says, "Inherent in the very definition of 'wilderness' is contained the gulf between the understandings of the two cultures. Indians do not see the natural world as a wilderness" (1992: 281).
6.   Contrast this approach with that taken by the Israeli Knesset in the Israeli Holy Places Law of 1967:

> 1) The Holy Places shall be protected from desecration and any other violations, and from anything likely to violate the freedom of access of the members of the various religions to the places sacred to them, or their feelings with regard to those places, and, 2) whoever desecrates or otherwise violates a Holy Place shall be liable to imprisonment for a term of seven years. [In Nabokov, 1981: 5.]

CHAPTER 7. THE ONE WHO FLIES ALL AROUND THE WORLD

1.   The mythological synopsis below is based primarily on Yurok narratives contained in Kroeber's *Yurok Myths* (1976), collected between 1900 and 1907. "Great Money" was not often spoken of on the Klamath in the years I spent there, in the 1970s–80s. Since the early years of the twentieth century, the trickster-creator Wohpekumew has increasingly been spoken of as *the* Creator, the other mythical world-makers becoming increasingly obscure.

2.   Florence Shaughnessy remembered her foster father's descriptions of Yurok men skipping gold coins across the Klamath River in the 1860s, both in contempt of *wo·gey ci·k* and because they were pretty, flashing in sunlight before sinking into the mud.

3.   "Headdress" isn't used much locally. People say, "We don't wear dresses on our heads!"

CHAPTER 9. MELANCHOLY

1.   The emergence of prominent male doctors, whose traditional roles Kroeber had notably underplayed, and the replacement of sucking by various forms of touch both were interpreted by ethnologists as signs of cultural disintegration and a resulting cultural "slovenliness" in twentieth-century Indian doctoring in northern California (Spott and Kroeber 1942; DuBois 1940: 97, 103).

2.   This understanding of an entire hypothesized people as both fitting subjects for Freudian analysis and as developmentally arrested went largely unquestioned until the mid 1970s, when John and Donna Bushnell began to critically examine the cultural presuppositions that underlay the entire debate (Bushnell and Bushnell 1977). Even so, psychopathological analyses of native northwestern Californian cultures as "crying children" remained common into the 1980s, when Richard Keeling described their ritual singing as based in "hysterical" weeping (1982b). It was not until the 1990s that Erikson's wholesale "infantilization" of American Indians—Yuroks and Pine Ridge Lakotas in particular—was closely examined and critically deconstructed (Elrod 1992).

3.   See Valory 1970: 2. On the discourse on "hysteria" contributing to "a form of sexual theater" in which 1) native shamans of both genders are compared to Western women and, thus, 2) the reality of their pain trivialized and questioned, see Morris 1991: 112.

4.   Fanny Flounder was considerably older than Robert Spott, and Spott would seem to be quoting a secondary oral source and speaking interpretatively here and in the following.

5.   *New York Times Book Review,* February 16, 1997: 24.

6.   Hamlet II:2. Quoted by Freud (1917–25) in a footnote.

7.   Note Carlos Castaneda's bowdlerization of this familiar metaphor in his best-selling shamanic fiction, *A Separate Reality* (1971).

8.   *teloget* incorporates the stem *tel-*, "to be ill."

CHAPTER 10. THE SHAKER CHURCH

1.   The comparison was at least in part based on an interesting similarity: Wohpekumew tried to kill his Immortal son, Kapuloyo, imprisoning him high in a tree, and blinded his own grandson, Kewomer. Wohpekumew did not try to sacrifice Kapuloyo and Kewomer to save humanity, however, but to facilitate his own seductions of women. Happily, Kapuloyo resurrected himself by his own wits and restored Kewomer's sight. Together they went to the spirit world, abandoning Wohpekumew (Kroeber 1976).

2.   The English term "half doctor" alluded to the fact that, although the new doctors had been spiritually called and trained, they had either failed to cap their training by passing an "examination" in the mountains or had not danced the doctor dance in their villages successfully. Thus they had done only half of what was traditionally required—as a person who married without the exchange of full bridewealth was once said to be "half married."

3.   A parallel may be found in the rejection by many younger Indian people in the Southwest and elsewhere of the Peyote Way and the Native American Church of their fathers and grandfathers.

CHAPTER 11. JUMP DANCE

1.   This ongoing effort seems reflected in Julian Lang's understanding that, when the human jump dance is finished, the Spirit People immediately begin their own jump dance in the Spirit World. Whether this reflects a Karuk understanding only, or whether Yuroks share it, I do not know.

References

Aaland, Mihkel
    1978   *Sweat*. Santa Barbara: Capra Press.

Abu-Lughod, Lila
    1991   Writing against culture. In *Recapturing Anthropology: Working in the Present,* edited by Richard G. Fox. Santa Fe, N. Mex.: School of American Research Press.

American Anthropological Association
    1979   *Anthropology Newsletter* (October): 4.

Appadurai, Arjun
    1991   Global ethnoscapes: Notes and queries for a transnational anthropology. In *Recapturing Anthropology: Working in the Present,* edited by Richard G. Fox. Santa Fe, N. Mex.: School of American Research Press.

Arnold, Mary Ellicott, and Mabel Reed
    1957   *In the Land of the Grasshopper Song*. New York: Vantage Press.

Axtell, James

1981   *The European and the Indian: Essays in the Ethnohistory of Colonial North America.* New York and Oxford: Oxford University Press.

Bakan, David

1968   *Disease, Pain, and Sacrifice: Toward a Psychology of Suffering.* Chicago: University of Chicago Press.

Bakhtin, Mikhail

1981   *The Dialogic Imagination: Four Essays,* translated by C. Emerson and M. Holquist. Austin: University of Texas Press.

Barnes, R. H.

1984   *Two Crows Denies It: A History of Controversy in Omaha Sociology.* Lincoln: University of Nebraska Press.

Barnett, Homer G.

1957   *Indian Shakers: A Messianic Cult of the Pacific Northwest.* Carbondale: Southern Illinois University Press.

Bean, Lowell John, and Thomas C. Blackburn, eds.

1976   *Native Californians: A Theoretical Retrospective.* Socorro, N. Mex.: Ballena Press.

Benedict, Ruth

1934   *Patterns of Culture.* Boston: Houghton Mifflin.

Berg, Peter

1978   *Reinhabiting a Separate Country: A Bioregional Anthology of Northern California.* San Francisco: Planet Drum Books.

Berman, Howard

1982   A Supplement to Robins's Yurok-English Lexicon. *International Journal of American Linguistics* 48(2): 197–222.

Beyer, Sylvia

1933–34   Untitled MS on Yurok doctoring. Kroeber Papers, carton 7. Archives, Bancroft Library, University of California, Berkeley.

Bierhorst, John, ed.

1983   *The Sacred Path: Prayers & Power Songs of the American Indians.* New York: William Morrow.

Biolsi, Thomas

1997   The anthropological construction of Indians: Haviland Scudder McKeel and the search for the primitive. In *Indians and Anthropologists: Vine Deloria Jr. and the Critique of Anthropology,* edited by Thomas Biolsi and Larry J. Zimmerman. Tucson: University of Arizona Press.

Blackburn, Thomas C.

1976   Ceremonial integration and social interaction in aboriginal California. In *Native Californians: A Theoretical Retrospective*, edited by Lowell John
Bean and Thomas C. Blackburn. Socorro, N. Mex.: Ballena Press.

Bledsoe, A. J.

1885   *Indian Wars of the Northwest: A California Sketch*. San Francisco: Bea-
con.

Bourdieu, Pierre

1978   *Outline of a Theory of Practice*, translated by R. Nice. Cambridge:
Cambridge University Press.

Bruner, Edward M.

1986   Ethnography as narrative. In *The Anthropology of Experience*, edited
by Victor Turner and Edward M. Bruner. Urbana: University of Illinois
Press.

Buckley, Thomas

1976   The "High Country": A summary of new data relating to the
significance of certain properties in the belief systems of northwestern California Indians. In Environmental Statement, Six Rivers National Forest, Gasquet-Orleans Road, Chimney Rock Section, edited by Douglas R. Leisz. San
Francisco: USDA Forest Service.

1978   Sacred sites as commodities: Federal definition of cultural
resources. Paper presented at the Annual Meeting of the American Anthropological Association, Los Angeles. Typescript, Special Collections,
Humboldt State University Library, Arcata, Calif.

1979   Doing your thinking: Aspects of traditional Yurok education.
Parabola 4(4): 29–37.

1980   Monsters and the quest for balance in native northwestern Califor-
nia. In *Manlike Monsters on Trial: Early Records and Modern Evidence*, edited by
Marjorie Halpirn and Michael M. Ames. Vancouver: University of British
Columbia Press.

1982   Reply to Miller. FES: Chimney Rock Section, Six Rivers National
Forest. San Francisco: USDA Forest Service.

1984a   Living in the distance. *Parabola* 9(3): 64–79.

1984b   Yurok speech registers and ontology. *Language in Society* 13(4):
467–88.

1986   Lexical transcription and archaeological interpretation: A rock feature complex from northwestern California. *American Antiquity* 51(3):
617–18.

1987   Dialogue and shared authority: Informants as critics. *Central Issues
in Anthropology* 7(1): 13–23.

1988   Menstruation and the power of Yurok Women. In *Blood Magic: The Anthropology of Menstruation*, edited by Thomas Buckley and Alma Gottlieb. Berkeley and Los Angeles: University of California Press.

1989a   Kroeber's theory of culture areas and the ethnology of northwestern California. *Anthropological Quarterly* 62(1): 15–26.

1989b   Suffering and the cultural construction of others: Robert Spott and A. L. Kroeber. *American Indian Quarterly* 13(4): 437–45.

1991   Kroeber, Alfred L. In *International Dictionary of Anthropology*, edited by Christopher Winters. New York: Garland. Pp. 364–67.

1996   "The little history of pitiful events": The epistemological and moral contexts of Kroeber's Californian ethnology. In *Volksgeist as Method and Ethic: Essays on Boasian Ethnography and the German Anthropological Tradition*, edited by George W. Stocking. History of Anthropology 8. Madison: University of Wisconsin Press.

Bushnell, John
1968   From American Indian to Indian American: The changing identity of the Hupa. *American Anthropologist* 70: 1108–16.

Bushnell, John, and Donna Bushnell
1977   Wealth, work, and world view in native northwest California: Sacred significance and psychoanalytic symbolism. In *Flowers of the Wind*, edited by Thomas Blackburn. Socorro, N. Mex.: Ballena Press.

Castaneda, Carlos
1971   *A Separate Reality*. New York: Simon and Schuster.

Chadwick, David
1994   *Thank You and OK! An American Zen Failure in Japan*. New York: Penguin.

Champaigne, Duane
1998   American Indian studies is for everyone. In *Natives and Academics: Researching and Writing about American Indians*, edited by Devon A. Mihesuah. Lincoln: University of Nebraska Press.

Chartkoff, Joseph L., and Kerry K. Chartkoff
1975   Late period settlement of the middle Klamath River of northwestern California. *American Antiquity* 40: 172–79.

Chatwin, Bruce
1981   *The Songlines*. London: Jonathan Cape.

Clifford, James
1988   *The Predicament of Culture: Twentieth Century Ethnography, Literature, and Art*. Cambridge: Harvard University Press.

Cody, Bertha Parker
    1942   Some Yurok customs and beliefs. *Masterkey* 16(5): 81–86.

Cook, Sherburne F.
    1976   *The Conflict between the California Indian and White Civilization.*
    Berkeley and Los Angeles: University of California Press.

Count, Earle
    1934   Interview with Robert Spott. MS in Kroeber Papers, carton 7.
    Archives, Bancroft Library, University of California, Berkeley.

de Angulo, Gui
    1995   *The Old Coyote of Big Sur. The Life of Jaime de Angulo.* Berkeley, Calif.:
    Stonegarden Press.

de Angulo, Jaime
    1950   Indians in overalls. *Hudson Review* 3(3): 237–77.

Deloria, Vine, Jr.
    1969   *Custer Died for Your Sins: An Indian Manifesto.* New York: Avon.
    1981   Identity and culture. *Daedalus* 110(2): 13–37.
    1992   Trouble in high places: Erosion of American Indian rights to
    religious freedom in the United States. In *The State of Native America:
    Genocide, Colonization, and Resistance,* edited by M. Annette Jaimes. Boston:
    South End Press.
    1997   Conclusion: Anthros, Indians, and planetary reality. In *Indians and
    Anthropologists: Vine Deloria Jr. and the Critique of Anthropology,* edited by
    Thomas Biolsi and Larry J. Zimmerman. Tucson: University of Arizona
    Press.

Deutsch, Eliot, trans.
    1968   *The Bhagavad Gita.* New York: Holt, Rinehart, and Winston.

Dolgin, Janet L., David S. Kemnitzer, and David M. Schneider, eds.
    1977   *Symbolic Anthropology: A Reader in the Study of Symbols and
    Meanings.* New York: Columbia University Press.

Driver, Harold
    1939   Culture elements distribution vi: Northwest California. *Anthropo-
    logical Records* 1(2): 52–154.

Drucker, Philip
    1937   The Tolowa and their southwest Oregon kin. *University of California
    Publications in American Archaeology and Ethnology* 36(4): 221–300.

DuBois, Cora
    1940   Wintun ethnography. *University of California Publications in Ameri-
    can Archaeology and Ethnology* 36(1): 1–148.

Durkheim, Émile

1938   *The Rules of the Sociological Method,* translated by S. A. Solovoy and J. H. Mueller. New York: The Free Press. [1895]

Eaglewing, Chief, and Mrs. Eaglewing

1938   *Indian Legends of California: Peek-wa Stories.* Los Angeles: B. N. Robertson.

Eliade, Mircea

1964   *Shamanism: Archaic Techniques of Ecstasy,* translated by Willard R. Trask. Bollingen Series 76. Princeton: Princeton University Press. [1951]

Elmendorf, William W.

1960   *The Structure of Twana Culture, with Comparative Notes on the Structure of Yurok Culture by A. L. Kroeber.* Monograph Supplement 2, *Research Studies* 28(3). Washington State University.

Elrod, N.

1992   *500 Years of Deception, A Classic Case in the Twentieth Century: Erik H. Erikson's Portrayal of the Native Americans,* translated by C. Brooks. Zurich: Althea Verlag.

Erikson, Erik H.

1943   Observations on the Yurok: Childhood and world image. *University of California Publications in American Archaeology and Ethnology* 35(10): 257–302.

1963   *Childhood and Society.* New York: W. W. Norton. Second edition. [1950]

Falk, Donald

1958   Lyng v. Northwest Indian Cemetery Protective Association: Bulldozing First Amendment protection of Indian sacred lands. *Ecology Law Quarterly* 16(2): 515–70.

Field, Les

1999   Complicities and collaborations: Anthropologists and the "unacknowledged tribes" of California. *Current Anthropology* 40(2): 193–201.

Field, Margaret A.

1993   Genocide and the Indians of California. M.A. thesis, Department of History, University of Massachusetts, Boston.

Flaherty, Gloria

1992   *Shamanism and the Eighteenth Century.* Princeton: Princeton University Press.

Fogelson, Raymond D.

1974   On the varieties of Indian history: Sequoyah and Traveller Bird. *Journal of Ethnic Studies* 2: 255–63.

1989   The ethnohistory of events and nonevents. *Ethnohistory* 36(2): 133–47.

Fox, Richard G., ed.
1991   *Recapturing Anthropology: Working in the Present.* Santa Fe, N. Mex.: School of American Research Press.

Frank, Jerome
1974   *Persuasion and Healing: Comparative Study of Psychotherapy.* New York: Schocken.

Frederick, Paula
1996   Review of *Disciplined Hearts: History, Identity, and Depression in an American Indian Community* by Theresa DeLeane O'Nell. *Harvard Graduate School Alumni Association Newsletter,* Summer.

Freud, Sigmund
1917–25 Mourning and melancholia. In *The Standard Edition of the Complete Psychological Works of Sigmund Freud,* edited and translated by James Strachey et al. London: Hogarth Press. [1953]

Friedman, Lawrence J.
1999   *Identity's Architect: A Biography of Erik H. Erikson.* New York: Scribner.

Geertz, Clifford
1973   *The Interpretation of Cultures.* New York: Basic Books.

Gibbs, George
1854–57 Observations on the Indians of the Klamath River and Humboldt Bay, accompanying vocabularies of their languages. Bureau of American Ethnology MS 196-b.

Gifford, E. W.
1958   Karok confessions. *Miscellanea Paul Rivet Octogenario Dictata,* Vol. 1. Mexico City: Universidad Nacional Autonoma de Mexico.

Gill, Sam
1988   *Native American Religious Action: A Performance Approach to Religion.* Columbia: University of South Carolina Press.

Goddard, Pliny E.
1903–4 Life and culture of the Hupa. *University of California Publications in American Archaeology and Ethnology* 1(1): 1–88.
1914a   Texts of the Chilula Indians of California. *University of California Publications in American Archaeology and Ethnology* 10(6): 265–88.
1914b   Notes on the Chilula Indians of California. *University of California Publications in American Archaeology and Ethnology* 10(6): 290–380.

Goldman, Irving
1975   *The Mouth of Heaven: An Introduction to Kwakiutl Religious Thought.*
New York: John Wiley & Sons.

Goldschmidt, Walter
1940   A Hupa calendar. *American Anthropologist* 42: 176–77.
1951   Ethics and society: An ethnological contribution to the sociology of
knowledge. *American Anthropologist* 53(1), part 1: 506–24.

Goldschmidt, Walter R., and Harold E. Driver
1940   The Hupa white deerskin dance. *University of California Publications
in Archaeology and Ethnology* 35(8): 103–42.

Gould, R. A., and Furukawa Theodore Paul
1964   Aspects of ceremonial life among the Indian Shakers of Smith
River, California. *Kroeber Anthropological Society Papers* 31: 51–67.

Graves, Charles S.
1929   *Lore and Legends of the Klamath River Indians.* Yreka, Calif.: Press of
the Times.

Gurdjieff, G. I.
1968   *Meetings with Remarkable Men.* New York: E. P. Dutton.

Haley, Brian D., and Larry B. Wilcoxon
1997   Anthropology and the making of the Chumash tradition. *Current
Anthropology* 38: 761–94.

Harrington, J. P.
1932   Tobacco among the Karuk Indians of California. *Bulletin of the Bureau of American Ethnology* 94.

Hawking, Stephen
1988   *A Brief History of Time: From the Big Bang to Black Holes.* New York:
Bantam Books.

Heffner, Kathy
1983   Ethnohistoric study of the Trinity Summit, Humboldt County, California. Eureka, Calif.: Six Rivers National Forest. Duplicated.
1984   "Following the smoke": Contemporary plant procurement by the
Indians of northwest California. Eureka, Calif.: Six Rivers National Forest.
Duplicated.
1985   The Ferris cabin in the Salmon Trinity Alps wilderness. Eureka,
Calif.: Six Rivers National Forest. Duplicated.
1986a   Contemporary-historic Yurok ethnographic data for the proposed
Simpson Timber Company land exchange with Six Rivers National Forest in
Klamath, California. Eureka, Calif.: Six Rivers National Forest. Duplicated.

1986b   "Trail of the blue sun": Cultural resource interviewing for the Cro-
gan Compartment, Lower Trinity Ranger District, Six Rivers National Forest.
Eureka, Calif.: Six Rivers National Forest. Duplicated.

1986c   "Shadow of the rocks": Cultural resource interviewing for the Waterdog Timber Sale, Orleans Ranger District. Eureka, Calif.: Six Rivers
National Forest. Duplicated.

Heizer, Robert F.
1974   *The Destruction of California Indians.* Salt Lake City: Peregrine Smith.

Heizer, Robert F., ed.
1972   The Eighteen Unratified Treaties of 1851–1852 between the California Indians and the United States Government. Berkeley: Archaeological Research Facility, Department of Anthropology, University of California.

Heizer, Robert F., and Alan J. A. Almquist
1971   *The Other Californians: Prejudice and Discrimination under Spain, Mexico, and the United States.* Berkeley and Los Angeles: University of California
Press.

Heizer, Robert F., and John C. Mills
1952   *The Four Ages of Tsurai: A Documentary History of the Indian Village
on Trinidad Bay.* Berkeley and Los Angeles: University of California Press.

Hennecke, Edgar, and William Schneemelcher, eds.
1963   *New Testament Apocrypha*, Vol. I: *Gospels and Related Writings*, translated by R. McL. Wilson. Philadelphia: The Westminister Press.

Hinsley, Curtis M.
1981   *The Smithsonian and the American Indian: Making a Moral Anthropology in Victorian America.* Washington: Smithsonian Institution Press.

Holt, Catherine
1946   Shasta ethnography. *Anthropological Records* 3(4): 320–37.

Hurston, Zora Neale
1942   *Dust Tracks on a Road: An Autobiography.* Urbana: University of Illinois Press. Second edition, 1984.

Hurtado, Albert L.
1999   *Intimate Frontiers: Sex, Gender, and Culture in Old California.*
Albuquerque: University of New Mexico Press.

Jackson, Stanley W.
1985   Acedia the sin and its relationship to sorrow and melancholia. In
*Culture and Depression: Studies in the Anthropology and Cross-Cultural Psychia-
try of Affect and Disorder,* edited by Arthur Kleinman and Byron Good. Berkeley and Los Angeles: University of California Press.

Jones, Delmos J.

1970   Towards a native anthropology. *Human Organization* 29(4): 251–59.

Jorgensen, Joseph G.

1980   *Western Indians.* San Francisco: W. H. Freeman.

Keeling, Richard

1982a   Kroeber's *Yurok Myths:* A comparative re-evaluation. *American Indian Culture and Research Journal* 6(3): 71–81.

1982b   The "sobbing" quality in a Hupa brush dance song. *American Indian Culture and Research Journal* 6(1): 25–41.

1992   *Cry for Luck: Sacred Song and Speech among the Yurok, Hupa, and Karok Indians of Northwestern California.* Berkeley and Los Angeles: University of California Press.

Kleinman, Arthur

1977   Depression, somatization, and the new cross-cultural psychiatry. *Social Science and Medicine* 11: 3–10.

Kleinman, Arthur, and Byron Good, eds.

1985   *Culture and Depression: Studies in the Anthropology and Cross-Cultural Psychiatry of Affect and Disorder.* Berkeley and Los Angeles: University of California Press.

Kleinman, Arthur, and Joan Kleinman

1985   Somatization: The interconnections in Chinese society among culture, depressive experiences, and the meaning of pain. In Kleinman and Good 1985.

Knudson, Peter H.

1975   Flora, shaman of the Wintu. *Natural History* 84(5): 6–17.

Kristeva, Julia

1989   *Black Sun: Depression and Melancholia.* New York: Columbia University Press.

Kroeber, A. L.

1900–1907   Papers, cartons 6, 7. Archives, Bancroft Library, University of California, Berkeley.

1917a   California kinship systems. *University of California Publications in American Archaeology and Ethnology* 12(9): 336–39, 374–76.

1917b   The superorganic. *American Anthropologist* 19(2): 163–213.

1921   Review of *To the American Indian* by Mrs. Lucy Thompson. *American Anthropologist* 23(2): 220–21.

1925   *Handbook of the Indians of California.* Bureau of American Ethnology Bulletin 78.

1934   Yurok and neighboring kin term systems. *University of California Publications in American Archaeology and Ethnology* 35(1): 15–22.

1940   Psychosis or social sanction. In Kroeber 1952, pp. 310–19.

1948   *Anthropology: Race, Language, Culture, Psychology, Prehistory.* New York and Burlingame, Calif.: Harcourt, Brace & World. Fourth edition.

1952   *The Nature of Culture.* Chicago: University of Chicago Press.

1959   Ethnographic interpretations, 7–11: Yurok national character. *University of California Publications in American Archaeology and Ethnology* 47(3): 236–40.

1976   *Yurok Myths.* Berkeley and Los Angeles: University of California Press.

Kroeber, A. L., and S. A. Barrett

1960   Fishing among the Indians of Northwest California. *Anthropological Records* 21(1): 1–130.

Kroeber, A. L., and E. W. Gifford

1949   World renewal: A cult system of native northwest California. *Anthropological Records* 13(1): 1–155.

Kroeber, Theodora

1959   *The Inland Whale: Nine Stories Retold from California Indian Legends.* Bloomington: Indiana University Press.

1961   *Ishi in Two Worlds: The Biography of the Last Wild Indian in North America.* Berkeley and Los Angeles: University of California Press.

1970   *Alfred Kroeber: A Personal Configuration.* Berkeley and Los Angeles: University of California Press.

Kroeber, Theodora, and Robert F. Heizer

1968   *Almost Ancestors: The First Californians.* San Francisco: Sierra Club.

Lake, Medicine Grizzlybear

1991   *Native Healer: Initiation into an Ancient Art.* Wheaton, Ill.: Quest Books.

Lake, Robert G., Jr.

1982   *Chilula: People from the Ancient Redwoods.* Washington: University Press of America.

Lang, Julian

1989   Pay panau'ararahih: Our Indian language. *News from Native California* 3(3).

1990   How they almost killed our songs. *News from Native California* 4(2).

1994   *Ararapíkva, Creation Stories of the People: Traditional Karuk Indian Literature from Northwestern California.* Berkeley, Calif.: Heyday Books.

Laski, Vera

1959   *Seeking Life*. Austin: University of Texas Press.

Lear, Jonathan

1990   *Love and Its Place in Nature: A Philosophical Interpretation of Freudian Psychoanalysis*. New York: Farrar, Straus & Giroux.

Lindgren, Axel

1983a   Churey Trinidad trails: How my ancestors became doctors, part 1, by Louisa Lindgren. *Trinidad News and Views*. December 1.

1983b   Churey Trinidad trails: How my ancestors became doctors, part 2, by Louisa Lindgren. *Trinidad News and Views*. December 15.

Marcus, George E.

1998   *Ethnography through Thick and Thin*. Princeton: Princeton University Press.

Marcus, George E., and Michael M. J. Fischer

1986   *Anthropology as Cultural Critique: An Experimental Moment in the Social Sciences*. Chicago: University of Chicago Press.

Margolin, Malcolm

1978   *The Ohlone Way: Indian Life in the San Francisco–Monterey Bay Area*. Berkeley, Calif: Heyday Books.

1994   Introduction. *News from Native California* 8(1).

Marsella, Anthony J., et al.

1985   Cross-cultural studies of depressive disorders: An overview. In *Culture and Depression: Studies in the Anthropology and Cross-Cultural Psychiatry of Affect and Disorder*, edited by Arthur Kleinman and Byron Good. Berkeley and Los Angeles: University of California Press.

Mattthiessen, Peter

1984   *Indian Country*. New York: Viking.

Mauss, Marcel

1954   *The Gift: Forms and Functions of Exchange in Archaic Societies*, translated by I. Cunnison. Glencoe, Ill: The Free Press.

McGuire, Randall H.

1997   Why have archaeologists thought real Indians were dead and what can we do about it? In *Indians and Anthropologists: Vine Deloria Jr. and the Critique of Anthropology*, edited by Thomas Biolsi and Larry J. Zimmerman. Tucson: University of Arizona Press.

McNickle, D'Arcy

1972   American Indians who never were. In *The American Indian Reader: Anthropology*, edited by Jeanette Henry. San Francisco: American Indian Educational Publishers.

Medicine, Bea
    1972   The Anthropologist as the Indian's image maker. In *The American Indian Reader: Anthropology,* edited by Jeanette Henry. San Francisco: American Indian Educational Publishers.

Merkin, Daphne
    2001   The black season. *New Yorker,* January 8.

Mihesuah, Devon A.
    1998   *Natives and Academics: Researching and Writing about American Indians.* Lincoln: University of Nebraska Press.

Moratto, Michael J.
    1971   An archaeological overview of Redwood National Park. *National Park Services Publications in Anthropology* 8.

Morris, David B.
    1991   *The Culture of Pain.* Berkeley and Los Angeles: University of California Press.

Nabokov, Peter
    1981   Native land claims: Speaking of practicable things. *Anthropology Resource Center Newsletter* 5(4): 4–5.

Nelson, Byron, Jr.
    1978   *Our Home Forever: A Hupa Tribal History.* Hoopa, Calif.: The Hupa Tribe.

Norton, Jack
    1979   *Genocide in Northwestern California: When Our Worlds Cried.* San Francisco: Indian Historian Press.

Office of the Federal Register
    1977   Guidelines for implementing and documenting traditional cultural properties. *National Register Bulletin* 38.
    1993   Parker, Patricia L., and Thomas F. King. Documenting traditional cultural properties. *National Register Bulletin* 38, revised.

O'Nell, Theresa DeLeane
    1996   *Disciplined Hearts: History, Identity, and Depression in an American Indian Community.* Berkeley and Los Angeles: University of California Press.

Palmquist, Peter E.
    1976   *With Nature's Children: Emma B. Freeman (1880–1928): Camera and Brush.* Eureka, Calif.: Interface California Corporation.

Pearsall, Clarence E., ed.
    1928   *History and Genealogy of the Pearsall Family in England and America,* Volume III. Privately printed and held.

Peters, Christopher
    n.d.   The first "concept" paper. Duplicated, held by author.
Pettitt, George Albert
    1946   Primitive education in North America. *University of California Publications in American Archaeology and Ethnology* 43(1): 1–182.
Pilling, Arnold R.
    1969   Yurok law-ways and the role of Yurok medicine men: Final Summary Report. NIMH Grant BMS-11. MS, held by National Institutes of Mental Health, Bethesda, Md.
    1970   The ethnography of Christian and/or historical Indian burials (Yurok Indians of northwestern California). Paper presented at the meeting of the Society for Historical Archaeology, Toronto.
    1976   Yurok systems of social stratification. Paper presented at Northwest Coast Conference, Simon Frazer University. Vancouver, B.C.
    1978   Yurok. In *Handbook of North American Indians,* Volume 8, edited by Robert F. Heizer. Washington: Smithsonian Institution.
Pilling, Arnold R., and Patricia L. Pilling
    1970   Cloth, clothes, hose, and bows: Nonsedentary merchants among the Indians of northwestern California. In *Migration and Anthropology: Proceedings of the 1970 Annual Spring Meeting of the American Ethnological Society.* Seattle: University of Washington Press.
Posinsky, S. H.
    1956   Yurok shell money and "pains": A Freudian interpretation. *Psychiatric Quarterly* 30: 598–632.
    1957   The problem of Yurok anality. *American Imago* 14: 3–31.
Powers, Stephen
    1976   *Tribes of California.* Berkeley and Los Angeles: University of California Press. [1877]
Rabinow, Paul
    1991   For hire: Resolutely late modern. In *Recapturing Anthropology: Working in the Present,* edited by Richard G. Fox. Santa Fe, N. Mex.: School of American Research Press.
Raphael, Ray
    1985   *Cash Crop: An American Dream.* Mendocino, Calif.: The Ridge Times Press.
Rawls, James
    1984   *Indians of California: The Changing Image.* Norman: University of Oklahoma Press.

Robins, R. H.
1958   *The Yurok Language: Grammar, Texts, Lexicon.* University of California Publications in Linguistics 15.

Roheim, Geza
1950   *Psychoanalysis and Anthropology.* New York: International Universities Press.

Sapir, Edward
1909   Takelma texts. *University of Pennsylvania Publications of the University Museum* 2(1): 160–95.

Sapir, Jean
1921   Yurok tales. *Journal of American Folklore* 41(160): 250–73.

Schieffelin, Edward L.
1985   The cultural analysis of depressive affect: An example from New Guinea. In *Culture and Depression: Studies in the Anthropology and Cross-Cultural Psychiatry of Affect and Disorder,* edited by Arthur Kleinman and Byron Good. Berkeley and Los Angeles: University of California Press.

Seiter, H. D., and T. Williams
1959   *Prince Lightfoot, Indian from the California Redwoods.* San Francisco: Troubadour Press/H. D. Seiter Books.

Sexton, Anne
1966   *Live or Die.* Boston: Houghton Mifflin.

Sieber, R. Timothy
1990   Selecting a new past: Emerging definitions of heritage in Boston Harbor. *Journal of Urban and Cultural Studies* 1(2): 101–22.

Slagle, Allogan
1985   Tolowa Indian Shakers and the role of prophecy at Smith River, California. *American Indian Quarterly* 9(3): 353–74.

Smith, Marian W.
1954   Shamanism in the Shaker religion of northwest America. *Man* 54: 119–22.

Spott, Robert
1926   Address by Robert Spott. *The Commonwealth* 21(3): 133–35.

Spott, Robert, and A. L. Kroeber
1942   Yurok narratives. *University of California Publications in American Archaeology and Ethnology* 35(9): 143–256.

Steward, Julian H.
1961   Alfred Louis Kroeber 1876–1960. *American Anthropologist* 63(5, part 1): 1038–59.

1973   *Alfred Kroeber.* New York: Columbia University Press.

Stocking, George

1968   *Race, Culture, and Evolution: Essays in the History of Anthropology.*
New York: The Free Press.

1974   *A Franz Boas Reader: The Shaping of American Anthropology.* Chicago:
University of Chicago Press.

1977   The aims of Boasian ethnography: Creating the materials for traditional humanities scholarship. *History of Anthropology Newsletter* 4(2): 4–5.

1992   *The Ethnographer's Magic and Other Essays in the History of
Anthropology.* Madison: University of Wisconsin Press.

Strong, Pauline Turner

n.d.   To forget their tongue, their name, and their whole relation: The
contest of kinship in North America. Duplicated ms., held by author.

Styron, William

1990   *Darkness Visible: A Memoir of Madness.* New York: Random House.

Thompson, Lucy

1916   *To the American Indian.* Eureka, Calif.: Cummins Print Shop.

1991   *To the American Indian: Reminiscences of a Yurok Woman.* Foreword
by Peter E. Palmquist, introduction by Julian Lang. Berkeley, Calif.: Heyday
Books. [1916]

Thornton, Russell

1987   *American Indian Holocaust and Survival: A Population History since
1492.* Norman: University of Oklahoma Press.

Trigger, Bruce

1969   *The Huron: Farmers of the North.* New York: Holt, Rinehart and Win-
ston.

USDA/FS (U.S. Department of Agriculture: Forest Service)

1975   A Report on the Significance of Certain Properties Associated with
Traditional Ideological Beliefs and Practices of Northwestern California by
Donald S. Miller. Final Environmental Statement, Eight Mile–Blue Creek
Units, Six Rivers National Forest. USDA-FS-R5-DES (Adm)-75-9. Appendix
K. Duplicated.

1976   Environmental Statement, Six Rivers National Forest, Gasquet-Orleans Road, Chimney Rock Section, edited by Douglas R. Leisz. San
Francisco: USDA Forest Service. Duplicated.

1977   Draft, Forest Service Manual. Duplicated.

1978   Draft Environmental Statement, Chimney Rock Section, Blue Creek
Planning Unit, Six Rivers National Forest. Duplicated.

1979a   Cultural Resources of the Chimney Rock Section, Gasquet-Orleans Road, Six Rivers National Forest. Dorothea J. Theoderatus, principal investigator. Contract No. 53-9158-8-6045. Six Rivers National Forest, Eureka, Calif.: USDA Forest Service. Duplicated.
1979b   Final Report, Blue Creek Planning Unit, Six Rivers National Forest. Duplicated.

USDI (U.S. Department of the Interior)
1978   The National Heritage Program. Duplicated.

USDI/BLM (U.S. Department of the Interior: Bureau of Land Management)
1976   Cultural Resource Management. Duplicated.

Valory, Dale Keith
1966a   The focus of Indian Shaker healing. *Kroeber Anthropological Society Papers* 35: 67–111.
1966b   Humanity, what is it? An interview with Claude Lévi-Strauss. *Kroeber Anthropological Society Papers* 35: 41–53.
1968   Ruth Kellett Roberts 1885–1967. *Kroeber Anthropological Society Papers* 38: 1–9.
1970   Yurok doctors and devils: A study in identity, anxiety, and deviance. Ph.D. Dissertation, Department of Anthropology, University of California, Berkeley.

Vizenor, Gerald
1994   *Manifest Manners: Postindian Warriors of Survivance.* Hanover, N.H.: University Press of New England.

Wallace, A. F. C.
1956   Revitalization movements. *American Anthropologist* 58: 269–81.

Wallace, M.
1987   The politics of public history. In *Past Meets Present: Essays about Historic Interpretation and Public Audiences,* edited by J. Blatti. Washington: Smithsonian Institution Press.

Wallace, William J.
1947   Hupa child training. *Educational Administration and Supervision* 33.

Waterman, T. T.
1920   Yurok geography. *University of California Publications in American Archaeology and Ethnology* 16(5): 174–314.
1924   The "Shake Religion" of Puget Sound. *Smithsonian Institution Annual Report for 1922:* 499–507.
1951   All is trouble along the Klamath: A Yurok idyll. In *The California Indians: A Source Book,* edited by R. F. Heizer and M. A. Whipple. Berkeley and Los Angeles: University of California Press. [1925]

Waterman, T. T., and A. L. Kroeber

1934   Yurok marriages. *University of California Publications in American Archaeology and Ethnology* 30(1): 1–14.

1938   The Kepel fish dam. *University of California Publications in American Archaeology and Ethnology* 35(6): 49–80.

Weathers, Diane, with Janet Huck

1979   A fight for rites. *Time* Magazine (April 9).

Weber, Max

1958   *The Protestant Ethic and the Spirit of Capitalism,* translated by Talcott Parsons. New York: Charles Scribner's Sons.

Whiteley, Peter M.

1998   *Rethinking Hopi Ethnography.* Washington: Smithsonian Institution Press.

Wolf, Eric

1981   Alfred L. Kroeber. In *Totems and Teachers: Perspectives on the History of Anthropology,* edited by Sydel Silverman. New York: Columbia University Press.

Zitkala Sa

1921   *American Indian Stories.* Washington: Hayworth.

Acknowledgments of Permissions

Substantial portions of several chapters in *Standing Ground* first appeared elsewhere in different forms:

Chapter 1 *Encyclopedia of Native Americans in the Twentieth Century*. New York: Garland, 1994.

Chapter 2 Sergei Kan, ed. *Strangers to Relatives: The Adoption and Naming of Anthropologists in Native North America*. Lincoln: University of Nebraska Press, 2001.

Chapter 5 Lowell John Bean and Sylvia Vane, eds. *California Indian Shamanism*. Menlo Park, Calif.: Ballena Press, 1992.

Chapter 7 *Parabola* 13(2), 1988.

Chapter 8 *Parabola* 16(1), 1991.

Chapter 10 *American Indian Quarterly* 20(2), 1997.

Chapter 11 Lawrence E. Sullivan, ed. *Native Religions and Cultures of North America*. New York: Compendium Books, 2000.

I thank all of the editors concerned and their publishers for kind permission to re-cast these essays. I also thank the following for permission to use quotations that appear in this book: Delacourt Press (Kurt Vonnegut, Jr., *Breakfast of Champions,* 1973); HarperCollins (John Bierhorst, *The Sacred Path: Prayers and Power Songs of the American Indian,* 1983); Houghton Mifflin (Anne Sexton, "Menstruation at Forty," *Live or Die,* 1966); Random House (Ford Madox Ford, *Parade's End,* 1961).

Index

Compositor:	Impressions Book and Journal Services, Inc.
Text:	10/14 Palatino
Display:	Bauer Bodoni, Univers Condensed Light
Printer and Binder:	Sheridan Books, Inc.